Praise for

The Death of Santini

"A painful, lyrical, addictive read that his fans won't want to miss."
—*People* (3½ out of 4 stars)

"Conroy has fashioned a memoir that is vital, large-hearted and often raucously funny. The result is an act of hard-won forgiveness, a deeply considered meditation on the impossibly complex nature of families and a valuable contribution to the literature of fathers and sons."

—*The Washington Post*

"*The Death of Santini* instantly reminded me of the decadent pleasures of [Conroy's] language, of his promiscuous gift for metaphor and of his ability, in the finest passages of his fiction, to make the love, hurt or terror a protagonist feels seem to be the only emotion the world could possibly have room for, the rightful center of the trembling universe. . . . Conroy's conviction pulls you fleetly through the book, as does the potency of his bond with his family, no matter their sins, their discord, their shortcomings."

—*The New York Times Book Review*

"Conroy remains a brilliant storyteller, a master of sarcasm, and a hallucinatory stylist whose obsession with the impress of the past on the present binds him to Southern literary tradition."

—*The Boston Globe*

By Pat Conroy

The Death of Santini

DIAL PRESS TRADE PAPERBACKS
NEW YORK

Pat Conroy

The Death *of* Santini

THE STORY OF A FATHER AND HIS SON

Library of Congress Cataloging-in-Publication Data
Conroy, Pat.
The death of Santini: the story of a father and his son/Pat Conroy.
p. cm
ISBN 978-0-385-34352-7
ebook ISBN 978-0-385-53085-9
1. United States. Marines—Military life—Fiction. 2. Fathers and sons—Fiction.
3. Conflict of generations—Fiction. 4. Dysfunctional families—Fiction. 5. Life
change events—Fiction. 6. Teachers as authors—Fiction. 7. Domestic fiction. I. Title.
PS3553.O5198D43   2013
813'.54—dc23   2013019095

This book is dedicated with love and gratitude to my brothers and sisters:

Carol Ann, the Conroy family poet and fabulist, the great explainer of it all;

Mike, the keystone, the calm in the midst of the family storm, the center that always holds;

Kathy, the family nurse, Santini's caretaker and confessor, the azalea crafted with iron;

Jim, our brightest, most brilliant sibling, also our dark and hilarious commentator on the flawed clan;

Tim, the kindest and sweetest Conroy, a compassionate worker with special needs kids who brought joy into the lives of all he taught;

Tom, our lost boy and baby brother whose suicide was the mortal wound to the heart of the family and reminded us how bad it really was.

Contents

The Death of Santini

Prologue

I've been writing the story of my own life for over forty years. My own stormy autobiography has been my theme, my dilemma, my obsession, and the fly-by-night dread I bring to the art of fiction. Through the years, I've met many writers who tell me with great pride that they consider autobiographical fiction as occupying a lower house in the literary canon. They make sure I know that their imaginations soar into realms and fragments completely invented by them. No man or woman in their pantheon of family or acquaintances has ever taken a curtain call in their own well-wrought and shapely books. Only rarely have I drifted far from the bed where I was conceived. It is both the wound and foundation of my work. But I came into the world as the son of a Marine Corps fighter pilot as fierce as Achilles. He was a night fighter comfortable with machine-gun fire and napalm. He fought well and honorably in three wars and at one time was one of the most highly decorated Marine aviators in the corps. He was also meaner than a shit-house rat, and I remember hating him even when I was in diapers.

For a long time, I thought I was born into a mythology instead of a family. My father thundered out of the sky in black-winged fighter planes, every inch of him a god of war. My mother's role was goddess of light and harmony—an Arcadian figure spinning through the grasses and wildflowers on long, hot summer days. Peg Peek and Don Conroy brought the mean South and hurt Ireland to each other's bloodstreams.

Peg came from snake-handling fundamentalists in the mountains of Alabama, while Don brought the sensibility of rosary-mad Chicago into a family that would be raised on military bases through the South. But the myths of our lives had no stories to support them. I've no memory of my father sharing one story about his growing up in Chicago, while my mother would simply make up stories of her own privileged upbringing in Atlanta. There, she was the belle of the ball during the seasons of society when the Pinks and Gels crowded into the ballrooms of country clubs before World War II. This was fantasy and an untruth. My mother was dabbling in fiction long before I tried my hand at that slippery game. Mom was always writing a plot where she was a daughter of wealth and privilege. Her actual South was utterly unbeautiful, but we never knew it, because my mama wrote her own mythology, making it up as she went along. My childhood was storyless except I was being raised by an Irish god of fire and a Georgian goddess of the moon. Their marriage was composed of terror and great violence, storm-tossed and seasoned with all the terrible salts of pain.

Both of my parents were larger-than-life to me. Dad prepared me for the coldheartedness of tyrants, for the spirit of Nero contained in the soul of every man, for the Nazi with his booted foot on the Jew's throat, for the mass slaughters of the Tutsis by the Hutus, the collective roar of the ayatollahs—for the necessity of understanding the limits of cruelty as well as the certain knowledge that there are no limits at all.

In the myth I'm sharing I know that I was born to be the recording angel of my parents' dangerous love. Their damaged children are past middle age now, but the residues of their fury still torture each of us. We talk about it every time we get together. Our parents lit us up like brandy in a skillet. They tormented us in their own flawed, wanton love of each other. This is the telling of my parents' love story—I shall try to write the truth of it the best I can. I'd like to be rid of it forever, because it's hunted me down like some foul-breathed hyena since childhood.

My childhood taught me everything I needed to know about the dangers of love. Love came in many disguises, masquerades, rigged card tricks, and sleights of hand that could either overwhelm or tame you. It was a country bristling with fishhooks hung at eye level, man-traps, and poisoned baits. It could hurl toward you at breakneck speed or let you dangle over a web spun by a brown recluse spider. When love announced itself, I learned to duck to avoid the telegraphed backhand or the blown kiss from my mother's fragrant hand. Havoc took up residence in me at a young age. Violence became a whorl in my DNA. I was the oldest of seven children; five of us would try to kill ourselves before the age of forty. My brother Tom would succeed in a most spectacular fashion. Love came to us veiled in disturbance—we had to learn it the hard way, cutting away the spoilage like bruises on a pear.

It took a world war to arrange my parents' accidental meeting on Atlanta's Peachtree Street in 1943. Don Conroy was a hall-of-fame basketball player at St. Ambrose College in Iowa when he heard about the Japanese attack on Pearl Harbor. He left the gym that day, walked down to the recruiting office in Davenport, and joined the Marine Corps. He learned to fly at the Naval Air Station Great Lakes. After practicing a series of aerial acrobatics over Lake Michigan one day, he returned to his squadron and announced, "I was better than the Great Santini today." It earned him his first and only nickname among these fighter pilots, who would compose his circle of fierce brotherhood. These pilots could kill you and do it fast. The original Great Santini had been a charismatic trapeze artist who performed in a circus act my father had seen as a boy. In his death-defying somersaults, the Great Santini had seemed fearless and all-powerful—with a touch of immortality in his uncanny flair—as he vaulted through the air on a hot Chicago night, always working without a net.

I hated my father long before I knew there was a word for hate. My mother would later claim that I refused to learn the word "Daddy" until after my first birthday. From the start he was a menacing, hovering presence, and I never felt safe for one moment that my father loomed over me. I don't think it occurred to him that loving his children might be part of his job description. He could have written a manual on the art of waging war against his wife and children. I can't remember a house I lived in as a child where he did not beat my mother or me or my brothers; nor do I believe that he would've noticed if both his daughters had run away from home. My mother raised me, the oldest child, to be the protector of her other kids, to rush them into secret hiding places we had scouted whenever we moved into a new house. We learned to hide our shame in the madness of our day-to-day lives so that the nuns and priests who ran our parishes everywhere we went considered us an exemplary Catholic family.

Sometimes on the long car trips we spent rotating between Southern air bases, my father would tell the romantic story of his chance encounter with Peggy Peek as she drifted out of Davison's department store on Peachtree Street. He said, "I was in Atlanta getting some extra training before they shipped me out to the Philippines. I asked a barber where I could hunt up some broads and he told me the best place was down on Peachtree, right in the middle of the city. So I hopped a bus and got off and started walking around, sort of scouting the place out. Then your mother came out of a store in a red dress, carrying some shopping bags. Man, what a package. What a figure. I mean, this was one fine-looking Southern girl. So I followed her across the street. She was walking with two other girls. They were sisters, but I didn't know that then. I started up a conversation with her. You know. Showed her some suave moves of a Chicago boy. Told her I was a pilot—getting ready to go to war. Back then, it was always a sure pickup line with the broads. But I couldn't get your mother or her sisters to even talk to me. I mean, talk about three cold fish! But they'd never met a Chicago boy, especially one as charming as me. So I kept going, ratcheting up the pressure, throwing out my best lines. I told Peg I was heading off to war, would probably be dead in a month or two, but was willing to die for my country, and wanted to live long enough to bomb Tokyo. Then I saw a bus coming up to the stop and watched in panic as your mother and her sisters got on. No air-conditioning back then, so all the windows were raised. Jesus Christ, I was starting to panic. Your mother sat by the window. So I started begging, begging, which I'm not ashamed to admit. I begged her for an address, a telephone number, the name of her father, anything. We could go dancing, to a movie, maybe make out a little bit.

"The bus took off and I took off with it, running my ass off, pleading with this broad. I didn't even know her name and she hadn't said a word to me. The bus began to pull away from me and I felt like I had struck out big-time when your mother stuck her pretty head out of the bus window and said, 'BR3-2638.' Ain't it a bee-you-tu-ful story? And we lived happily ever after."

From the backseat of our station wagon, Carol Ann always wailed out into the night: "Tell him the wrong number, Mom. One digit. Just one digit and none of this had to happen. None of us would've been born. Tell him the wrong number, Mom. Please. For all of us, tell him the wrong number."

In the driver's seat, my father responded to Carol Ann, "Shut your trap. I can always count on you to be Miss Negative."

I thought Dad would stop the car and beat her, but now I think he never gave much thought to what his daughter felt. That would change later.

What made Dad's temper dangerous was its volatility and unpredictable nature. Anything could set it off and no weatherman in the world could track its storm warnings. His blue eyes were born to hate. Because he was a fighter pilot of immense gifts, he was also born to kill. When I was four years old, my father was stationed at El Toro and my parents liked to take me and Carol Ann to the San Diego Zoo on family outings. The animal world held rapturous powers over my mother, and a zoo was one of the happiest places on earth to her. My mother was pushing Carol Ann in her baby carriage, with my father in charge of looking after me. When my father stopped to get a drink of water, I took off running, then heard my mother screaming for me to stop. Exhilarated, I ran faster and missed the moment my father sprinted into action behind me, unamused by my defection. Looking back I saw him lunging at me; then I fell hurtling down a long flight of stone steps that led to the big cats. When I reached the bottom step, Dad was on me in an instant and went crazy when he saw I was bleeding from a head wound I sustained in the fall. He started slapping my face harder than he ever had before. My screams and his slaps brought two sailors running to my rescue as Mom was crying from the steps above. When the sailors pulled Dad off me, he turned to fight the two intruders into his family business.

"Hey, squids," he said as he raised his fists, using the contemptuous name he used his whole life for members of the navy. "This is my kid and I'll do anything I want to him."

My mother got between Dad and the two sailors with Carol Ann in her arms and said to the sailors, "Please just leave. Everyone just leave and calm down."

Carol Ann and I both were screaming, and my dad started yelling that if my mother did not shut us kids up, he'd give us something to cry about. From that day, I carried a lifelong affection for sailors, a mortal fear of my father, and the selection of a dog, Chippie, from a litter of mongrel puppies. Chippie was my reward for surviving the fall and the beating at the San Diego Zoo. In a farmer's backyard, my mother and I examined a crush of puppies, but my eye was caught by the runt of the litter who was eyeing me from the back of the enclosure. I walked over and picked the dog up, who licked my face, beginning a fourteen-year love affair with the Great Dog Chippie.

. . .

My mother's physical beauty played counterpoint to my father's powerful fists. Her loveliness made her delicious cunning both possible and dangerous. In my mother, I caught glimpses of Becky Sharp, Lady Macbeth, Anna Karenina, and Madame Bovary long before I read those works that introduced them into world literature. My brothers and sisters do not all share in my adoration of my mother, for reasons both painful and legitimate. She could camouflage the blade of beauty in the folds of a matador's red cape. Often she was an unreadable woman who could use silence to declaw her ungovernable husband. When I was a boy, she used me as helpmate and confessor to let me know of her desperate unhappiness with her life with Don Conroy. At least once a week, she swore she was going to divorce him as soon as she saved up enough money. Almost every year, she found herself pregnant, leading me to wonder if my father ever saw a condom. Soon there were too many children to feed and not enough money to save. But my heart would leap like a jackrabbit every time Mom said she wanted to divorce my father. It gave hope to a childhood not filled with much. The last time I heard her say it was on March 10, 1956, when we lived on South Culpeper Street in Arlington, Virginia—one of the nightmare years.

It was my sister's birthday and Mom was lighting eight candles that had Carol Ann dancing around the table, waiting to blow them out. My father was reading the sports section of the *Washington Post* in the living room and kept refusing to come to the table to sing "Happy Birthday." The barometer within me felt the pressure in the room changing, and I watched my father's eyes turn predatory.

"You're going to sing 'Happy Birthday' to your daughter, Don," my mother said, the register of her voice rising a pitch.

"Shut up," Dad said. "And don't make me tell you again."

Carol Ann began crying, which brought Dad to the boiling point of his sulfurous rage. He got up and backhanded my mother to the floor, the first overture in the long dance of my childhood. Over the years the choreography of this musical set piece hardened into grotesque and mistimed rhythms. My steps had been easy to learn, but they darkened my whole life because I had to learn them. As Mom struggled to rise, I ran and got between my parents. He knocked me with another backhand that sent me sliding across the living room floor. All the kids were screaming and the pandemonium unleashed in that house had reached a pitch of hysteria. When Dad pulled Mom to her feet to resume the beating, he shoved her into the very narrow kitchen. When I got between them again, there was barely room for all three of us as I pounded my fists against Dad's chest before he slapped me out of the kitchen with his right hand. Somehow, I got the feeling during those years that my mother's love for me depended on how many times I placed myself between them when Dad was beating her. Taking an ugly turn, the beating became the worst one I ever witnessed. From my vantage point it looked to me like my father was going to beat my mother to death. I was hitting against him as hard as I could, now crying and screaming loudly, joining the tribal wail of my brothers and sisters, in a house undone by pure bedlam. Looking up, I saw my father's hated face getting ready to slap the living hell out of me when I saw something else rising into the air above him. It was a butcher knife. I saw its flashing blade slashing in the artificial light. A jet of blood hit my eyes and blinded me. I had no idea if it was the blood of my mother or my father.

When my mother began wiping the blood out of my eyes with a moistened towel, I saw the bloody knife in her hand. I caught a glimpse of my wounded father trailing blood as he made his way to the staircase. The kids were all going nuts, and Carol Ann seemed traumatized to the point of psychosis.

"Pat, get the kids out into the car," Mom said. "We've got to make a run for it." Mike, who was five, and Kathy, age four, were already running to the front door. I made a grab for the toddler, Jimbo, as I blew out Carol Ann's birthday candles and helped walk her to the car. She babbled in a strange patois that seemed like a form of madness itself. Although Dad had bloodied my nose and Mom was bleeding from the mouth, she drove us away from that unhappy house, everyone in the car weeping and terrified. Mom drove us to the Hot Shoppe in Fairlington Shopping Center, where she cleaned everyone up, then bought us ice-cream sodas. She kept saying, "I'll never go into that man's house again. I'll not subject my children to that kind of life. All of you deserve better than that. I'll divorce him and go live with Mother in Atlanta. It's just a matter of time before he kills me or kills you, Pat. Why's he so mean? What makes him so goddamn mean? No matter, I'll never enter his house again. None of us will. That's a promise and I'd swear my life on it."

An hour later we drove back to the house on South Culpeper Street in Arlington, Virginia. I don't remember the next year of my life.

My siblings freely admit that they made frequent use of denial and repression in their growing up. My problem was different. I seemed to remember almost every violent thing, and the memories tortured me. But I shut it all down as a seventh grader in Blessed Sacrament School. Although Sister Bernadine was my teacher, I don't recall a thing she taught me, but she complained to my mother that she found me drifting, unserious, and remote. She told my mother I was unpopular and didn't even try to make friends. I can't recall a single name of my classmates that year, though they sprang to life again when I entered Sister Petra's penal colony in eighth grade. I know I played on a football team and a basketball team, but I couldn't venture a guess at the names of those teams. We moved up the street sometime after the stabbing incident, but I have no memory of the move. I can't conjure that year out of darkness or bring it up to the light. Because I'd been blinded by my father's blood, I had to battle my way back to being a seer and recorder of my own life. I learned about grief covered by the forgetfulness of havoc.

My sister Carol Ann sustained the most ruthless collateral damage in that blood feud between our parents. When I was writing *The Great Santini* I thought about putting that scene into the book as the final assault in the tempestuous marriage of Col. Bull Meecham and his wife, Lillian. But I ran into an obstacle I could not overcome, one that I had not expected to encounter. Though it didn't surprise me when both Mom and Dad denied any knowledge of the bloody scene on Culpeper Street, it shocked me when Carol Ann agreed with them and claimed it was part of my overwrought imagination. Neither Mike nor Kathy had any memory of the ordeal, and Jim had been too young. Even though I remembered every detail of the event down to Mom's anguished soliloquy at the Formica table at the Hot Shoppe, I was uncomfortable being the only witness who carried the memory of that dreadful day.

Several years after *The Great Santini* came out, Carol Ann called to tell me she had gone through a most extraordinary therapy session in which she recalled those long-ago crimes committed during the lighting of her birthday candles. Because of her lousy childhood, Carol Ann had spent her days tormented by voices and visions and hallucinations. She was the clear winner in the Conroy siblings' sweepstakes for human lunacy until our youngest brother, Tom, made a last-minute lunge at the finish line and leaped to his death from a fourteen-story building in Columbia, South Carolina.

Carol Ann's voice was slow and shaken as she told me what she had revealed to her therapist. Carol Ann loved her birthday parties better than any of the other kids. All during her girlhood she would look at the presents piled up for her and she would cackle, "Every present on the table's for *me*. You other kids get nothing. I love that you get nothing and I get everything. This is my favorite day of the year, by far. Pat, you get zero. Mike, look all you want but don't touch, midget boy. Kathy, I may share something with you, but probably not."

I had always been Carol Ann's most supple interpreter in the family, and her oddball view of the world struck me as hilarious. But on that day in 1956, she had hardly slept the night before because of her rising excitement over her party. When the fight broke out, it was so violent and bloodthirsty that she had the first psychotic break of her life. She looked up into the kitchen and saw Mom and Dad locked in what seemed like mortal battle; she hallucinated two wolves slashing at each other's throats with their cruel and lethal fangs. She remembered the bloodcurdling curses and my terror-induced runs to get into the middle, which sent me flying out of the kitchen onto the living room floor. Then, for the first time, she heard the initial hisses of the voices that would corrupt all possibility of untroubled thinking for her.

The voice was cruel and satanic: "My name is Carol-Wolf. I'm going to be with you for a very long time. And I'm going to hurt you. That's a promise. I'll hurt you."

So my sister's lifetime of madness was born in the wavering light of birthday candles, and she would speak for the rest of her life in fiery tongues of poetry to fight off that pack of wolves on the hunt in her psyche.

In my father's sock drawer, he kept a deadly looking knife that fighter pilots carried into battle with them if they ever got shot down. As the men made their way back to friendly lines, the knives could sever the throats of the enemy or stop their hearts. It had a blade curved like a serpent's lips. Each time we moved, I made sure I knew where to find that knife. Whenever Dad was on a night flight or away on maneuvers, I would study the edges and point of that frightening weapon. If I ever witnessed a beating of my mother like that again, I planned to sneak into their bedroom at night, unsheathe the knife, and drive it into his throat at the windpipe, trying to sever all the way through the backbone. I knew I would have to be swift and silent and remorseless. A glancing blow or a missed thrust would get me killed, and I wanted to be the killer that night. I longed to remove that malignant aviator from my mother's bed. My father had succeeded in turning me into a murderous, patricidal boy. I never regretted these deplorable visions of making an abattoir of my father's bed, nor ever confessed these sins to any parish priest. The only thing about that knife in my father's drawer that struck me as strange was that I would never leave such a deadly weapon near a woman who had once stabbed me with a butcher knife.

I don't know what happened to that knife, but it brought me comfort in a wife-beater's house.

When I was thirty years old, my novel *The Great Santini* was published, and there were many things in that book I was afraid to write or feared that no one would believe. But this year I turned sixty-five, the official starting date of old age and the beginning countdown to my inevitable death. I've come to realize that I still carry the bruised freight of that childhood every day. I can't run away, hide, or pretend it never happened. I wear it on my back like the carapace of a tortoise, except my shell burdens and does not protect. It weighs me down and fills me with dread.

The Conroy children were all casualties of war, conscripts in a battle we didn't sign up for on the bloodied envelope of our birth certificates. I grew up to become the family evangelist; Michael, the vessel of anxiety; Kathy, who missed her childhood by going to sleep at six every night; Jim, who is called the dark one; Tim, the sweetest one—who can barely stand to be around any of us; and Tom, our lost and never-to-be-found brother.

My personal tragedy lies with my sister Carol Ann, the poet I grew up with and adored. She has spent much of her adult life hating me with a poisonous rage she can't control. Her eyes turn yellow with the fury of a leopardess whenever I walk into a room. For a long time I endured her wrath with a stoic forbearance because I was an eyewitness to her forlorn life as a girl. I watched Mom and Dad coax her to madness and I grew up applauding her wizardry with the English language. She was the original truth teller in the family and she force-fed me the insider information that our parents were crazy. Her perspicacious voice formed the anthem of my own liberation. Don and Peg devastated a sweet kid and smothered her like a firefly in a closed-up bottle.

My books have always been disguised voyages into that archipelago of souls known as the Conroy family.

When *The Prince of Tides* was published, my father said, "I hear you made me a mean shrimper in this one." I replied that my father couldn't catch a shrimp with a fork in a seafood restaurant. When *Beach Music* made its appearance in 1995, Dad said, "Hey, I'm a drunk judge in this one. And as mean as shit again. Folks are gonna get the idea that your old man is something of a monster. Let's face it, Pat, you can't write down the word 'father' without my face hovering over you. Admit it."

It was superb literary criticism. I realized its truth when I wrote down the word "mother" on a blank sheet of paper and my mother's pretty face appeared in the air above me. Once, I wrote that my father and mother always appeared like mythical figures to me, larger-than-life Olympians like Zeus and Hera. For many years, because of the house they created, I've wished I'd never been born. I've felt like I was born in a prison yard and would never be eligible for furlough or offered safe passage into a cease-fire zone. My family is my portion of hell, my eternal flame, my fate, and my time on the cross.

Mom and Dad, I need to go back there once again. I've got to try to make sense of it one last time, a final circling of the block, a reckoning, another dive into the caves of the coral reef where the morays wait in ambush, one more night flight into the immortal darkness to study that house of pain a final time. Then I'll be finished with you, Mom and Dad. I'll leave you in peace and not bother you again. And I'll pray that your stormy spirits find peace in the house of the Lord. But I must examine the wreckage one last time.

PART ONE

. . . .

CHAPTER 1 ·

The Promise

On June 4, 1963, I walked off the graduation stage of Beaufort High School without a single clue about where I was attending college next year or if I'd be attending one at all. My parents had driven me mad over this subject and neither would discuss it with me further. I had planned to get a job at the tomato-packing shed on St. Helena Island to earn some money if my parents somehow managed to enroll me in a college. But my father received orders to Offutt Air Force Base in Omaha, Nebraska, for the following year. I didn't want to leave Beaufort, and I sure as hell didn't want to move to Nebraska, a place where I didn't know another human being. I wanted to go to college.

My father had the car packed and ready when I turned my graduation robe in to my teacher Dutchen Hardin, hugged my other favorite Beaufort High teachers and classmates, then fled in tears toward my life in Nebraska. Before I entered the car, I composed myself, dried my eyes, and got in the shotgun seat. The motor was running and Dad threw me a map, saying, "You're the navigator, pal. Any mistakes and I whack you." Before a single graduation party had begun, we were already crossing the Savannah River into Georgia. Our journey took us on back roads and through scores of towns that we hurtled by in their sleep. It was the age before interstate highways were common, so most of our trip would take us through the rural South and the farmlands of the Midwest. To my shock, Dad planned to make it a straight-through shot to Chicago, pausing only for pit stops and gas.

"Dad, you sure you want to do this?" I asked.

"Hey, jocko, you a detective?"

"That's a lot of driving. It might be too much for you."

"That's why you're on guard duty, pal," he said. "I start nodding off, you rap me on the shoulder to keep me awake."

During the twenty-four-hour drive, my father fell asleep three times, and I knocked his right shoulder, hard, three delicious times. Once in Indiana, he had failed to follow the curve of the highway and drove the station wagon over a cow guard and into a field heavily populated with Black Angus cattle. When I punched his shoulder, he woke suddenly, dodging fifty cows on his way back to the highway.

"You'd get a court-martial for that one, navigator," he said.

"I kept all of us alive, Dad. This is getting dangerous."

We arrived at Uncle Willie's house on Hamlin Drive, where my mother had flown to the day before with her two youngest sons. Willie lived in a Polish neighborhood that looked like an elaborate card trick to me. The houses going up and down the street from Willie's were exact duplicates of one another as far as the eye could see. Variation was forbidden, and this neighborhood stretched for miles in all directions. You could sleepwalk out of Willie's house at night and find yourself lost as you tried to find your way back through a labyrinth that seemed to run on forever. It was an ugly house, as charmless as a Rubik's cube.

The Conroy kids were sent to the basement, where Uncle Willie had put pillows on the carpet and mattresses all around so we could camp out during our two weeks there. It turned out to be a deadly long visit, with tension breaking out unintentionally between my mother and grandmother, who lived nearby. Grandma Conroy was a harsh-voiced, unstylish woman who could have played a walk-on shrew in some of Shakespeare's lesser comedies. I never saw her wear makeup or try to prettify herself, and her dresses all looked like she had bought them from castaway bins at the Salvation Army. To her Southern grandchildren, she seemed to be yelling at us all the time.

"Don't do that. Get out of the way. Go back to the basement," she would say to us. It became a joke to my brothers and sisters that

Grandpa and Grandma Conroy had no idea what our names were and little curiosity in remedying this lack of knowledge. My father and his brothers played pinochle every day, then went out to catch a Cubs or White Sox game in the evening. My mother was left behind with her seven kids. Since she was terrified of getting lost in Chicago traffic, she could not use the car. When she asked my father to take her and the kids to the art museum, he refused. A fearsome argument broke out and I could feel Mom's fury rising as each day passed. Dad's neglect of Mom and her kids and his abandonment of his family by night and day were not sitting well with our pretty mother. The claustrophobia alive in that sad household was turning into a troubled, living thing.

It was Uncle Willie who set off the fuse. I had always liked my uncle Willie, because he was a schoolteacher and had no problem being around kids. He was the smallest of his brothers by far and looked like half a Conroy man as he stood in the middle of his platoon of tall brothers. His nose had been broken so many times in street fights that it gave him the appearance of a harmless bulldog. He was a droll man with a great sense of humor and we'd become golfing buddies on his visits to Beaufort. But Willie had a deep fear of my father that I could sense whenever Dad turned prickly. In his own house, Willie ignored my presence and barely spoke to me. When I offered to go golfing with him, he shrugged his shoulders and said he'd think about it. Three days later he took Dad golfing with some high school buddies of my father's, but didn't ask me to come. I never thought the same about Uncle Willie again.

But Willie did ask the combustible question that I think helped to get me into college. I was lingering after dinner as my grandfather and uncle were arguing about Chicago politics. Carol Ann had already joined the kids watching television in what she called "Dante's Inferno" in the basement. There was much talk about Mayor Richard Daley and the efficiency of his machine. My grandfather was a block captain for Mayor Daley and told a story of a man on his block who balked about promising to vote for the mayor in the next election. "He called Mayor Daley a corrupt Irish son of a bitch," my grandfather said, laughing at the memory. Grandpa Conroy reported it to the mayor's people and the man received no garbage pickup for three straight weeks. After his neighbors complained about the stench of his garbage overflow, the poor man appeared on the doorstep to beg for my grandfather's intercession with the mayor. He even added a small contribution of twenty-five dollars for the mayor's reelection campaign. His garbage was collected the following day, compliments of Mayor Daley.

"What a great story, Grandpa," I said. "Dad used to tell us about the great Daley machine, but I never knew how it worked."

"Are you interested in politics, Pat?" my grandfather asked. I was grateful he knew my name.

"Yes, sir, I sure am. I'm interested in everything," I replied.

Uncle Willie asked the question that ignited my parents' unspoken rage at each other yet again. "Where are you going to college, Pat?"

"That's a really good question, Willie. Where is Pat going to college next year?" Mom said in a voice that was pure acid.

"Shut up, Willie," my father growled. "It's none of your beeswax."

"None of my beeswax?" Willie echoed, not interpreting the signal flares of war lighting up my father's eyes. "Hell, college starts in two months' time, Don. If he's not enrolled in college now, he's not going."

"Drop it, Willie," my father warned again, but now my mother was in the middle of it.

"Pat hasn't even applied to college because the great wise one over there hasn't allowed him to do so," she said.

"Is your kid a dope, Don?" Willie said, studying me for signs of imbecility. "You can still get him into trade school."

"Shut your yap, Willie, or I'll shut it for you," Dad said.

"Shut my yap about what, Don?" Willie yelled back. "I teach school for a living. Pat should've been applying to colleges last fall. Our parents didn't have shit, and they sent all nine of their kids to college. Don't those Southern idiots have college counselors in their shitty schools?"

"We've got college counselors, Uncle Willie," I said.

"You shut the fuck up and get downstairs with the kids where you belong, asshole," Dad said to me.

"Let me know how the college search goes, Mom," I said.

"I told you to shut up," Dad said, then slapped me as I walked by.

"I will, Pat. That's a promise," Mom said. Dad slapped her in her face as my grandfather watched in wordless silence.

That night a fight between my parents rocked through the whole house. Five of us kids were watching TV in the basement when the screaming commenced. I went over and turned the TV off, then turned the lights out and said, "If Dad comes down here, pretend you're asleep. Otherwise, he'll start hitting."

The shouting ended thirty minutes after it began; then the door opened at the top of the stairs and Dad turned on the lights and came halfway down the stairs. When he satisfied himself that we were all asleep, he shut the door noiselessly, so as not to wake us up. The next day, we left Chicago for Iowa as the end of my boyhood moved insanely on.

Dad drove his family to the blue-collar town of Clinton, Iowa, where another of his brothers, Fr. Jim Conroy, served as chaplain in the local Catholic hospital. Uncle Jim was a gregarious pink-faced man who grew temperamental when he was tired and was rumored to pick fights with every bishop he served under during his embattled career as a priest. He became famous for saying the fastest mass in the Midwest, and Catholics flocked to his services when he took over Holy Family parish in Davenport at the end of his career. In my lifetime of listening to lusterless sermons by Catholic priests, I knew Uncle Jim was famous for being the worst public speaker in the Iowa diocese. I never trusted him after he'd slapped me around for a nightmarish six weeks when I went on a fishing trip with him to Minnesota, and I made sure that none of my brothers went anywhere near him.

But I rode with Uncle Jim from his hospital to his home on the Mississippi River that would be the Conroy family home until our quarters were ready for us to move into at Offutt Air Force Base. Uncle Jim confessed to me that his brother Willie had called and begged him to get those seven kids out of his house.

"You guys really got on Grandpa and Grandma Conroy's nerves," Father Jim said. "They were driving Willie crazy complaining about the mess you were making."

Uncle Jim drove across the Mississippi and turned north on a country road that paralleled the river, carrying us through beautiful Illinois farm country. We rode for twenty miles before he turned off to a dirt road, passed several farms, then pulled into the driveway of an insubstantial shack that looked both isolated and forlorn. The house sat on a hill above a tributary of the great river completely clogged with lily pads. You could fish all day and not get your hook wet.

When my mother toured the house, she erupted into another argument with Dad. "This is just great, Don. You're going to leave your wife and seven kids in this run-down dump with three beds, one toilet, no air-conditioning, no car, no stove, in the middle of goddamn nowhere. Real good thinking, Don. Great planning," she said, unhinged and wrathful. "There is no TV set, no radio, not a toy for the little kids to play with, not a bottle of milk or a loaf of bread or a jar of peanut butter. Jim, what were you thinking, having us here?"

"Not much, Peggy," Uncle Jim said. "I've never had a family. I just didn't think it through."

Dad said, "Okay, kids. Attention to orders. Start getting this place polished up. There'll be a formal inspection at fifteen hundred hours."

Of all the disconsolate summers the Conroy family spent following our Marine from base to base, everyone agrees that our summer on the Mississippi River was the most soul-killing of all. We sweltered in a summer heat that was brutal, and the house was so small and inadequate for our tribe that we stumbled over one another and got in each other's way from morning till night. In the mornings, we woke with nothing to do, and went to sleep because there was nothing to do at night, either.

Uncle Jim was solicitous and as helpful as he could be and provided our only lifeline to civilization and to groceries. Several times a week he would take us all for a swim at a public lake in a nearby town. It was the summer I thought my mother's mental health began to deteriorate, and I think my sister Carol Ann suffered a mental breakdown caused by that ceaseless drumbeat of days. Carol Ann would turn her face to the wall and weep piteously all day long. Mom appeared sick and exhausted and slept long periods during the day, ignoring the many needs of my younger siblings. The days were interminable and Mom grew more weakened and distressed than I had ever seen her. I asked what was wrong and how I could help.

"Everything!" she would scream. "Everything. Take your pick.

Make my kids disappear. Make Don vanish into thin air. Leave me alone."

. . .

In July I got a brief respite when I took a Trailways bus on a two-day trip to Columbia, South Carolina, to play in the North-South all-star game. I'd not touched a basketball since February, was out of shape, and played a lackluster game when I needed to have a superlative one. After the game, Coach Hank Witt, an assistant football coach at The Citadel, the military college of South Carolina, came up to tell me that I had just become part of The Citadel family, and he wished to welcome me. Coach Witt handed me a Citadel sweatshirt and I delivered him a full, sweaty body hug that he extricated himself from with some difficulty. In my enthusiasm, I was practically jumping out of my socks. By then, I'd given up hope of going to any college that fall and had thought about entering the Marine Corps as a recruit at Parris Island because all other avenues had been closed off to me. My father never told me nor my mother that he had filled out an application for me to attend The Citadel. I danced my way back into the locker room below the university field house and practically did a soft-shoe as I soaped myself down in the shower. In my mind I'd struggled over the final obstacles, and there were scores of books and hundreds of papers written into my future. Because I'd been accepted at The Citadel, I could feel the launching of all the books inside me like artillery placements I'd camouflaged in the hills. The possibilities seemed limitless as I dressed in the afterglow of that message. In my imagination, getting a college degree was as lucky as a miner stumbling across the Comstock Lode, except that it could never be taken away from me or given to someone else. I could walk down the streets for the rest of my life, hearing people say, "That boy went to college." And then it dawned on me that the military college of South Carolina did not preen about being a crucible for novelists or poets. Hell, I thought in both bravado and innocence, I'll make it safe for both.

I returned to our exile on the Mississippi with great reluctance and thought Mom looked even more haggard and spent. She looked like a sleepwalker going through her morning chores. I was still disturbed by her appearance when Dad rang the house for his weekly phone call.

"I'm worried about Mom," I said, trying to sound every inch the adult. "She doesn't seem to be herself. She's totally exhausted."

"Worry about something you can do something about, pal. Give your mother the phone. You're wasting my time and money."

"Hey, Mom," I yelled to her in the grassless yard. "Dad's on the phone."

It was the summer I tackled some of the great Russian novelists, such as Dostoyevsky and Turgenev. I entered the soul of Russia while swinging in a hammock with the Mississippi River visible in the distance. Mom and Carol Ann read *The Brothers Karamazov* after I did and I remember discussing the book and what it meant to us. We were breaking camp and moving into our new quarters in the middle of August. Not one of us looked back at that miserable cottage when we left it; nor did any of us ever see it again. We had been banished there for two months, and none of us remembers having a good day there in rural Illinois during the summer that never seemed to end.

It was two weeks before I left for The Citadel when we moved into our new house on Offutt Air Force Base. Mom took me to the PX to buy the socks, underwear, T-shirts, and military shoes The Citadel required. Dad had given me his trunk, which he had taken with him to World War II. Before my grand departure, my mother took me out to the officers' club for lunch, which she had never done before. It was the first time I ever considered how a mother must feel when her oldest child goes off to college. It seemed like some essential rite of passage that moved me more than I could express to her. I don't think I would have survived my trial by father had she not been there every step of the way. I tried to tell her how much she meant to me and how I adored everything about her. I told her I wanted to do things in the world that would make her proud to be my mother.

My mother took my hand and said that I'd made her proud already. I had survived Santini and provided a great example to my younger brothers and sisters. Then she told me a secret she had kept from the rest of the family. She had just discovered that she had cancer and had to have a massive hysterectomy sometime in the near future. There was a real possibility that she would die on the operating table. She wanted me to promise her something. I told her I would promise her anything, and would fulfill that promise.

My mother said, "If I die because of the operation, Pat, I want you to promise me you'll quit The Citadel and come home to raise your brothers and sisters. I'm afraid your father would end up killing them all."

"He may start off with me," I said.

"He thinks you're a match for him," she said.

"Not yet. But I'm getting there, Mom."

"Then promise me."

"If you die," I said, starting to cry just mentioning the words, "I'll quit The Citadel and come home to raise my brothers and sisters."

"Get Tim and Tom in high school," she said, "and then you can start your life all over again."

"I promise," I said, through tears.

On September 2, 1963, I left the city of Omaha by train to walk into the fearful mouth of The Citadel's plebe system. Even my father had not prepared me to encounter such ferocious abuse. I hated it from the moment I walked into the barracks until the time the upperclassmen recognized me the following spring. It was a nightmare from beginning to end, and I found nothing ennobling about it. I'd been brought up in the United States Marine Corps and my military education was complete the day I entered the barracks. In the Marines, you fed your men first, and then the officer in charge ate only after his men were fed. At The Citadel, the cadets hounded and brutalized and starved the plebes. The Romeo company cadre was especially savage and feral. I've not quite found it in my heart to forgive them almost fifty years later.

As a novelist, however, I thought I was blessed with my Citadel education. It gave me wider knowledge of the nature of atrocity and mankind's capacity for infinite cruelty. I believe The Citadel plebe system prepared me quite well for the setbacks and disappointments of life—it even prepared me for the savagery and jealousies of my brother and sister writers. It gave me a narrative of darkness that I could move through my life's work. It gave me a story line that was action-packed and adrenaline-fueled, since my plebe system was not like your day in the eating clubs of Princeton. I've ended up writing about my college as much as any writer in American history. It became my crucible of origin, whose anthems were all warlike and barbarous and wild. I'd been tested by American males as few writers had ever been, and I was the handiwork of the school's grim codes. They sensed my weakness, my disabling emotional frailty, and they hardened me into the likeness of themselves, made me pretend to be one of them. It took me many years to understand I *was* actually one of them. It took The Citadel much longer to accept me into its own staunch brotherhood.

Soon after I entered college, my mother was operated on for her hysterectomy, and the doctors made a mess of it. As she predicted, she almost died on the operating table. For a long, agonizing month, she was in the hospital with her life in danger the whole time. I would have been frantic but the plebe system was giving me more than I could handle and I was fighting for my survival every day. When I went home to Omaha on the Christmas break, Mom was there, but I was anxious about her and asked Dad so many questions about her health that I annoyed him.

"Hey, you her doctor, sports fan? She's fine. She's still a little weak, but she's getting there," Dad said.

When I burst through the door in my excitement to see my family, I did what I had done since I was a five-year-old boy and went down on one knee to receive the delirious charge of the Great Dog Chippie, who would fly into my arms. This time there was no charge; there was nothing to pet; there was no Great Dog Chippie.

Mom came out of the kitchen to watch me and said, "I had to put the dog down. It was for the best."

I hugged my mother furiously and kissed her a dozen times. She pushed me back, rather brusquely, I thought, and looked at me with eyes I did not recognize and said in a voice that was not my mother's voice, "You can sleep downstairs in the basement with Mike, Kathy, and Jimbo. You don't have a bed now, Pat, so we borrowed one for you."

"What do you mean, I don't have a bed?"

"You don't live here anymore," she said.

Somewhere during the course of that hysterectomy, in the scrimmage of blood and hormones and the great shock of estrogen shutdown that my mother suffered during her morbid ordeal, I had lost part of the mother who raised me, the sweet girl, the smiling one. She had left part of herself on that operating table and a darker Peg Conroy made her way forward in the world, an angrier one, and I think a more treacherous one. My brothers and sisters fight me on this and say that Mom always was the same mother she was in the end. Though hormonal mysteries have always been beyond the realm of my understanding, I still hold to the claim that there was a significant change in my mother's personality after her operation. My brothers and sisters hoot in derision over this and accuse me of worshiping a mother who was my own creation or invention. My version of Peg Conroy rings hollow and untrue to them, and they're not shy about letting me know it. To them she was vain, cheap, and had grown bone-tired with the exhaustion of motherhood.

In despair, I flew back to The Citadel to complete my abysmal plebe year. That was my job now and I was going to do it. But I faced it with a damaged mother and a Chippie-less world I could never repair.

CHAPTER 2

Fun and Games at The Citadel

After the holidays, I left the city of Omaha yet again for a two-and-a-half-day journey back to Charleston. Liberated from my father's house at long last, I felt my adventure in life had finally begun. During the train trip, I entertained extravagant fantasies of becoming a writer. I pretended I was the young Thomas Wolfe gorging on the images of small towns and cornfields as I returned to the South. I wrote an earnest poem about two-stoplight villages. As passive as a lamb, I was traveling back to a slaughterhouse for boys, where I would have to kill the poet in me as an act of survival. I'd never encountered another college student who was as mismatched and insufficient for the test of his chosen college. Though I was heroically unprepared for my immersion into this final, unsurpassable test of manhood, The Citadel was my only chance to earn a degree, and I planned to make the most of it.

When I entered The Citadel in the fall, I thought I was going to college. This delusion was quickly dispelled. What I entered was the plebe system. I hated it from the moment I walked into the barracks. Even my father had not prepared me for such ferocious abuse. What I hadn't factored in was the peerless cruelty of the training cadre. That the plebe year would prove its worth as an inflammable touchstone, a worthy successor to my father's trial by fire, came as a great surprise to me. I thought I'd endured the great tempestuous tests of manhood by surviving my father's fists and becoming a letterman in every sport I participated in during high school. I had forged my soul in a fire pit of cruelty and discipline and was not expecting those darkling, black winds that The Citadel threw at me for the next four years. Desperately, I wanted to be a writer and didn't see how my immersion into the annihilating white noise of suffering was going to help me in my quest.

Though I survived the plebe system, I did not distinguish myself during that rite of passage. For the first three months, I lived in terror that my mother might not recover from the botched hysterectomy that had her lingering near death for several days. On the rare occasions I was allowed to call home, I talked to Stanny, my maternal grandmother, who was often drunk and lugubrious as she reported on my mother's condition. "Yo' mama's dying and that's the honest truth, Pat," she'd say to me. "You might as well quit that school and come home to raise your brothers and sisters. You'll be doing it sooner or later anyhow. She's getting weaker every day. Pray hard for your mama, Pat. She's not going to make it. Our girl's dying, son, just dying."

Then Stanny would hang up or pass out with the phone in her hand, and I would sit in a phone booth shivering with despair. My future was all paralysis and grief to me. The plebe system had gotten the better of me, and my time on the basketball team brought me close to a physical breakdown. I was not strong enough to face a world without Peg Conroy. I staggered my way toward June.

The cadre tried to turn me into a mirror image of them, and they trained me to torture plebes as they had molested me and my classmates. When I was going to sleep at night, I promised that I wouldn't model myself after a single member of Romeo company. If I ever led a platoon or squadron, I planned for my men to love and respect and follow me. They would eat before I ate and sleep before I went to bed. I would try to be more courageous in battle than I asked them to be. My battalion who loved me would slaughter your battalion who hated you was the summation of my military philosophy long before I entered the gates of The Citadel. I developed that philosophy as the son of the Marine Corps because I knew many Marines who hated serving with my father. The Citadel's plebe system taught me nothing about leadership and everything about humiliation. It was never to be for me, then or now. I was not one of them.

I did discover, however, the joys and mysteries of The Citadel's library, which for most cadets was as remote and undiscoverable as an oasis below the Atlas Mountains. For four years, I would enter the library and find a welcoming world of solitude and books awaiting my inspection, and in their mute attentiveness, I heard those same books trying to call out my name as I wandered through their marvelous stacks at my leisure. There, at the Daniel Library, I found the college education I was looking for, and I would carry piles of books across the parade ground at night, and bring back the books I'd finished reading the next afternoon. Without my knowledge, the faculty wives began to call me "the boy with the books," even though they couldn't put a name to my face until I began to play well as a basketball player. In the classroom, my English teachers were all Southern white men both conservative and kindly, but they were helpful in my attempt to become a writer and did everything they could to nurture that uncommon ambition in a member of the Corps of Cadets. When I wrote drivel, they claimed it showed promise. When I wrote with mediocre results, they calmly instructed me to make it better with more of an eye toward craft. When I turned in something good, they told me I was on my way. They never slapped me down or ridiculed me or heaped derision on me, because I believe they saw the impossibility of the task I'd set up for myself. Col. John Doyle wanted me to be "The Citadel's Faulkner." Col. James Carpenter chose Dickens for my emulation. James Harrison wanted me to shoot for a slot near Henry James. As impossible as those goals were, I learned that it is lovely for a writer to receive such validation at so young an age by the men who led him or her by the hand to an appreciation of the world's greatest novelists. Every day I found myself thrust into a building of fifty thousand books famished for readership. By slow degrees my writing was getting better, more hard-nosed and less abstract. It was plain to me I lacked genius when it came to my ambition to write books, but I could ingest all of the writings of those born with the gift.

My father did not attend my graduation at The Citadel; nor did he ever see me outfitted in the full dress of a Friday parade. During my four years there, he never made a single appearance on campus and never took any interest in my college life. I remember calling Dad for help only one time, and his response to me played a large part in shaping my entire life.

During my sophomore year, I enrolled in air force pilot training that would begin the following summer. It was 1964 and the conflict in Vietnam was escalating at an alarming rate. My father would be sent to that war zone the following year. Patriotism was religion at The Citadel, where I didn't hear a radical or discordant note about America's participation in the war. At evening mess, they began to recite the names of Citadel grads who had lost their lives in battle. By my senior year, I knew grads whose names were called. I would lose eight of my classmates, including four boys I loved. The Vietnam War still stings in my memory.

I arrived at The Citadel as patriotic as any boy in America. That is how my parents raised me, and I'm still comfortable with that honorary designation. I came to college thinking I would one day take off from a carrier deck as a hotshot pilot in my father's squadron. Already I'd developed a fascination for military tactics and the infinite patience it took to form a plan of battle. I had walked the battlefields of Gettysburg, First Manassas, Vicksburg, and Kennesaw. In high school, a beloved teacher, Joseph Monte, had gotten me to read Thucydides on the Spartan battle of Thermopylae. I shivered with delight when I read the quote of the Spartan commander: "They have the numbers; we, the heights."

It was the first bit of military tactics I memorized, and it resonated like poetry with me. But my attraction to the rules of battle did not contribute to the flow of another habit I brought to the world of ideas—my need to read everything written down about a subject before I could render a judgment on it. The Citadel's library served up a slender, inauspicious collection of books on Vietnam, but I stumbled on the works of Bernard Fall, who introduced me to his assessment of French colonial warfare in Vietnam. In a public speaking course, I wrote up and delivered a speech on Dien Bien Phu, a classic battle where the French forces found themselves overrun and defeated by a Vietnamese army in the highlands. Several cadets told me that my speech had nearly put them to sleep because no one in the class had ever heard of the battle of Dien Bien Phu. Both The Citadel and America would soon learn you shouldn't fall asleep when you're receiving information about Ho Chi Minh and the military generals he put into the field.

As part of my air force training, I accompanied several busloads of my classmates out to receive our physicals for flight school. I remember my excitement as we drove onto the base. I was surrounded by classmates such as Charlie Buzze and Johnny Sams, who went on to have distinguished careers as air force pilots. Unlike me, they were excellent cadets filled with a fervent spirit for The Citadel I could not even pretend to match. But I thought I would one day outfly the best of them, that I'd one day fly in my father's squadron, and that I would take to the air against him and kick his ass during a maneuver that involved simulated air-to-air combat. These were the dreams I took from the fighter pilot's household.

My physical was going fine as I performed the tasks that were simple for any college athlete. Then I lined up with a whole herd of boys for an exhaustive series of eye tests that were the most essential part of a pilot's physical exam. In the first exam, the doctor shocked me by saying, in front of my classmates, that I was so nearsighted I'd never qualify for a pilot's license. Trembling, I stumbled into the next booth, where I was tested for color blindness. I flipped through a book with pages blotched with different colors, but revealing a number hidden away in the fields of color. I got the first five numbers right, then turned the page and didn't see any. The doctor announced that I was red-green color-blind, the kiss of death for a fighter pilot. In the next test, they discovered I had the worst case of depth perception ever seen at a testing of Citadel men who had received the call to be pilots.

"No wonder I can't shoot a basketball," I said to myself.

When I left the Charleston Air Force Base that day, I had flunked every single eye test that a man could use to his advantage as he flew through enemy air corridors. I was a washout even before I got started. Devastated, I returned to campus.

But I held on to a single, last-minute hope. The next day I called my father at his desk at the Pentagon, where he now worked, and told him what had happened to me at the physical. Though I despaired initially, I had held on to the many times when my father had made phone calls on behalf of other aviators' sons to get them waivers for their failed tests. He had made it look easy when fighting for the other flyboys' kids, but he wouldn't even make a call for his own son. He thought Marine aviation would be a much better place without me up in the air with my color-blind ass.

"Dad, just get me a waiver. That's all I'm asking," I pleaded.

"Negative," he said, infuriating me.

"You've done it for other Marine kids, Dad. I've heard you do it."

"You've got bad peepers, son," Dad said. "I don't want anyone in my squadron who's got bad peepers. And you got the worst I've ever heard of. You've got your mother's eyeballs. Too bad for you. But good for the corps."

"I wanted to fly like you did," I said.

"Tough titty, winkie dink," Dad said. "Look, you might be able to make it in the infantry. You'll never be a fighter pilot. But hey, if you're a grunt fighting on the ground, I might do you a big favor and dip my wings to say howdy when I pass overhead."

My military career ended at that moment.

. . .

My father quivered with joy over my failure to become a fighter pilot. He had always referred to me as a "shit basketball player," even though I became captain and most valuable player in my senior year at The Citadel. When I made gold stars in academic achievement, he mocked my 3.8 GPA as a demonstration of my love for pussies and faggots who wrote froufrou poetry. Where I was concerned, he remained unimpressible, but I don't think I ever stopped trying to please him. My father treated me with a permafrost persona, making him as approachable to me as an Alp. He was all snowdrift and glacier without a demilitarized zone in his makeup. But he taught me how to hate. My God, he taught that lesson well.

But the Vietnam War was a battle I had to wage inside myself, and I read everything I could about it. The zeitgeist swept me up in the gun sight of anxiety that was fixing America in its crosshairs. At The Citadel I didn't hear a discouraging vowel uttered against the war, and I found this intellectually repellent. I couldn't find a good reason for the search-and-destroy missions; nor have I heard of one since. My father had taught me the doctrine of the folly of fighting a land war in Asia, and the Vietnam War stood in as a substitute for a petri dish, proving his theory. In my AF ROTC class, I devised an air battle plan where I took out every dam and wharf in Hanoi, but was told that my targets were off-limits. Though I would have the city of Hanoi swimming and their water supply destroyed, I flunked the assignment because I'd not followed the rules of engagement. Finally, I could see no difference between the Vietnamese trying to control their own destiny and the American colonists rebelling to decide their own fate. Even though I've had harrowing second thoughts about my actions during that war and wished I'd gone in as a Marine lieutenant, I don't think I was wrong about the futility and fatuousness of that conflict. Smart governments fight only wars they intend to win. Fifty thousand names on that slab of immemorial marble in D.C., and I can't blow up the dams and harbors around Hanoi? I should've served my country, but did not. But if America could not convince a military brat like me that it was doing the right thing, it was going to have to come up with a hell of a sales pitch for the rest of the country. I said no to the war, and it makes no difference if I think I was right or wrong. I marched in peace demonstrations in five cities as eight of my classmates were being cut up and outfitted for body bags in Vietnam. The war gleams like a bloody wound on my generation's soul, and I'm scarred by both sides.

I left the graduation stage at The Citadel and took a job teaching psychology at Beaufort High School, where I'd graduated four years earlier. In Beaufort, I rented a small cottage, since my parents were now living in Hawaii. I fell in love with teaching, and thought I'd be doing it for the rest of my life. The students I met in the next two years changed my perception of myself, since they found me hilarious, and not bad to look at (according to my female students). I'd never known either of those things about myself.

At night I wrote poetry in my cottage that overlooked the Beaufort River and did some innocent, though fixable, damage to the English language. In the American Government course I taught, I brought in Marines who'd fought in battles around Vietnam, as well as antiwar activists who were eloquent in their refusal to accept the premises of that war. The debates were fierce and stimulating. I thought a class functioned best as an honorable field where all ideas were welcome visitors.

In those years following my graduation, Citadel classmates began to argue with me about the wrongness or rightness of the Vietnam War. By then several of them were veterans of battle. Steve Grubb, for example, had been severely wounded in the foot, so that I had to help him into my house as he struggled with his crutches. Steve, who had been president of the honor court, a member of the sword drill, and a battalion major voted most likely to succeed, had been my model of the perfect cadet when I was at The Citadel. Although I revered him, we argued long into the night about the war. As low tide changed to high and the sun rose, we were still tossing ideas back and forth. When I helped him out to the car, we hugged each other hard, and I thanked him for his visit.

I didn't think to thank Steve Grubb for his service to his country, however. It never crossed my mind to thank him for shedding his blood, and the numerous medals he had won for valor. That's how a gentleman and a son of the South, a Citadel man and a true liberal, would've handled that most delicate situation.

Four months after my meeting with Steve Grubb, I walked into my new job on Daufuskie Island, where I became the first white person to teach black children in that part of the Jim Crow South. Already, the sixties had me by the throat.

CHAPTER 3

Daufuskie Island

My childhood was but prelude and crucible for the mess I was about to make of my adult life. On October 10, 1969, when I married Barbara Jones, a Vietnam War widow with two small children, I was in my first months of teaching on Daufuskie Island, a position I took after two years teaching at Beaufort High. I was proud of the job and aware of its historical significance, and was starting to make some headway with children who had been intellectually murdered at birth. None of the Daufuskie kids or their parents were told that a white teacher was coming to the Mary Fields School that September. It had shocked the island when I stood waiting as the school bus pulled up on the first day. Later, some of the kids admitted they thought the school board might have sent a deranged Klansman to torment them and spy on their families. It was a job that would unsettle my life and cause me to take stock of my centrifugal attraction to storm and battle. I was an impulsive, combative young man lacking any skills for compromise and diplomacy.

Because my wife, Barbara, would not consider raising her two young daughters on an isolated South Carolina island that housed witch doctors but no licensed MDs, and lacked paved roads, telephones, or a store of any kind, we had to buy a house in Beaufort.

I owned a house before my parents did. Barbara and I purchased a two-story, many-columned, slightly run-down house on the "Point," what Beaufort's historic district is called. Because of the Marine Corps, I had grown up in house trailers and Quonset huts and Capehart housing from El Toro to Camp Lejeune. No one ever wanted to own a house more than I did. To me, our house was a mansion, even though it was built around the turn of the century and lacked the panache of the antebellum homes that flanked both sides of 403 Hancock Street. On the day we moved in, Barbara and I lifted wineglasses to each other as we sat on the second-story balcony hidden from the street by the feathery stutter of palmetto fronds shaken by a salt wind off the river. I felt like I had bought a palace for my wife, my children, and for me, and I still think that over forty years later.

The following summer, my entire family came to Beaufort to stay with Barbara and me at our new house while waiting for their own house to be ready, not too far from mine. Dad had received orders for his second tour of Vietnam, and they were returning to the States after being stationed in Hawaii. My mother had rented a house on East Street, only three blocks away, but repairs on it would not be completed for three weeks. I could not wait for everyone to see the extraordinary house we had bought and begun to fix up. Famous among my friends for lacking the skills of a handyman, I had become somewhat sufficient in minor repair work and was astonished to realize my favorite store in town had become Fordham's Hardware. My brothers and sisters had never seen me hold a tool in my hand, and I could not wait to hammer a nail for them. That my family was going to be staying with me pleased me beyond all reckoning. By buying this house, I had discovered that I had a gift for hospitality. Barbara and I loved inviting people to our home for rest and conversation, for good food and drink and safe harbor. When they arrived, my family was stunned by the house's size and grandeur. I kissed my mother, and she whispered, "Careful, Pat. Your father's on the warpath." And of course, she was right.

My father was leaving that July for his second tour of duty in South Vietnam, and he never had a meaner summer in his violent, disgraceful life. From the moment he entered my house, I thought Don Conroy and I would come to blows every time we passed each other in that spacious, wonderful home.

"My, my, you must think you're quite the Southern gentleman," he said, the only time he referred to the house.

He was on the prowl and dangerous, and my mother's hatred of him was now an open wound between them. They could barely utter a civil word to each other except when Barbara was around. Then they would playact as though the Conroys were an upstanding family and not the American tragedy we insiders knew us to be. My mother's beautiful face had a haunted, frantic look, and my father's eyes were withering and cruel. In the family lore, the Conroy children will often try to select my father's worst and most out-of-control years, and 1970 always rears its violent head and captures a couple of votes. My contempt of him was now a wordless, unsigned agreement between us. I looked at him with loathing and he returned it with equal and passionate measure.

All this the Conroy family had managed to hide from everybody. Barbara became the latest victim of the elaborate opera of evasion. She thought my family was hilarious and rambunctious and fun to be around. But that would come apart on the night known in the annals of my brothers and sisters as movie night with the Conroy family. Mom and Dad had taken the four kids—Kathy, Jim, Tim, and Tom (Carol Ann and Mike had gone off to college by then)—to the movies over at Parris Island. I felt the tension in the house subside when my father went out the front door and pulled his car down the street, his family silent around him. He looked mean enough to carry claymore mines in his cheeks, and I was happy to see him gone. In a week, he would leave for Vietnam, which made me like the war, because it took him off to Asia every couple of years, and I knew my mother and the kids were safe from his fists.

I was asleep at eleven thirty when I heard the ancient, ordained noises below. Like an aroused lion, I awoke to the sound of my mother's sobbing and of a hand slapping her face. Then I heard my brothers and sisters trying to suppress their own weeping while my father whispered for them to shut up. Here I came, a deadly young man of twenty-five, and a game one, too. I slipped into my jeans and Docksiders, and I came down the steps noiseless as a serpent. I witnessed the next slap to my mother, and something snapped in me, became unglued, and I drove my shoulder into my drunken father like a linebacker taking on a fullback in a dive play. I drove him out of the foyer, through the screen door, and laid him out on the floorboards of the first-floor veranda. Rising fast, I kicked my drunken father down the steps and across the front yard. Then I lifted him up, punched his ugly face, placed him behind the wheel of his car, and said, "You ever touch my mother again and I'll kill you. You ever touch my brothers and sisters again and I'll beat you with a tire iron until your heart stops and my arm gets tired. You get it, you worthless son of a bitch? That's the last time, pal. The last time in this lifetime. Got it? Now, you get your drunken, worthless ass out of my yard, and never darken the door of my house again."

"Kiss my ass," my father said, slurring his words.

I punched him in the face and said, "Get out of here, Colonel."

When I returned to the house, my mother, three brothers, and sister did everything but throw me a ticker-tape parade. I walked through the front door and whispered to them, "Family life. Don't you love it?" They surrounded me and hugged me and held on to me as a gladfulness and keen elation filled me up. I knew the things David knew when he brought Goliath crashing to the ground. Then all of us were frozen when we heard Barbara screaming from where she stood, alone on the upstairs banister: "What is going on down there? Something terrible is going on!"

I went to the stairs and said in a hearty voice, "It's nothing, dear. Nothing at all. One of the kids tripped and got hurt. But it's fine now. Go back to bed."

"You're lying to me! Something awful is going on in my house, and I demand to know what it is."

"It sounded a lot worse than it was, Barbara," I said. "It's all been taken care of."

"Peg, are you there?" Barbara called out. "Your son's a goddamn liar, Peg, but not a very good one. Please tell me!"

It was at this moment that the Conroy family sense of humor betrayed me. My brother Jim started to laugh, and he set off Kathy, then Tim, and finally Tom. When Tom began giggling, my mother lost it. She began laughing, though she still had blood on her lips. Barbara came down the stairs in her robe and slippers, and by then we were all laughing uncontrollably in the vestibule beneath the stairs.

"Is this family completely nuts?" Barbara asked me, and my siblings began to sink to the floor, doubled up in laughter.

When we returned to bed, I told Barbara the whole story of my father's long, debilitating war against his family. I had never revealed to another soul that he had been beating my mother since I was conscious of being alive, and that I remember hating him when I was in a high chair, my face burning with shame and humiliation that I could do nothing to protect my mother. My father could sense my hatred of him, and he began to beat me with some regularity when I was still in diapers. He always went for the face. Don Conroy was not the "pop you on the fanny" kind of dad. My brother Jim once told me that his first memory as a child was my father having me by the throat, beating my head against the wall. When my father laughed and denied it, I informed him that I could show him the wall.

For hours, I talked to my wife and told her of savage beatings that I had received over a lifetime. "But you're such a nice boy, Pat," Barbara said.

"Yes, I was," I answered in the darkness.

"Do you think it will ever stop?" she asked.

"I think it stopped tonight."

After Barbara drifted off to sleep, I began to worry about my father. In my last glimpse of him, he was driving down Hancock Street, weaving and out of control. He was far drunker than I had imagined.

Again, I lifted myself out of bed and dressed in the darkness. Lightly, I skipped down the stairs and went out to the front yard, where I looked down Hancock Street for any sign of Dad. I began to jog down the street, now badly shaken by my violent encounter, and guilt-ridden that I was the source of that violence. I regretted kicking him, and wished I had fought him straight up, but I had kicked him across the yard, and that's what I had to live with the rest of my life.

Dad had not gotten far. I found his car on the Green, a park-like acre in the middle of the Point surrounded by stately antebellum homes. He'd passed out on the grass and was lying on his back six feet away from the car, its motor still running. I switched off the engine and walked over to sit down beside my father. I thought, as I studied his face, what a horrible thing it is for a boy to hate his father, how it harms that boy and damages him, how it makes him afraid and cowering every waking moment, how it debases and haunts his nightmares, and how the fighter pilot dives for his son even in his sleep. There is nowhere a boy can run to, no one who can help him. As I studied my father's face in the moonlight, I realized I would always be serving a life sentence without parole because of the unpardonable cruelty of this one man. Now, on this night, my father had proffered his final gift to me—because I had kicked him across the lawn and beat him with my fists, I sat studying him at my leisure, deep in thought on the first night I ever thought of myself earning my natural birthright as a violent man. I was devastated. All during my childhood, I had sworn that I would never be a thing like him, and here before me, drunken and beaten, was living proof that I was the spitting image of Don Conroy.

But, in telling Barbara my story, I had felt a great lifting of the spirit, a cleansing and scouring and airy rising of the soul toward light. I felt what truth tasted like, and it rolled like honey off my tongue. I could change my life as a man if I could just quit pretending I came from a normal American family, if I could grant myself permission to hate my father with every ounce of loathing I could bring to the surface. If I was going to be truthful as a writer, I had to let the hate out into the sunshine. I owed it to myself to let my father know how much I hated every cell of the body that had brought mine to life.

I reached over and shook him. Turning over slowly, he tried to rise to his knees, and I helped him get to his feet. I put his left arm around my shoulder and we staggered toward the car together. I was going to tell him what I thought about him, but the words got confused in the passage, jumbled in the inexact translation as often happens in the strange world inhabited by fathers and sons. As I groped for the proper words, they formed by themselves—truth-telling words that could not be censored or slowed down, life-changing words for a bruised soul. In utter shock, I heard myself say out loud to the fighter pilot, "I love you, Dad."

My father looked startled, as though I held a hand grenade up to his eyes with its pin dangling between my lips. He took off running, but drunks don't run well, and I was beside him in a flash. I whispered in his ear, "I love you, Dad." He lunged in the opposite direction, where

I pursued and caught up with him and turned him like a steer with the taunting yet magical four words that the Great Santini, a disgraceful father, could not bear to hear. Every time I said the words, he would stagger away from them as though I were pouring acid into his eardrum.

When I wrote *The Great Santini*, I wrote about the drama on the Green exactly as it happened, and my father hated that scene more than anything I ever wrote. He told every journalist who would listen to him that I had made the whole thing up. "My son has a bit of an overactive imagination, as the critics have pointed out," he said.

When they filmed the movie in Beaufort, the actors Robert Duvall and Michael O'Keefe performed the scene with such brilliance and accuracy that I would have sworn they had been eyewitnesses to the event itself. Of course, Hollywood filmed it on the Green, at the exact spot of its provenance.

But that was all in the future. That night, after exhausting my father by chasing him around the Green, I helped him into the car and drove him back to my house and put him to bed on the living room couch. I went into the kitchen and put on a pot of coffee. When the sun came up I was drinking a cup of coffee on the front steps of my house, every cell of my body ablaze with astonishment and wonder and the full knowledge that I had just lived through the most amazing night of my life.

. . .

When I took Dad to the Marine Corps Air Station to begin his second tour of duty in Vietnam, it was only a few days after the night I would always think of as movie night with the Conroys. Dad and I did not speak a word to each other on the way to the base, but he grabbed my arm and squeezed it until it hurt and said, "Hey, asshole, never get yourself killed in a politician's war."

As I drove home that morning I realized that I would have to turn myself into a cunning translator of my father's indirect, sclerotic use of the language. In his own rough way, I thought Dad had just taken baby steps toward some future day in the sun when he could actually say he loved his children.

So my father went off to war for the last time in his life, and a month later, Walter Trammell, the superintendent of schools, fired me from my job on Daufuskie Island, after a scant nine months on the job. He fired me for gross neglect of duty, insubordination, being AWOL, and conduct unbecoming to a professional educator. After a recommendation like that, I would never teach again. The following day, I received my notice that I'd been drafted and was to report to Fort Jackson in ten days. I had reaped the whirlwind at last and placed my family in the most perilous situation imaginable.

Looking back, I can see how strange I must have seemed to a town like Beaufort, a white Southern boy who was a pain-in-the-ass liberal who believed in every part of the civil rights movement, welcomed the stirrings of feminism, and protested against the Vietnam War. My own zeitgeist had ambushed me in the streets, and the sixties changed everything about how I thought. Because I was raised on Hollywood movies, it wasn't difficult to tell the good guys from the bad guys when the fire hoses were turned on black people in Alabama who were singing songs about freedom. A different kind of white Southerner was forming all over the South, but we were young and our own voices had not been heard yet and would not be fully voiced until the elections of Jimmy Carter and Bill Clinton. Though I wanted to be part of this momentous change, I arrived a bit late to the dance.

My firing became a small news item across the state. When Joe Cummings of *Newsweek* came to file a story about the incident, it became a syndicated item in papers across the nation. Hollywood began calling, and Beau Bridges, the actor, came and spent the night at our house and fed my new daughter, Melissa, her two-o'clock bottle. A telegram to the selective service bureau in Washington slowed my induction until an inspection could be done by the South Carolina selective services director. Neighbors began writing letters to the draft board protesting that Barbara Conroy had already lost one husband to Vietnam and now was in danger of losing a second. Our house was in an uproar from morning until night, filled with friends who came up to help in whatever way they could—the scene was hip, inspirational, argumentative, and fast-talking, the nearest thing to the sixties revolution that ever happened to the white folks of Beaufort.

Then I lost the trial to get my job back, and the sixties were over for me. My first book, *The Boo*, was published the same week of the trial, and my mother planned an elegant party for me at her house on the Point. As my teaching life began to fade into the distance, the secret life of writing began to assert itself once more in my aggrieved psyche. I had begun to write about my year on the island and how that year had transformed me by demonstrating the shameful atrocities committed against black children in the South. "Separate but equal" is the most contemptible line ever spoken by a Southern tongue, and it was spoken a million times by a million liars all over the Southern states. With my time on Daufuskie, I thought I'd discovered some lost island made backward because of its isolation from the mainland. By accident, I'd discovered America, and the great tragedy would soon be clear to all, that America turned its hateful eye on the poor kids in the country— from sea to shining sea. I wrote *The Water Is Wide* in a white-hot fever, letting my rage pour out in burning funnels of lava. I wrote both day and night as I tried to re-create a magical year where I steered my boat, happy as a river otter, through weeds and rivers and vast miles of emerald marsh as I taught eighteen kids eager to learn about the world I set before them. Now my task was to tell the world about those kids, and I kept filling up page after page with words.

But I was a young man with no idea what being young meant. When I began to write *The Water Is Wide*, I was twenty-five years old and could not yet write about all the things I felt in my heart. I found my own voice elusive, and I harbored the melancholy dread of the amateur writer that every word I put down on paper was worthless and of no interest to anyone else. Still, I persisted, and the manuscript began to grow, and the yellow legal pages began to pile up on my desk. Somewhere in the middle of the passage, I realized that I had a story to tell, and one that had never been written by a white boy in my part of the world. Though I'm sure they were terrified doing so, Barbara and my mother were like lionesses protecting me from intrusions from the outside world.

In January, the selective service in Columbia requested my presence for a meeting at state headquarters. A friend named Zach Sklar prepared me for the meeting with exquisite care. I had met Zach because he had been one of the "California boys" who had spent a semester on Daufuskie for the sociology program. His father was a novelist and playwright; his mother had danced with Martha Graham's troupe in New York, and years later Zach would receive an Academy Award nomination for adapting the screenplay for *JFK*. A low-key intellectual, Zach possessed one of the sharpest political minds I've ever encountered as he prepared me for what could be a life-changing ordeal.

In my mind I'd gone over every possible scenario imaginable as I thought of the possibility of my getting drafted into the army. I thought about going to Canada, but that was the coward's way out to me and not the way I was raised. Another option: A Marine sergeant whose family was rumored to have Mafia connections claimed that his cousin owned a judge in New Orleans. The sergeant told me to go to his hometown and refuse induction there while wearing nothing but a bra and women's panties, and the judge would take my case from there. I also thought about signing up for Officer Candidate School, or fulfilling my natural destiny by going to Quantico and joining the Marine Corps. I thought of everything but could decide on nothing.

Before I left Beaufort, I received a Citadel haircut from Harvey's Barber Shop on Bay Street. I spit-shined my inspection shoes from The Citadel and dressed in the blue suit I wore to my wedding. Out of nervousness, I spun my Citadel ring, which was always on my right hand. Barbara was so upset that day, I don't even remember telling her goodbye. My mother hugged me at the back door and said, "You were raised to do your duty to your country, Pat. Never forget that."

"I know, Mom," I said. "I just don't know what form that duty is going to take."

In Columbia, I entered the office of a colonel who had taken temporary command of the selective services after his retirement from the armed services. He was a fine-looking, muscular man in impeccable shape, and gentlemanly to his core. I liked him the moment I saw him, and he flashed me a friendly smile as we sat down. I had spent a lifetime in the brotherhood of colonels.

His first move startled me. He was staring at a thick file of articles and letters when he looked up at me, tapped his ring on the table twice, and said, "The Citadel"; then he cited the year of his graduation.

Thinking that this could be very good news—or possibly catastrophic—overwhelmed me, but I recovered enough to tap my own ring on his desk and I said, "Citadel, 1967."

"So, you're the young man who's been causing all the fuss," he said as he waded through newspaper clippings.

"Yes, sir. I'm afraid I am."

"Are you a conscientious objector, Mr. Conroy?"

"I most certainly am not," I said.

"If this country was attacked by an enemy nation, what would you do?"

"Throw me a rifle, sir."

"If I draft you today, what will you do?"

"Be a good soldier, sir."

"When did you decide that?"

"On the trip up here," I said.

He took out a piece of paper and studied it with great interest. He read the page again slowly; then he said to me, "The superintendent who fired you? He thinks he may have had a drink or two. He called a member of the draft board, who also admits that he too may have had a drink or two. The superintendent said he had just fired you, and a letter drafting you was sent out the next day. It's the worst case of collusion I've ever encountered. Son, these people not only wanted to fire you, they wanted to kill you. It's disgraceful."

"I irritate people, Colonel," I said. "I get it from my father."

"Your father's in Vietnam. Your wife's first husband died in Vietnam. How did he die?" the colonel asked.

"He was flying close air support for troops on the ground when he was shot down," I said.

"You adopted the two children he left behind?"

"Yes, sir. Jessica and Melissa."

"I've received over fifty letters from your neighbors protesting the fact that you received a draft summons."

"They worry about Barbara, not about me," I explained.

"These are some of the most moving letters I've ever received. They're remarkable. One is by a Marine wounded at Okinawa who says he is a member of the John Birch Society. Why would he write a letter on your behalf?"

"That's Dr. Charles Aimar. He's always loved me. He doesn't want to, but he just can't help it."

Then the colonel opened a drawer and placed a book from it on his desk. It was a copy of my first book, *The Boo*, which had been self-published a month earlier. I had never seen a loose copy of this book floating around anywhere. I was speechless as I stared at a photograph of the Boo's head on the jacket of my book.

"My son bought it for my Christmas present. We both loved it," he said.

"My God, what if you'd hated it?"

"Mr. Conroy, you got railroaded. I'm ashamed of the conduct of the Beaufort draft board—but here is one thing I promise: You'll never hear from us again. You walk out of here a free man."

"Sir, can I ask you a favor?"

"Of course."

"Can I kiss you?"

"No, I wouldn't like that," he answered.

"Then that's the only reason I won't do it," I said.

In jubilation, I drove back to Beaufort, taking all the back roads out of Orangeburg. The meeting had held much terror and uncertainty for me and my family, but I was struck by the wonder of it all. I had met a colonel in the last moment of my overmilitarized life that I would have followed toward any machine-gun nest in the world or fought with in any war. This colonel, whose name I never knew, permitted me a last glimpse of a kind of soldier I always fell in love with—dutiful, fair, and just—and issued me my walking papers. He returned me to the middle of my own life.

In the winter of 1971, three of the children I had taught on Daufuskie had moved in with Barbara and me in our spacious home. Margarite Washington, Jackie Robinson, and Alvin Smith lived with my family in the very year of my firing from Daufuskie. All of them were sweethearts and a pleasure to be around, and they provided fresh eyewitness accounts of my time on the island. I learned that it was after the trip to Beaufort for Halloween that their parents started to trust me, and that my over-the-top performance as Scrooge in the Christmas play convinced the mothers of the island that I should quit teaching and go act in a soap opera. But the clincher was the school trip to Washington over the Easter break. The whole island got to send their children off to an enchanted place where presidents lived, and the islanders understood that I was trying to bring the world to the island or take their children out to discover that world for themselves.

"What did you like best about Washington, Margarite?" I asked her afterward.

"The bed that our hostess Judy Hanst let me sleep in," she said. "God, that was nice."

"What about you, Jackie?"

"The Smithsonian," he said. "You scared us to death with that big elephant in that big hall. You told us that elephant was alive. That he was just resting and was going to stomp us all."

"That doesn't sound like me," I said.

"It sounds just like you," Margarite said. "It is you."

I wrote *The Water Is Wide* that winter. The chapters came fast and I tried to control the immense anger and hurt I felt inside me. But the words began to speak out for me, and I recognized my own voice and realized I was discovering the voice I would be using for the next fifty years. I trained it to be a strong voice, a resilient and bold one—yet I longed for suppleness, for clarity, for laughter and beauty. I trained myself to be unafraid of critics, and I've held them in high contempt since my earliest days as a writer because their work seems pinched and sullen and paramecium-souled. Yes, it was that fruitful winter that I made the decision to never write a critical dismissal of the works of another brother or sister writer, and I've lived up to that promise to myself. No writer has suffered over morning coffee because of the savagery of my review of his or her latest book, and no one ever will.

It was the same winter I drove to Columbia twice a week to a poetry workshop taught by James Dickey. Though his poetry has had an electrifying effect on my writing, it helped me more as a human being to take his measure as a man. I found it dangerous for a poet's soul to be surrounded by achingly beautiful coeds who were openly flirtatious with the poet and enamored of his work. I never wanted a column of grad students trailing behind me like a line of newly hatched goslings as I made my way from class to class.

Also, Mr. Dickey alerted me to the dangers of the company of other writers. Although I admired his body of work extravagantly, I never entertained the thought of becoming his friend. He was competitive, hostile, and carnivorous in his relationships with other writers when he was with them on the speaking circuit. When writers gathered, I felt as though I'd been thrown into a tank of moray eels. From the beginning, I distrusted the breed and made a vow to avoid them for the rest of my life. Though I've made some great friends among writers, I've stayed away from most of them and it's made for a better and more productive life. I would've loved being able to write like Jim Dickey, but didn't want to be anything like him as a man. His life was a force field of chaos—just like mine would turn out to be.

But my luck had changed and my future had brightened. I was writing well and starting to average a chapter a week as I recounted that year when I was a teacher who learned far more than he taught to the children of a cutoff Gullah nation. Eventually, I failed my kids completely because I ran my mouth and got myself fired by throwing myself into the fray of Southern racial politics. Southern politics was a fanged and poisonous thing that always ate its young. But the island had changed me, and I would never go back to being that young man who arrived on Daufuskie the previous September. I had to go to a small sea island to learn the lessons of a great, bright, and sometimes ruthless world.

In that cold season, the elegant literary agent Julian Bach wrote me a life-changing letter when he agreed to represent *The Water Is Wide* for publication. Then Houghton Mifflin quickly bought it, and later, *Life* magazine would publish an excerpt of it, and 20th Century Fox bought the movie rights. Even though I had brought my family to the point of financial ruin, I could finally breathe again. Barbara lost that look of mourning and fear she had carried with her since the night I was fired. News of the book began to spread through Beaufort, unsettling the town, disturbing the dreams of school board members.

When the book was published in 1972, it caused a firestorm in South Carolina. It produced such a furor in Beaufort that I knew I would soon be moving from the prettiest town on earth. While a student at Beaufort High School, my sister Kathy was called "the nigger lover's sister," and Jim, also a student there, was called "the nigger lover's brother." I didn't care what anyone on earth thought about me, but I didn't want my family suffering for it. My mother was getting into fusses all the time with citizens who accosted her on the streets. Mom was articulate and polite, but she was a warhorse in her spirited, fiery defense of her oldest son. But Beaufort had hurt me deeply, and no longer seemed like the place I could spend the rest of my life. The city of my birth, a more liberal place, began to call out to me. Barbara and I sold our home to my mother and father, who planned to make it their retirement home. We moved to Atlanta in 1973 and toward the disastrous motions of the rest of my life.

When the book was published, I traveled with friends and family over to Daufuskie for the last time. I took four cartons of my book to my kids and their parents. Ricky Pollitzer and Larry Rowland sat in the wheelhouse of their shrimp boat. They had let me work as a striker on this same shrimping boat when I'd lost my job teaching. A crowd had gathered on the public dock to meet us. The men were piling shovelfuls of blue crab and boiled shrimp onto newspaper covering weathered picnic tables. There was a lot of hugging and kissing and laughter as we all ate lunch—there is nothing that tastes better than fresh crab and shrimp just taken from a salt creek that morning.

After lunch, I started to open the boxes of books and give them out to the children and other islanders. The day was both emotionally exhausting and bittersweet for me. There were times I could barely speak as I said good-bye to my kids. When the shrimp boat pulled away from the dock and the people of Daufuskie waved farewell, I teared up and thought I was saying good-bye to something of infinite value, to a job that had meant something to me, to kids I'd fallen in love with, and to a youth and a bright take on life that was darkening fast behind me. As I waved to my kids for the last time, I felt great loss, but also an immense joy. Those children on the dock had managed to place their story in front of the whole world. Their photographs had appeared in the pages of *Life* magazine, and a script was being written in Hollywood as the shrimp boat entered the waters that would take it past Hilton Head and into Port Royal Sound. Although Daufuskie had let me know everything I needed to know about myself and the man I was planning on becoming, I never stepped foot on Daufuskie Island again.

There are three more stories I want to tell about my time on the island, and three only.

Sallie Anne Robinson, who is shown on the jacket cover of *The Water Is Wide*, was a sixth-grader when I taught her. She was a bright and pretty young girl who has turned into a beautiful, articulate woman who writes cookbooks for a living. I wrote an introduction for her first cookbook, *Gullah Home Cooking the Daufuskie Way*, and I was proud as a Carolina gamecock when it came out. One of the greatest moments of my life was when Sallie and I signed her cookbook together at the Bay Street Trading Co. in Beaufort, where I'd signed every book I'd written since 1970.

In 2010, Sallie sent me an e-mail after a trip she took to Washington, D.C. She told me she had never been back there since I had taken her and her classmates over the Easter break in 1970. She remembered my excitement in taking the Daufuskie children to the Smithsonian, and she recalled my showing the kids the Hope Diamond and the dinosaur skeletons. Then she stunned me with the news that she had just come back from signing her cookbook after a speech she delivered at the Smithsonian Institution. As I read her joyous message, I closed my eyes and let myself be enkindled by the miraculousness of Sallie Anne's written words. She added that everyone had loved her and that the crowd had been huge at the signing. I was sixty-five years old when I learned that Sallie Anne Robinson had a book signing at the Smithsonian Institution. It was a very good day in my life.

Several months later, I was sitting in the May River Grill in Bluffton when a feisty, combative man approached my table. I rose to introduce myself to him. He had the terrific Southern name of Cloide Branning and told me his wife wanted to give me a copy of her new cookbook, *Shrimp, Collards & Grits*.

"It has my name written all over it, Cloide," I said. His table came over to my table, and his wife, Pat, signed one of her books for me—a beautifully bound and boxed book that would look handsome in any kitchen. Their pretty young daughter had begun her teaching career on Hilton Head and had just finished reading *The Water Is Wide*. I told the young teacher that I was twenty-five years old when I started writing that book and had reached the age when I did not listen to anything a twenty-five-year-old, snot-nosed kid had to say.

"You had a lot to say and you said it well," she replied.

"Thank you so much," I said.

"I played golf once a week with Walter Trammell," Cloide said, with mischief in his eyes.

"I hear my superintendent was a very good golfer," I said.

"He used to beat me every time we played," he said. "Then you came along."

"I don't understand what I had to do with his golf game," I said, puzzled.

"Well, you ruined his whole life. That's just for starters. When your book and movie came out, he became one of the most hated men in America. The same school board that fired you fired him a couple years later—what you did to him haunted him to his death."

"I used to have nightmares about Walter Trammell," I said.

Cloide said, "You whipped his ass, and Trammell knew it and so did the whole town."

"Good. I couldn't be happier. But his golf game?"

"Every time we went out to a golf course, he would get ready to tee off on the first hole," Cloide explained. "Walter would begin his backswing, and I'd say, 'Pat Conroy,' and his arms would palsy up and begin shaking—they would actually spasm when I said your name. It ruined his golf game."

And finally. A month later, I attended a black-tie affair when Penn Center announced that I was one of the two inductees into the 1862 Circle, a prestigious fellowship that usually goes to one of the pillars of the black community around Beaufort. The circle is named in honor of the dedicated band of Quaker teachers who left their homes in Philadelphia to teach slaves freed from local plantations. The Beaufort slaves were the first freedmen in the former Confederate state, and the Penn School became the center of the Geechee-Gullah culture in the low country. Penn Center was begun in 1862 in what was known as the Port Royal Experiment.

Sallie Anne Robinson surprised me by showing up to introduce me, and she gave a moving and elegant talk about our time on Daufuskie when I was a young man and Sallie Anne was a child. I had been her teacher forty-one years ago and I still could remember how she combed her hair and what clothes she'd wear to class.

It was a night of deep reconciliation for me, because when I was fired from Daufuskie, I expected Penn Center would throw their support to me. After all, I had practically spent my high school years going to seminars and workshops over there. At Penn Center, I'd met Martin Luther King Jr. and the entire leadership of the Southern Christian Leadership Conference. In addition, I had taught the first Afro American history course at the former all-white Beaufort High School.

Though Penn Center did not inform me of their decision, I walked into the Hampton courtroom that day in December of 1970 and my knees nearly gave way beneath me when I saw the board of Penn Center sitting on the side of the board of education and Walt Trammell. When I saw black friends of mine sitting beside white administrators who would tell the court under oath that I was a worthless teacher, a liar and a cheat, a book thief, and a clear danger to children. No one from Penn Center would look, speak to, or acknowledge me. Julia Johnson, the black woman who taught in the next room to me, whom I pulled off two of my kids when I found her beating them with a leather strap, was sitting next to the head of Penn Center, and they were in the middle of an animated talk. Someone had sabotaged the boat that was bringing a group of islanders as my witnesses. I didn't have a single witness from the island.

My Beaufort High English teacher, Gene Norris, rushed to my side.

"Why would Penn Center do this to me, Gene?" I asked. "They practically raised me."

"I've told you that race is one of the most dangerous subjects in the world," Gene said. "The board of Penn Center decided it was more important to back up a black teacher than to defend a white one. It's despicable, Pat, but sometimes it's the way the world works."

I've never written about this betrayal before and would not write about it now if the past had not risen up, snake-headed and mean-spirited, to remind me of those wretched times. On the night of the Penn Center induction all those years later, one of those old board members hunted me out to say, "I remember you from those Daufuskie days, Pat. I never saw such a hothead in my life."

I let it go because I had to stand up and make my thank-you speech before the crowd, but words can sometimes sink down and catch in my throat, making it hard to swallow. I got up to do my speech, which was a happy one as I went over my life in Beaufort and my life at Penn Center.

"When I first drove into this town," I said, "black people were not allowed to enter and buy a meal in any restaurant in town or rent a room in a single hotel. There were separate water fountains in the Greyhound bus station, and separate bathrooms, and it was against the law for a white kid to go to the same school as a black kid. Look at us on this magical night, five hundred black people in their tuxedos and gowns, one hundred and fifty white people dressed in their Sunday finest! We're gathered in a hotel where any of us could pay good money to spend the night. Tell me the South hasn't changed, and changed for the better. I had a former board member of Penn say tonight that he had never seen such a hothead as I was. It startled me to hear a young Southern white boy being called a 'hothead' by a civil rights leader. But I thought about it and have considered it deeply. I've come to the conclusion that I was not a hothead. Penn Center, I've come to the conclusion that I was right. I thought I was right then and I think it even more today. And, Penn Center, you who honor me tonight, please tell me something—those mean-ass white folks who fired me—tell me I didn't get those sorry sons of bitches back!"

I sat down to a standing ovation. I looked at the award I was given on May 7, 2011, welcoming me to the fellowship of the 1862 Circle. It said I was being honored for being an author, a Gullah culture advocate. Finally, it said, "Educator." I swear it did. It said, "Educator."

At long last, that circle closed.

CHAPTER 4 ·

The Writing of *The Great Santini*

After the publication of *The Water Is Wide*, I began work on what would become my first novel. *The Water Is Wide* had enjoyed more success than I'd dreamed of having my entire lifetime, yet that success filled me with far more dread than confidence. Since I was a little kid, I've always been comfortable with disaster and catastrophe and wary of triumph of any kind. Bad news is a comfort zone for me, the fields of brawling where I'm most at home.

I was setting forth into dangerous waters, and no one knew it better than I did. But I also thought I was getting ready to write the book I was born to write. Because I had studied the biography of Thomas Wolfe with such meticulous attention, I thought I knew all the pitfalls and fly traps into which I could fall by writing on such an incendiary subject as my own family. When I began to write the book, I had never heard the phrase "dysfunctional family." Since the book came out, that phrase has traveled with me as though a wood tick has attached itself to my armpit forever.

The shadow looming over this book was the figure of my Thor-like father. As I began to write, my rage at Dad was a disfiguring thing even to me. My portrait of my father was so venomous and unforgiving that I had to pull back from that outraged narrative voice and eventually decide to put the book into third person. But even then, the words flowed like molten steel instead of language.

When I sent three or four chapters off to my beloved editor, Anne Barrett, she wrote back a very kind note. The essence of her letter explained that my descriptions of Col. Bull Meecham troubled her profoundly. No reader could expect to believe that such an unsavory man could exist without a single virtue to recommend him. To make him credible, I had to include scenes that displayed a softer and kinder man.

So I took my walking orders from Anne Barrett, and had Bull Meecham give his son a flight jacket for his eighteenth birthday and take him out to the officers' club for his first drink. On the night of his prom, Bull sent his daughter a dozen red roses. Both scenes were fictional and would never have occurred in my father's house. To make my father human, I had to lie. Because Anne did not believe his violence against his wife and family, I softened up my hard-nosed, take-no-prisoners father.

One day, I was sitting around with my brothers and sisters and I asked them, "Did Dad ever do anything nice for us when we were kids—ever?"

They thought about it for a while, and then Mike said, "Nope. Not a single time."

But I persisted. "Did he take us out to get us a hot dog or a root beer?"

"Are you nuts?" Jim said.

"Never happened," Tim said. "Hey, I've got a question for you. Now, I've never had an insight into Dad's behavior in my life, but I finally had one. Question: When was the only time you knew for certain that Dad was going to hit you?"

"When he was drunk," Jim said.

"No," Tim said. "Sometimes he passed out."

"After he hit Mom," Mike offered.

"No," Kathy said. "Sometimes he'd just hit her."

"When he was breathing?" Carol Ann suggested.

"Nope, sometimes he went for days without backhanding us."

"I don't remember those," Jim said. "I think he brain-damaged me."

"There was one thing that would set Dad off and he'd belt us every time. He would always hit us when he spotted us having a really good time," Tim said.

We hollered and laughed and gave Tim a round of applause. He stood and bowed deeply in appreciation. Then he recalled a night when the family gathered in the stands to watch me play a basketball game at Beaufort High School. It was halftime when six-year-old Tim ran down to join a group of kids his age who were leaping high and laughing on the trampoline. Tim was bouncing and grinning and enjoying his time with little strangers when Dad backhanded him while Tim was in midair. Tim bounced once on the trampoline, then flew through the air and landed on his back, careening off the polished gym floor. In the ancient family dance, Tim went running to Mom screaming with hurt and fear. Her part in the game came swiftly as she comforted her son and turned a murderous eye on our father.

Dad said, "Trampolines are dangerous. The kid could've gotten hurt."

The happiest years of my childhood were when Dad went to war to kill the enemies of America. Every time my father took off in an airplane, I prayed that the plane would crash and his body be consumed by fire. For thirty-one years, this is how I felt about him. Then I tore my whole family apart with my novel about him, *The Great Santini*.

Looking back, I can see that I made many mistakes in the field during my rookie season as a novelist. The writing of the book had taken an emotional toll on me that included a breakdown months before the book was in the stores. I had done almost no preparatory work on my family, no plowing the fields to ease their way into a country they did not realize was their native land. To Dad, I'd given more hints about what I was up to, and for the simple reason that he lived in Atlanta then, where Barbara and I had moved. Dad would visit the house often—too often for me, but Barbara had come to adore Dad, and our daughters rejoiced in his visits. It both moved and disturbed me to see my children scrambling around on my father's lap like some comely litter of kittens.

I would often say things like, "Hey, Dad, why don't you break all their facial bones? Then they'd know what it was like to be raised by you."

"Don't listen to him, girls," Dad would respond. "Let me take you out for ice-cream cones. This weekend I'll take you to Six Flags."

Before he would whisk the girls off to Baskin-Robbins, he would say, "Visit the head before we leave, girls—no waterworks. Waterworks are strictly off-limits." When he arrived on Friday to take my daughters to Six Flags Over Georgia, I had the first intuition and sense of dread and said to myself, "Oh, God—that damn book is coming out soon. How's my family going to feel about it?"

When Dad first came to live in Atlanta, I had just committed the most unforgivable crime against him. I had refused to attend his retirement parade that took place in the summer of 1973. I did it with all the purposefulness and cunning of a man who knew how to cut deepest and wound another man. I was a son gifted in the art of patricide. Though I had loathed my father, I fell in love with the mystique and sense of fraternity I grew up with as the son of a Marine Corps officer. The corps stood for excellence and a code of honor that burned in me for life. I was raised in the mythos of the corps, and I knew about Belleau Wood, Iwo Jima, Guadalcanal, Okinawa. I took great pride in my dad's gallant fighting at the Chosin Reservoir, when he provided air support for a brutal Marine retreat through entrenched Chinese lines. Don Conroy was a proud member of "the Chosin Few," yet his oldest son did not go to his retirement parade. It sickens me to write those words.

To make matters worse, my family and I arrived for a visit the day after his retirement party, and I walked into a house touched with nothing but malice. I could feel the hatred in that house that I had sold to my parents so that they could enjoy a peaceful and fruitful retirement. My brother Mike told me that our mother had not spoken to Dad for days, not even on the day of his retirement ceremony. To Mike, their relationship had never been this poisonous. It now had turned into a disaster area.

When Barbara was out with the girls, I assembled all the powers of diplomacy I possessed. Unknown to me, it would be the last day when that melancholy alliance of Don and Peg would exist. They had come to the final days of their marriage, but none of us knew it then.

I entered Mom's kitchen and she ran up and hugged me hard. She was crying, and because I am a Conroy male, I never learned the necessary set of skills to comfort a weeping female. But I managed to mouth a few ineffectual words intended to soften her sense of outrage. Something had snapped in her.

"I can't stand it for another day, Pat," she said. "It repulses me to look at him. Or speak with him. You've got to get him to leave this house." She was begging me now. "One of us has to go. I want it to be him."

"I'll do my best," I said. "But the boy's got a stubborn streak."

"If he doesn't leave, then I want you to play guard duty and stand between Don and the car when I load up the kids."

"No, Mom. You're not going to involve the kids. If you leave, load them in the car and tell Dad that you're going shopping at Piggly Wiggly. Just lie to him."

"You mean my oldest son, who witnessed everything, won't lift a finger to help his own mother?" she cried, appalled.

"Of course I'll help. Just let me talk to him first."

I found Dad in the living room watching a baseball game on TV, but I could tell that he'd been shaken up by the events of the past couple of days. His eyes had the wounded look of a predator limping back to his den.

"Hey, Dad, who's playing?" I asked.

"Cubs and the Phillies. The game sucks," he answered, not looking up to greet me. Then he said, "Retirement is harder on women than it is on the Marine. That's a known fact."

I said carefully, "Dad, I think Mom's planning to leave you."

Suddenly he looked away from the ball game and stared at me with such ferocity that I braced for a charge.

"She can't do that," he said. "We're Roman Catholic. We took vows to each other."

"Them vows don't seem to be worrying her much," I said. "Look, Dad, let me help you develop a plan."

"I got a plan," he said. "I'm staying here. This is my home. Where I belong."

"If it doesn't work out, come to Atlanta to stay with me, Barbara, and the kids. Mom looks bewildered, terrified, and even a little crazy.

Your being away would give both of you some time to think things over."

"There's nothing to think over."

"The offer is there," I said.

"Thanks for nothing," he answered.

"It was my pleasure. How does it feel, Dad? We just had our first conversation."

"It sucks. It's lousy. It's shitty. Let's never have another one again," he said, red faced and angry.

Even for the Conroy family—as battle-scarred veterans of our own journey through the Peg and Don wars—that Memorial Day holiday of 1973 was as melancholy as any we had endured. It seemed as if both our parents had simultaneous breakdowns, and the retirement parade had only exacerbated the tension between them.

When we packed up the car to head back to Atlanta, I made one final attempt to get my father to consider a visit.

"Negative," he said. "This is where I belong. I'm the head of this household."

"You could just visit for a couple of weeks," I said. "To give you and Mom a cooling-off period."

"Negative. Do I have to draw you a picture?"

"You might even enjoy it," I suggested.

"Negative. If you need me, you can find me in my quarters," he said.

After Barbara and I unloaded the car back in Atlanta, she gave the girls their baths upstairs, and I heard a knock on the front door. I went to the door and opened it to find my very distraught father standing there. I couldn't have been more surprised to find the Archbishop of Canterbury.

"Can I buy you a beer, son?"

When we entered Manuel's Tavern, a legendary bar on Highland Avenue, I waved to Larry Woods and Paul Hemphill, two writers I had recently met. My father had not spoken in the short ride to the tavern. To me he seemed ready to launch off a carrier, but I'd respect his silence and talk when he needed to talk. Dad had never bought me a beer. As far as I could remember, he had never bought me a present, ridden me around any town he'd been stationed in, nor taught me any of the social skills necessary for a boy to make his way into an unforgiving world. I found myself strangely excited by this distinctive moment that I had read about in novels and seen depicted in movies—a father and son getting to know each other. The owner, Manuel Maloof, brought the two draft beers I'd ordered on the way in.

"Talk about it, Dad," I said.

A look of bitterness engulfed his face. He was in an agony that was as authentic as it was vitriolic. In his newly minted despair, Colonel Conroy did the most terrifying thing: He laid his head on his powerful arms and burst into tears. The most pitiless of men had imploded on himself and felt the soft tissues of his emotions for what must have been the first time in his life. His cries began with stifled weeping, but soon turned to explosive sobs, attracting the curious attention of every patron in the bar.

Manny Maloof came rushing over to see what was wrong.

"He all right?" Manny asked. "Should I call an ambulance?" By now Dad was howling and blubbering and creating a scene that became increasingly alarming.

"He'll be okay, Manny," I said. "He just hates your fucking beer."

"Buy him another one, Pat," Manny said, staring at my distraught father. "Hell, it's on the house."

"Naw, I just had to tell him his mother died," I said. "He was very close to his mother."

Dad bawled and wailed for several minutes before he calmed himself and raised his sheepish face to survey the room. He said, "These people must think I am a fucking lunatic."

"Yeah, most of them do," I said.

"My mother ain't dead, thank you very much," he growled.

"I was just practicing," I said.

"Practicing for what, sports fan?"

"For the day she does die," I said. "You want to talk about Mom?"

At the mere mention of Peg, my father began weeping again, but his recovery was much faster this time. "Sorry. Sorry, son," he said, whimpering.

"I kind of love watching you cry, Colonel," I said. "It reminds me of a boy who once lived in your house."

This angered him. After wiping his eyes and face with napkins on the table and blowing his nose, he turned to face me. We both carried hard looks without much love being conveyed between us.

"You ever tell anybody what happened here tonight, I'll kill you. Got that straight?" he warned. Then he added a word he knew I hated: "Pal."

"Yeah, I got it, pal," I said. When he gathered himself together again, I asked him in a low voice, "Dad, do you understand *your* part in Mom's kicking you out?"

"Of course I understand it, son. I see it clear as a bell. I was just too good to your mother. I was good for so long when what I should've done a long time ago was to crack down on Peg and you kids. My kindness got me into trouble. I should've cracked down really hard on all of you."

Astonished, I said, "Crack down? Caligula couldn't've cracked down more than you cracked down. Genghis Khan looks like Woody Allen next to you. Dad, you ran a reign of terror in every house we ever lived in. You were a hideous father and husband. Your own children hate your guts. You don't know a single thing about any of us and you never seemed to care. You slap toddlers in the face. Little kids, Dad. Nice little boys like Mike and Jim, Tim and Tom. You hurt your whole family. You destroyed it. And what you got out of the whole experience was that you were too good, that you should've been tougher? My God. Dad, you don't know anything about yourself."

"Is the lecture over, padre?" he said, his fighting spirit restored by my outburst.

"For now, but it's going to continue for the next forty years," I said. "So get used to it."

. . .

During my parents' separation, my father made the most baffling decision of his world-traveling life—he became a citizen of Atlanta, Georgia, a city he had always held in contempt. He rented a two-bedroom furnished apartment in the Darlington—which had a sign in front of it tallying the population of Atlanta each day. Even though the place looked faded, if not shoddy, he lived in that apartment until his death twenty-five years later.

Soon enough, he found a routine that included breakfast at the Darlington Café while reading the *Atlanta Constitution*. For a while he kept a small notebook in which each day began with reveille and ended with taps. He made friends with a garrulous Jew named Lou Lipsitz, who was a neighbor in the complex. They would take daily walks through Atlanta that covered ten miles or more. In the late fall, he began courting Atlanta women around his age. They included some beautiful women who were nice to his kids. The company of pretty women helped him get out of his unfathomable moroseness after Mom kicked him out of her house.

Dad was a terrific dancer. Don and Peg Conroy had caused a sensation whenever they jitterbugged their way through any officers' club of the American South. Strangely, they never taught their children how to dance; nor did they try. The Conroy children approached a dance floor as though it had warning signs about copperheads.

During those months, Dad got into the habit of coming over for a cup of coffee before I started writing for the day. That morning ceremony solidified when I separated from Barbara after four years in Atlanta and moved into a small but well-placed apartment in the ethereal curves and gardens of Ansley Park. Each morning, Dad would knock on the door and I would rise to let him in, then plug in the coffeemaker. Mostly we made small talk about sports. But, unknown to my father, I was writing a fictional rendering of my life with him in the room next to the one we were sitting in, and it was taking an outrageous toll on my emotional life. I found it hard to write all day about the bastard who raised me, then drink coffee with him the next morning.

One morning I finally asked him, "Do I have to spend the rest of my life having coffee with your sorry ass?"

"Affirmative," Dad said. "Those are the orders of the day."

"I'd rather stick a wet finger in a wall socket," I said, then, "Don't you remember our first night in Atlanta? What I told you? Let's refresh. I hate you. I loathe you. I want to vomit when I hear you knock on my door each morning. That do the trick for you?"

"I told the kids you were trying to make me out to be some kind of ogre," he said, pronouncing the word as "o-gree." "Did you see where Hank Aaron hit two homers last night?"

"Yeah," I said. "I got it, Dad. I got it all."

Yet the manuscript for *The Great Santini* was growing day by day. I suffered writing it as I tried to explain to myself the bottomless terror I felt as a boy. Because we moved on an almost yearly basis, my childhood loneliness would stay with me until I got to Beaufort High School. Though I did not perceive it at that time, the book was taking me at a rapid speed toward another great breakdown of my life. The question that troubled me most was what my father got out of putting my mom and their children on the floor of every house we entered. In full Technicolor, I remember every beating that my father administered and I could take you to the exact spot where it happened in each of those small houses of his early Marine Corps career. I would grow heartsick when he walked in the den every afternoon after happy hour. I was afraid of him and it showed in my eyes. He had supreme contempt for my cowardice and sometimes he would backhand me because I dared to show fear.

Driving in his car, me riding shotgun, was the most dangerous place in the universe for me. After a Little League game, a backhand if I'd made an error; after a football game, a slap to the face for missing a tackle; after a basketball game, a bloody nose for playing on the losing team. A boy played a game at his own peril when the Marine was in the stands. We all played scared when the colonel was in the field house. Dad had an odd, unsettling habit of yelling out to the opposing team to put Conroy on the deck, or "Cut Conroy's legs out from under him!" When Mom would protest, Dad would say he was just trying to toughen me up. He wanted a street fighter and not the mama's boy he had on his hands.

But the story kept rolling, and I could not stop or impede its toll. I thought I was telling a story that had never been told in the history of American literature. There had been innumerable novels about soldiers and their wives and wartime, but I had never heard a word about their children. I was a proud member of an invisible tribe called "military brats," voiceless and unpraised as both children and adults. Because

I grew up encountering the restlessness of warriors during peacetime training, I had watched my father's visible disappointment when the Russian ships turned back during the Cuban Missile Crisis. Carol Ann said, "Can you believe Dad's pissed off because we didn't have a nuclear war?" My father laughed when he heard that our high school had a fallout drill and said, "Skip those drills. Because of Parris Island and the air station, Beaufort is ground zero. Drill all you want. You sports fans are going to be dust in five seconds."

Because of such insider information, when my father scrambled his squadron 331 off the runway in Beaufort and turned south toward Puerto Rico, he had horrified his children about the fate of his family if the flag went up. Being miles from the air station, we would be atomized in an instant. The whole East Coast as we knew it would disappear from the face of the earth. When Gene Norris announced that the Russian ships had turned back, an exultant cheer went up in the class—more relief than joy. Several kids in that class, including me, had men ready to take to the air against the Russian MiGs, and they feared for their fathers' lives. I was still praying for my father to die in his warplane, a disfiguring element I brought into my novel.

Yet there were many scenes that I was writing about a military family's life that seemed mystical to me. Originally, I began the novel with the Meecham family waiting for the arrival of their Marine Corps fighter pilot from a year spent on an aircraft carrier in the Mediterranean Sea. The scene was always emotional because my fear of the return outweighed the pleasure of seeing my father again. It had become clear to me that when Dad was gone, I was a happy young boy. When he was home, I became a melancholic, despairing one. Still, the return of the warrior was a rite of passage for every military brat on earth.

The night following his return, Bull Meecham drives his family from the house on Rosedale Road to their new quarters in Beaufort. My father always left at night with his kids sprawled uncomfortably on a mattress laid out in the back of our Ford station wagon. The move to a new town and a new base was always hard; Carol Ann and I were filled with a clanging anxiety at having to reinvent ourselves one more time. In the middle of the night, we moved with the virtuosity of bedouins as our father rotated through bases all across America.

Also I could write for the first time of the pride I felt in being the son of a Marine, proud of being connected to the corps, which represented excellence, fearlessness, a relentless drive for perfection; the corps trained to be the most fierce fighting force in the world. I was intoxicated by the love of country and the corps whenever I made a boyish salute on the fields of Camp Lejeune and Cherry Point. I grew up believing that the army, navy, and air force were pale imitations of the real thing. I learned the way of the warrior from the Marines. From a boyhood spent watching maneuvers, I learned that no one wanted to be on a beach when those guys showed up. It was the easiest way in the world to get dead.

The writing of *The Great Santini* began to feel like a case of battle fatigue. In my head, I was falling apart as I excavated one buried memory at a time. Since no one in my family knew what I was up to—and I include myself in that calculation—I issued no storm warnings or small-craft advisories. I was going at it alone, entering into strange and dangerous waters every time I wrote a page. Still, I wrote and wrote, fighting through those times when I found myself assaulted by the unforgivable crime of full disclosure. Guilt. Every time I found myself censoring the writer in me, I would write it anyway. Finally, it became a credo for my entire writing life—if I feared putting something on paper, it was a voice screaming from the interior for me to start writing it down, to leave out nothing.

So, I came to this illustrious moment I had dreamed about since I was a ten-year-old boy—I had arrived at the last chapter of the only first novel I'd ever write. Its doors were flying open and I knew where it was going and what was going to happen. I wanted that last chapter to put the readers on the floor with its power. There are other writers who try for subtle and minimalist effects, but I don't travel with that tribe. I like to make people look up and see me walking the high wire without a net. That's what I was born to do, and I almost ran to my writing desk every day, anxious and willing to have at it.

In the single most creative burst of my career, I completed that last chapter by writing almost nonstop for twenty-four hours. Every word seemed summoned and anointed with a limitless power over which I had no control. It delighted me, the ease with which the words appeared, with me as some involuntary instrument taking dictation from the stars. In that chapter, I put the Great Santini into his warplane, where he flew from Key West back to his home base in South Carolina. In the middle of the flight, his fire warning lights flickered on, and Bull Meecham fought to get his plane safely back in its hangar. He aborted his first landing when he saw the lights of family homes beneath him. He changed direction and his A-6 disappeared from the radar screen forever. They found the remains the next day. No one has ever loved writing his father's funeral scene more than I did. I relished every word of it.

Then, in the last two hours of this epiphanic night, I began an almost hallucinatory scene involving the God that eighteen-year-old Ben would pray to about his guilt-ridden relief over the death of his own father. I began creating that God from the spirits of different characters I had made up during the course of writing the novel. This part surprised me, because I'd not planned for this. I had wanted the novel to end with a trip, the way military families always rotate through bases. I needed the Meechams to set off on the highway toward Atlanta—the son now driving the family away from the town, just as the father drove the family into town at the beginning of the book. What in the hell was God doing there? But it felt right, so I went with it. Then I felt the surge, the rush of adrenaline, when I'm coming onto something larger than myself. I had Ben Meecham pray to this God he had just created out of his own imagination:

And can one boy who has said ten thousand times in secret monologues, "I hate you. I hate you," as his father passed him, can this boy approach this singing God and can he look into the eye of God and confess this sin and have that God say to him in the thunder of perfect truth that the boy has not come to him to talk about his hatred of his father, but has come to talk about mysteries that only gods can translate. Can there be a translation by this God all strong and embarrassed, all awkward and kind? Can he smile as he says it? How wonderful the smile of God as he talks to a boy, and the translation of a boy screaming, "I hate you. I hate you," to his father who can't hear him would be simple for such a God. Simple, direct, and transferable to all men, all women, all people of all nations of the earth.

But Ben already knew the translation and he let God off with a smile, let him go back to his song, and back to his flowers on River Street. In the secret eye behind his eyes, in Ben's true empire, he heard and saw and knew.

And for the flight-jacketed boy on the road to Atlanta, he filled up for the first time, he filled up even though he knew the hatred would return, but for now, he filled up as if he would burst. Ben Meechum filled up on the road to Atlanta with the love of his father, with the love of Santini.

When I finished this last line, I fell apart and wept for a long time. For several months, I believe that Barbara—acting on behalf of our children—could have had me committed to a mental institution, because I had traveled too far into the great wound that is my family. Instead of granting me a portion of strength and satisfaction, the novel felt like a bloodletting, an auto-da-fé, or a crown of thorns. Inchoately, I could feel it killing me from the inside out, making me desperate, suicidal, emptied out. Though I thought I had written a good book, I had pulled the pin of a hand grenade, then thrown my entire body over it, knowing it would kill me without harming anyone else. For six months I walked around Atlanta, bedbug crazy and tortured by anxiety and nightmares. At the end of the six months, I found a therapist, Dr. Marion O'Neill, who came in to save me. By this time, the book was in full production and would come out in the spring of 1976. Still, I had warned no one about its content or subject matter. The days passed slowly, but inexorably, like a firing squad assembling at dawn. I could not bear to think that I wrote a five-hundred-page novel just because I needed to love my father. It never occurred to me that I was born with a need to love my dad. It seemed like a madman's fantasy that my father could ever bring himself to love me. Then the book was published, and my problems really began.

CHAPTER 5

Publication of *The Great Santini*

When the postman delivered the first ten copies of *The Great Santini* to my house on Briarcliff Road, I knew that there was no escape in secrecy or vagueness or distortion. Houghton Mifflin was shipping my book to stores all across the country, and I'd soon be facing the judgment of family and critics. When the verdict was in, I far preferred the critics.

My father raced over from his aerie in the Darlington apartments. I had rarely seen him so animated. He shouted with joy when I handed him the book and he saw the title of my first novel.

"My God, son, you've named the book after me. What an honor."

"Dad, you might want to read the book before you start talking about it," I said, horrified that I had even kept the name of the book from my father. He opened the book and started thumbing his way through its pages, excitable and happy-faced as a King Charles pup.

"So, you dedicated this book to me and your mother." Suddenly moved, he added, "This might be the best day of my life."

At first, I had dedicated it to my mother alone, phrasing it, "This book is dedicated to Frances 'Peggy' Conroy, the grandest of mothers and teachers." When I wrote the dedication, I went to Ellen Harper's dress shop and asked Ellen to type it for me. She put on her reading glasses and started typing. I could feel her irritation at me. She was the mother of my best friend in high school and she'd been like a mother to me since I first walked into her house. She had exercised an editorial privilege that I had not authorized, but she was giving me a lesson I would long remember. Ellen had added the following words: "And to Colonel Donald Conroy, U.S.M.C. Ret., the grandest of fathers and Marine aviators."

"I thought I raised you right," Ellen said. "Wipe that frown off your face. I taught you to do the right thing, boy, to take the high road. Now get! Mrs. Aimar has come in to shop for a hat."

I left the words in and will be grateful to Sarah Ellen Harper until I draw my last breath. It was the only armor I took going into the wars that would soon erupt on both sides of the family. But the center of conflict was standing in my living room holding a novel I had written describing my withering contempt of him. It was an awful and existential moment in a young writer's life. My coming-of-age novel was taking on the grotesque trappings of a public beheading. My father danced down the driveway to his yellow '68 Volkswagen convertible I had given him as a retirement gift. He was buoyant while I was worried. When he drove off, I knew trouble lay ahead.

In two hours, the phone rang and I picked it up, knowing it would be my father.

"Why do you hate me, son?" he asked. "Just why do you hate me so goddamn much?"

"Keep reading, Dad; please keep reading. You've got to get to the last line. It's all in the last line."

"It's the shittiest book I've ever read," Dad said. "You ain't worth a crap as a writer. That's my humble opinion."

"Thanks, Dad. Just keep reading the book. Finish it."

Two hours later Dad called again. This time he was sobbing so badly I couldn't understand a word he was trying to say. He began hiccuping, then blubbering again, and finally broke into a high-pitched wail of indiscriminate anguish. The hardest, toughest man I had met in the Marine Corps roared out in unarticulated pain because of words I had hurled against him. Finally, he gained control over himself and whimpered, "What's my mother gonna think?"

"I don't know what your mama's going to think. I don't know the woman. I've seen her two or three times in my life. She's never written me, called me, asked me a question, or sent me a gift. She wouldn't know me if she passed me in the streets of Chicago. And that goes for your daddy, too. I don't know a single thing about any of your Chicago relatives. But I imagine I'll start hearing from all of them soon."

And hear from them I did.

I believe the first to check in was Father Jim Conroy, who was furious from the first word out of his mouth to the last. He called me a Southern sack of shit, and a perverted ingrate who had eaten one too many bowls of grits in my morose, father-hating life. He was going to send his copy of the book to my mother's people in Piedmont so they could use it in their outhouses. He wished my father had beaten me up a lot more, because I deserved it.

After his rant, I said, "Father Jim, remember that wonderful summer fishing trip you took me on when I was ten? You beat me more that summer than my dad did. I ain't ten anymore, Father Jim. Come beat me up now, big fella, and I'll send you back north in a body bag."

My grandmother called and bawled me out, followed by my grandfather, who told me if I really wanted to learn how to write to read James Fenimore Cooper. "It's all there, Pat. It's all there."

Sister Marge checked in, as did Aunt Mary, Uncle Willie, Uncle Jack—everyone but Uncle Ed, Dad's youngest brother.

To my complete astonishment, my mother and her family started checking in with their own barrage of literary criticism. My mother's reaction was the most devastating.

"Nice going, Pat. You managed to destroy your entire family's good reputation. Your father will walk like a leper in whatever town he is in. I won't be able to show my face in Beaufort for the rest of my life. Your brothers and sisters will have to move out of state and change their names. We're ruined, son. You stabbed your own family right through the heart."

"Mom," I said, "do you remember when we read Thomas Wolfe's biography, and what you said to me after his family and town went nuts about *Look Homeward, Angel*? You said you'd be proud if one of your children ever wrote about your family."

"You know I didn't mean it," she said. "I hate your portrait of me."

"If the book has one great flaw, it's that your character is flawless, way too good to be true."

"To me, Lillian Meecham was a sappy, tacky, spineless creature, not the fighter you know me to be. Lillian set my teeth on edge every time she opened her mouth."

"Listen to me," I pleaded. "I wrote about you the way I saw you as a boy. To me you were the most beautiful, loving woman on earth. That image of you got me through our god-awful family. I had to make Lillian perfect, because that's how I looked up to you as a boy."

"Then you're just a lousy writer. A shallow one, too," she said.

"My God, Mom," I said, flabbergasted by her blindside hit on everything that was most significant to me. Because my mother was so well read, she knew exactly how to wound the heart of a young, insecure writer, and her appraisal was uncompromising.

Finally, she ended her critique with a summing-up. "Here's why you really stink as a writer, Pat. You gave that book to *him*. You gave *him* center stage, the starring role. You had *him* rule that house. Let me tell you a secret, son—I ruled that house and everything that went on in it. I could make him dance like a puppet whenever I wanted. I was the power in that house. I was the boss and the chief of police in every town we entered. You just weren't a good enough writer to see who was really in charge."

"I know what you're saying. Since I grew up, I can see you as a much more complicated woman than I ever realized. I know that now. But for this book, I had to paint a flawless portrait of you. For me, just for me. I know about the enigmatic you, the dangerous you. I know all about that, Mom, and I promise that I'll deal with that darker woman sometime down the road."

Mom's mother, Stanny, checked in the next evening with her own dismissal of my novel. She began by telling me, "Pat, your father was the most wonderful husband and father I've ever met, and I've been on five world cruises. I've circumnavigated the globe five times."

"Not you, too, Stanny," I said, furious.

"Now, don't you forget it was me who bought you *The Complete Works of Shakespeare* when you graduated from high school. Also *Ulysses*, by Mr. James Joyce," she defended herself. "I got me some credibility in the old literary game."

"Tell me the truth. Did Dad call and whine to you?" I asked.

"You hurt him terribly," Stanny said. "He'll never get over it. What do your brothers and sisters say?"

"They haven't checked in yet. Thank God," I said.

"I loved one part of the book," she said.

"That's the first time I've heard these words. Tell me what pleased you."

"I loved every bit about Alice Sole, the sixty-three-year-old mother of Lillian Meecham, except her part is far too short. I think you should concentrate on her completely when you write the next book. I'd make a great novel."

"You're an egomaniac, Stanny. So you loved the part about you, but you join forces with my enemy family to torment me."

"Your mother called me too. I think she's angrier than Don. She thinks the whole book should've been all about her," Stanny said.

"My whole family is a bunch of narcissists," I said with a sigh.

Then my father disappeared from Atlanta, and it began to be a major concern for all his family as his self-imposed exile stretched to three days and counting. I called Jim Townsend, the founder of *Atlanta* magazine, and he put in calls to the police chief and the mayor. At night, I would drive around Dad's old haunts, and even ate breakfast with his running buddies at the Darlington to see if I could coax any stray information from them. But they were as deeply concerned as I was. Lou Lipsitz said, "You might as well face it, Pat: Your book probably made your dad go kamikaze. I bet he rented a Piper Cub and flew it into a mountain in North Georgia."

"Shut up, Lou," I said, and resumed my search, but that afternoon my uncle Willie called a second time. "Nice going, Pat. We think Don went off somewhere to kill himself."

My sister Carol Ann had read an earlier version of *The Great Santini* that I had brought her the previous summer that she had spent fighting off the madness that the family had bequeathed to both of us. When she finished it, she told me I had restored her childhood to her, that her own survival depended on repressing those same memories that I recorded in the novel. I had given her back a childhood voice that she had lost somewhere when we followed Dad from base to base. She thought I had captured exactly the way that terrible family felt as she was growing up in it—in the discordance and bristling tension of living an impossible life.

My brothers have always remained the solid citizens of my realm when it came to my defense of my portrait of Dad. I could not ask for more valiant safekeepers of my point of view. They were quick to the fight and articulate from the start. Mike, Jim, and Tim have faced a squad of doubters and naysayers about the accuracy of my memories. From the first, my brothers leaped to the front line of defense and backed me up a hundred percent from the day of publication until the present day. There may have been a lot wrong with my childhood, but I was born into a round table of knightlike brothers. It took my sister Kathy many years to make her own complex peace with the novel. Carol Ann's long rearguard war against me had not commenced, but she was already sharpening her arrows in secret and concealing weaponry in false drawers and hidden cupboards of her troubled soul. Carol Ann had developed a hazardous talent for searching out the most scrofulous shrinks on earth, who in their breathtaking banality would convince her of their superiority and genius. She let them cut her out of the family like the removal of a malignancy that could not be named. But that secret war was yet to begin, and there was still no sign of Dad.

The reaction of the Chicago Irish part of the family held no surprises for me, except it startled me that all of them seemed to have read the book. Chicago was uncharted territory for me. In some interior way, I knew this tempest was tribal in nature, but I had barely met the tribe and knew nothing about their customs and ceremonies. But their phone calls infuriated me, and that was when I was beginning to learn that I could plead ignorant to all things Irish, but Ireland lived deeply inside of me, a fierce and intransigent resident in my bloodstream. Ireland has always ridden coach to the South in my fog-bound family history. But I was learning all the anger and hurt of the Irish immigration as they banded up against me in defense of one of their own. Though I lashed back in fury, their loyalty impressed the hell out of me.

That my Southern family felt much the same affection for Dad and that no one but my brothers believed in my caustic portrait of him astonished me. Surely they had witnessed attacks on my mother and his kids over the years. But when I thought hard about it, I could come up with no instances when I could remember Mom getting slapped at Aunt Helen's dinner table or Dad knocking his sons around when we were visiting Aunt Evelyn's house in Jacksonville. Stanny or Grandpa Peek would visit for months at a time during my childhood, but I could come up with no centering image of violence when they were resident in our many different houses. I now believe that my mother invited Stanny and her father for extended visits because it provided a measure of safety for her and her kids.

Before my father returned from his long sulk, the calls in his defense came rolling in from all my Southern kin—Uncle Russ issued a complaint, as did Uncle Joe and my beloved Aunt Helen. It occurred to me that there was some uncanny genius at work in my father's perfection of child and spousal abuse. He did it in the dark, like a roach crossing the kitchen floor at night. He slapped Mom in towns where they knew barely a soul. I would most often get slapped when he picked me up from football, basketball, and baseball practices, but strangers rarely saw that, and a kid was the last person believed in the American society of the fifties. My father had kept his abuse secret by mostly confining it to the fortresses of family routine. But as the days wore on, the calls got harsher and harsher. It was my uncle Willie who first called me a liar, and I blasted him with a surge of vitriol that proved my own Irishness to him once and for all. But he'd hit the central nervous system with the phrase that would send me spinning out of control. I was a liar who had invented a series of lies to wound this good and tender man—some perversity inside me made me invent tales of wife beating and tantrums that never happened except in the imagination of a most ungrateful son. I'd made it all up and sold out my father for the price of a book.

My father returned to Atlanta a week after he left town. He had heard his family had turned on me hard, and he handed me a letter when I opened the front door to him at my house on Briarcliff Road.

"Read any good books lately?" I asked as we shook hands.

"A piece of worthless shit that I stomped on and threw across the room," he said. "Read my letter."

The letter was an open one sent out to all the members of his family and my mother's as well:

May 15, 1976

To the Magnificent Seven:
Let me start my epistle by simply stating that I was deeply touched by your oldest brother's latest literary endeavor. Pat is a very clever storyteller and I was totally absorbed and encountered every emotion as, reading very slowly, life with father unfolded in this work of fiction. It was as though I knew some of the characters personally.

Pat did a superb job in developing the character Mary Ann, excellent on Ben, Lillian, Karen, Matt, and, with all modesty, fell far short on Santini—which is quite understandable with such a dashing and complex character.

My absolute favorite parts, not necessarily in order, were: 1. Dave Murphy, 2. Mess night, 3. Toomer scenes, 4. Our trip to Beaufort, 5. Bull goes on base, 6. Opening chapter (mushroom soup incident), 7. Bull and Ben out to recruit depot, 8. Archaic word usage, 9. Mary Anne and Ben prom night, 10. Ben's basketball game—including one-on-one.

Characters which I enjoyed that were nonfamily were: Toomer, Dacus, Loring, Jim Don, Spinks, Sammy, Red, and the Hedgepaths, to name a few, but the setting for some was interesting and often amusing.

In all honesty, I read the first hundred pages, and I was furious; at page 222, not that the page is important, I was livid and put the book down; when I resumed reading it came easier for me, and now I look back, the writer had me, and many readers will feel much the same, in the palm of his hand. I laughed at some scenes, cried at others (figuratively speaking, of course), and you came away a better person having lived with the Meechams.

I thought the book was great and it should make a real terrific flick. But how do you go about the task of telling your son and his family that you are profoundly grateful and extremely proud of his latest literary endeavor. Particularly when I fell into his literary trap and could have choked him as often as twice a page early in the book; but he would only say, "Read on, Macbeth, read on." How true.

When you're Irish, dumb, and then stupid, it is a series of major obstacles to overcome. Each of you possesses an essential quality of greatness that cannot be explained as to the whys and wherefores, but I can only thank the Deity for His benevolence.

Pat's literary ability has never been excelled as in his plea with God in the last pages of the book. Maybe the reason I was so impressed was that it was in the area of religious discussions that I had my greatest concern and my gravest reservations. All of you should read these words; his informal prayer does pay great honor and glory to our Deity. We all take turns rejecting God for one reason or another; the spirit can never rest until you make your peace with your creator. And so the "Hound of Heaven" shall pursue each of you.

To Pat, my oldest son, may you forever wear the cloak of authority, as befitting the eldest Conroy, as a sign to all of our pride in you as Son and Brother. And may Barbara and your children have the patience to endure the idiosyncrasies of such a clan.

Lovable, likable Donald Conroy, U.S.M.C. (Ret.)

Cc: Pat Conroy, Carol Conroy, Mike Conroy, Kathy Conroy, Jim Conroy, Tim Conroy, Tom Conroy, Mr. & Mrs. J. P. Conroy Sr., Rev. J. P. Conroy, Mr. & Mrs. Herb Huth, Will Conroy, Sr. M. Conroy, Jack Conroy, Ed Conroy

"Nobody fucks with one of my kids," Dad said, when I finished the letter and put it down on the coffee table in front of me. "Nobody."

Once Dad's letter arrived in Chicago and among my mother's people, the criticisms ceased. I never heard a disparaging word from family members again. It took a longer time to soothe my father's ruffled feelings about the book. After some time, he learned to use the book to his great advantage and to turn his fictional self into a blissful second career.

"Dad, I'm sorry I hurt your feelings with the book," I said the day I read the letter. "I really am—but I want you to know that nothing I write can ever make up for my ruined childhood."

"You exaggerated everything," he said.

I answered, "I exaggerated nothing."

When my friend and bookstore owner Cliff Graubart threw me a book party for the publication of *The Great Santini*, my father was one of the first guests to arrive and the last to leave. It was the first time he had come to Cliff's Old New York Bookshop as a celebrity, and people gathered around him to question him about his response to the book. Then I saw someone make a request that would alter my father's world forever. A guest opened my book to the title page and asked my father to sign it.

At first, he hesitated, then shrugged his shoulders and began to inscribe the book in his lovely penmanship, but with the slight awkwardness of the southpaw. He signed many copies of *The Great Santini* that night, and his inscriptions became prized by many collectors. His first inscriptions were witty. He signed to one of my friends, Frank Orrin Smith, in the following way:

> To Frank, I hope you enjoy these weird fantasies of my oldest son. The boy was always a little goofy and there was nothing that Peg and I could do to help him. He obviously did not take discipline well at all.

He signed off as, "Yours truly, old lovable, likable Col. Donald Conroy, USMC ret."

The next day, I signed books in Rich's department store with a small crowd of readers in attendance. When I handed a book back to a woman who'd bought it, I saw my father watching from the back of the store, pretending to be shopping for cutlery. I waved for him to join me in the book department, and with feigned reluctance, he approached the signing desk. I introduced the real Great Santini to the twenty-some people who were in attendance, and they seemed thrilled to meet him. The request for an inscription happened again when a pretty customer asked my father to sign her book. My father hesitated, and I could see his old allegiance to protocol and the chain of command were making it unclear what he should do. I helped him by pulling out a chair beside me.

"Sit here, Dad," I said. "Sign away."

So, my father took his place beside me and, in many ways, he never left my side, nor I his, for the rest of our lives. Together we had forged a secret language made up of the blood and contentious harmonies that composed the music of our lives together. I marveled at my father's charm as he schmoozed with the readers and made them laugh and feel happy to be there. Two separate lines formed—one for me and one for the Great Santini. Dad's favorite part of the afternoon was when he looked up and I heard him say, laughing, "Hey, son, my line's longer."

My father learned to turn my portrait of him to his own favor. He would joke about my famous sensitivity, and how could he help having a son with such a spineless, emotional makeup who wilted in the face of lawful orders by a parent who flew fighter jets? On the Neal Boortz radio show in Atlanta, Dad became a frequent guest, and he would often give parents his unsolicited opinions about raising children. "Don't spare the rod. America is falling apart because parents are afraid of their own children. The father is the center of the family unit. He gives out the guidance and the punishment. He is judge, jury, and king. From him, all good things flow."

One day when Dad got home from Neal's show, he asked me what I thought, and I said, "The Great Santini giving advice about raising children. That's not exactly why I wrote my book. Jesus Christ! My dad, the Nazi Dr. Spock."

For the rest of his life, my father and I would sign all my books together. We signed for five hours in Atlanta when *The Prince of Tides* came out in 1986. When *Beach Music* appeared in 1995, we signed for seven straight hours in Charlotte. We made a vow to each other that no customer would ever leave these stores without books signed by us both. Though he often drove me nuts with his bullheadedness, his prejudices, his free-flowing narcissism, his awful Santininess, his letter had given me a way back to him. There was something in my father that the book touched, and it opened up a place in his heart that I thought had closed off long before I was born. So we began a journey together, set off on a voyage that would take us to many places and shared experiences that I never thought were possible with such an incomprehensible man. But that would come in bits and pieces and slow increments over the years. When I was on the modest tour for *The Great Santini*, I called my father on the road to give him a piece of news that would have a critical impact on both of us.

"Dad," I said, "Hollywood wants to do a film of *The Great Santini*."

CHAPTER 6

On the Set of *The Great Santini*

The making of movies from the books I have written has been one of the most surprising and unsettling parts of my adult life. When I first watched Jon Voight playing me in the movie *Conrack*, based on *The Water Is Wide*, I winced each time someone on the screen spoke my name, then went around for the next year feeling ugly. Harriet Frank and Irving Ravetch, the gifted screenwriters who delivered the script, could not imagine a white Southern man could bring himself to be nice to black people—it was inconceivable in the Hollywood I entered in 1972. When the folks I met there found out I was from South Carolina, they would look at me as though I raised police dogs to attack poor black people marching for their freedom. There's always a strong attraction and repulsion about the South in Hollywood, so the screenwriters felt like they had to make the Jon Voight character kind of goofy and disconnected as he performs those ditzy rituals in his first appearance on-screen. That I was born and raised in the South, and that the civil rights movement had a profound effect on me and thousands of other Southerners like me, did not make sense to anyone when I got to Los Angeles. Our image was set in stone. In the South, there were only fire-breathing white racists and wonderful, life-affirming black people hungry for their God-given rights.

The *Conrack* experience was a grand one for me and my entire family, and a troubling one for the town of Beaufort, South Carolina. When *The Great Santini* was sold to the movies, the complications became apparent after Bing Crosby Productions purchased the book. It had never occurred to me that Hollywood would ever play a leading role in my life, especially those years at The Citadel when I dreamed of being a poet.

Then I received a phone call from Charles Pratt, the producer of the movie, who told me two notes of interest about the film—one that thrilled me and one that sickened me. He informed me that the actor Robert Duvall had signed up to play Santini. I had followed Mr. Duvall's career since he played Boo Radley in *To Kill a Mockingbird*, and I thought he was on his way to a long and distinguished Hollywood career. Then Charles Pratt told me that they planned to make the entire movie in Beaufort. Instantly, I thought of the strategies I could employ to keep my parents from having a fistfight on the set, or to prevent encounters between them as they walked the streets of a very small town.

After their divorce, my mother and father's relationship became so rancorous and contentious that all seven children knew that there was no possibility of some peaceable agreement between them. When the divorce was final, Mom married a naval doctor, John Egan, and I thought there might be some cessation of hostilities between my parents. But Mom remained furious over the life she had lived with Dad, and I thought she had every right to be. Dad was hurt by the divorce, and I told him he had no right to those unexamined feelings.

The morning following my conversation with Charles Pratt, Dad arrived for coffee at my apartment in Atlanta, and I gave him the news as he was reading my copy of the *Atlanta Constitution*. I told him about Robert Duvall. He pretended to be disinterested in such a trivial piece of gossip, and then I heard, "Who's Robert Duvall?" Dad said it without lowering the paper.

"The Irish lawyer in the *Godfather* series," I said. "The guy who loves the smell of napalm in the morning in *Apocalypse Now*. Sounds like typecasting to me."

"I know that guy," Dad said as he lowered the paper. "What a role he just signed up for! This'll make his career."

"It's the modesty of your character that attracted Duvall to the role, Dad."

"Nah, I bet he's been waiting for a script with some meat on it for years. He's been a character actor."

"Charles Pratt told me that he felt like he had hired a young Humphrey Bogart," I said. "It's being filmed in Beaufort."

"Uh-oh. The land of your pissed-off mother. I smell trouble," he said. "Who's playing your mother?"

"Blythe Danner. A living doll and a great actress," I said.

"I bet your mother wet her britches when she heard the news," he said.

"She was pretty happy."

"Who's playing you?"

"A young actor named Michael O'Keefe. It's his first film. A young actress named Lisa Jane Persky is going to play Carol Ann," I said.

"What a family I produced," he said. "Who said a dumb-ass Irishman from Chicago could make a family like this? We're going to be in a fucking movie. It's a shame John Wayne is dead. Only he could've brought my virility and toughness to the silver screen."

"The silver screen?" I asked.

"That's what they call it, sports fans," he said. "A young Humphrey Bogart to play me—a nobody to play you. Kind of ironic, isn't it, son?"

. . .

A month before the film crew would arrive, I made an exploratory trip to Beaufort to gauge my mother's reaction to the gathering excitement that had elated the town with the arrival of the filmmakers. Mom had already spoken to Blythe Danner on the phone, and Mom was sure a deep friendship was in the making. Late one afternoon Mom and I walked down to the dock belonging to Billy Kennedy, a friend I'd made playing football in high school. It had a nice view of the bridge to Lady's Island and was across the street from Tidalholm, which the filmmakers had rented out as the Meecham family's Beaufort house—it was the purest fantasy of my military brat heart that I put my fictional family in the most impressive mansion in town. I had lived out a childhood in trailers and Quonset huts, while my younger siblings lived in much fancier quarters as my father accrued higher rank.

The pride was a powerful, nourishing one as my mother regaled me with the town's pleasure awaiting the coming of the film crew.

"You've made some people in this town mighty happy, son," she said.

"That's good to hear, after *Conrack*," I said.

"They've gotten over that," she told me, "at least most of them. Some people'll always be mad about that. But they're racist and we'll never care what they think, will we?"

"Mom? Dad wants to come down to watch a little of the movie being made."

"He can't come," she said.

"Yes, he can. Because I invited him," I said. "And Robert Duvall wants to meet him."

"I'll go to Florida if that happens," she said.

"Say hi to Aunt Helen for me," I answered, then added, "I'll keep him away from you. That's a promise."

It was a promise I was determined to keep, since my parents' divorce proceedings had an inescapable linkup with the publication of *The Great Santini*. Based on their reaction to the book, the whole family refused to believe that Mom and Dad could pull off a simple act of legal dissociation without all the excesses of grand opera spilling out, and they had been right.

In the month leading up to their divorce trial, Dad and I had met for lunch at the Varsity, a legendary hot-dog joint near the Georgia Tech campus. As we sat eating our chili-cheese dogs, I said, "You've got to hire a lawyer to represent you in your divorce trial, Dad."

"I've got rights," he said. "I'm defending myself. I'm telling the judge that I'm a Roman Catholic and my church doesn't believe in divorce. Your mother's got nothing to back her up, and I've got Thomas Aquinas on my side."

Putting my head in my hands, I said, "Dad, promise me you won't mention Aquinas in court."

"Yeah, that's just the start of it. There's Saint Francis of Assisi, you know—the bird guy. Saint Peter, who's the rock upon which my church was built. Saint Jude, the patron saint of lost causes. I might even recite the confiteor to let the judge know who he's dealing with."

"What would you have done without the Baltimore Catechism, Dad?"

"It's still my favorite novel, son."

"It's not a novel."

"Hey, it's a book. It looks like a novel to me. I still read it for pleasure," he said.

"You need a lawyer," I insisted.

"Negative."

I said, in slight despair, "You're going into court without one?"

"Affirmative." His jaw was set in defiance.

"I hired you one, Dad."

"I don't need one," Dad repeated, then, "Who is he?"

"Buster Murdaugh's son."

"Buster? I hate that Southern-ass name," Dad said. "I'm a Chicago boy. I like my lawyers to be called Mickey the Blade, Sharkey, or Opie the Jew Boy."

"Your lawyer's name is Randy Murdaugh. He's Buster's son."

"Tell me about Buster Murdaugh."

I remembered the time I met Buster quite well, and repeated it to my father. "At Hampton, during my trial to get my teaching job back, this older man sat in the jury box and laughed his ass off at several things I said. When the trial was over, Buster called me over and introduced himself. Smoking a cigar, he said, 'I'm the cock of the walk in this part of South Carolina, and, boy, you really know how to put on a show. You scared the living hell out of those bastards. But you're going to lose your ass.' 'What if I'd had you as a lawyer?' I asked. Buster took a puff of his cigar and blew a pillow of smoke in my direction before saying, 'You'd be teaching in that little school of yours tomorrow morning. But you ain't going to be teaching ever again. Let me send you to law school; then you come back and work for me. I'll make you the goddamnedest lawyer you've ever seen.'"

"I'll take Buster," Dad said.

I answered, "He's retired. You'll take his son Randy."

When my father walked into the Beaufort courthouse, his face registered shock when he saw my sister Kathy sitting at the same table as Mom. Prodded by her lawyer, both Mom and Kathy whispered and drew back in horror when they watched Dad's arrival. Their trembling and shaking in terror caused Mom's lawyer to approach the bench of Judge Donald Fanning to ask for a private conference in the judge's quarters. The judge asked Dad to join them. Mom's lawyer confided to the judge that my mother and sister feared Dad's uncontrollable temper and capacity for violence, and demanded that he be hand-searched for weapons. My father responded by bursting into tears.

The judge waited for Dad to calm himself, then asked him to swear Marine to Marine that he was not carrying a firearm or any other kind of weapon. Dad swore, and the two Marines shook hands.

In the courtroom, Mom took the stand and testified about every act of violence I described in *The Great Santini*, even though I'd made up most of those particular scenes, culling bits and fragments from a lifetime of mistreatment to fuel the fires. Mom used the book as her template and her proof of transit through her unlivable marriage. Kathy later said she told the judge she'd seen Dad hit Mom only once, and that was when she was in the fifth grade. Kathy's witness in all this has always been subject to interrogation and great doubt. Of all the children, Kathy reigns supreme as our most unreliable witness. Her only child, Willie, grew up telling his playmates: "Uncle Pat writes lies about my granddaddy."

The divorce was granted, and I called Dad that night. He was sobbing so hard he couldn't speak. When I called Mom, the same keening and wailing was going on at her house, but for a different reason. Mom did not receive a dime for alimony, and only a scant five hundred dollars a month for Tim and Tom, who were still in high school. When they left for college, she wouldn't receive another cent. Peg Conroy could not touch the generous retirement pay of my father's long career and was bitter about it for the rest of her life. A good military wife is a thing of treasured harmony on a base, and my mother was as good at it as any woman of her era. When she married Capt. John Egan a short time later, I'll always believe she did it as much out of financial necessity as love. The Marine Corps considered her life's work without recompense or worth.

When I pass in review and make astringent judgments about the life I've led, I'm still mortified that I didn't testify on my mother's behalf, despite her having begged me to do so. I find it weak-kneed, pusillanimous to my mother's time of greatest need. Even though I was going through a difficult phase of my own breakdown at the time, nothing should've kept me out of that court to testify for the woman who had pulled that son of a bitch off me since I was an infant. I earned the words my mother screamed at me when I refused to testify on her behalf. "Iscariot!" then again, "Iscariot!"

. . .

As the actors and screenwriters arrived in Beaufort to film *The Great Santini*, Peg Conroy became my eyes and ears, reporting everything that transpired. It was a time of enchantment for her. I had never seen her caught up so magically with her own life. Each night, she would call to tell me what happened on the set: that she taught Blythe Danner how to say the rosary, that Robert Duvall had winked at her, that she had talked to Michael O'Keefe about what I was like in high school, and that she told Charles Pratt the complications of moving a large family through the South. She would pass me delicious glimmers of gossip she had heard from Beaufortonians and the movie people.

The making of *The Great Santini* began a showy, extravagant season in my mother's life in Beaufort. When she walked the streets with a queenly hauteur, people would come out of shops on Bay Street to make a fuss over her. Later, she would tell me that it was one of the happiest times in her whole life. She felt like she was walking on clouds when she strutted out of her house each morning—whenever she could, she drove to the set to watch scenes being filmed, but I found out she mostly showed up when the elegant and lovely Blythe Danner was playing the seminal role of Peg Conroy in the same town the Conroy family had latched onto after leaving our nomadic, tumultuous life. Beaufort had soothed something in all of our souls and remains as much a symbol as it does a hometown heritage in the Conroy family story. I still walk its streets in wonder and gratitude, more than forty-five years after my arrival here. Its streets are distillations of roselike beauty, and the air shimmers with an elixir too lovely by half. The town of Beaufort did the most wondrous thing for me and my family—it brought repose to our nest of damaged souls.

Every night, my mother would call me in Atlanta to tell me about the gossip on the set or what she was hearing in her wanderings about Beaufort.

"Making a *movie* here, Pat, is the talk of the town. I saw Gene Norris today and he almost popped with pride when a tourist found out he was your English teacher. Walt Gnann was with Gene and told them that he was your chemistry teacher and that you were one of the worst chemistry students he ever taught."

Among my friends and family I'm famous for always being able to spot thunderclouds lurking on the brightest spring day. I distrust happiness, joy, or self-satisfaction because I've suffered the reprisals of wallowing in those enchanting emotions.

"Be careful, Mom," I said to her. "You're enjoying this far too much. Remember it's still Beaufort. It's still the South."

"Don't worry about your mama, Pat," she said. "I'm just enjoying the ride."

"We're newcomers to Beaufort, Mom, and we always will be," I warned.

"These people sure seem glad these newcomers came to town," she replied.

Beaufort struck back hard and fast. I was writing the middle section of *The Lords of Discipline*, called "The Family," and was about to break for the day when my phone rang. When I answered it, I couldn't have been more surprised when I heard the voice of John Trask Jr. The Trask family was one of the most respected, and certainly the wealthiest, families in Beaufort. I knew John and his pretty wife, Caroline, only because John's youngest brother, Freddie, and I had become close friends when we both taught during my second year as a teacher at Beaufort High School. Like me, Freddie was well read and he shared my ambition of becoming a writer. I think Freddie had the talent to become a very good writer if he had not been born a rich boy.

John Jr. told me he was throwing a party that weekend for the cast and crew at Orange Grove, their plantation on St. Helena Island, and inviting some people from town. Since I'd known and gotten to love Freddie, I'd spent a great deal of time out there, and it was as pretty as any plantation in the low country.

"Pat, the guests of honor are going to be Robert Duvall, Blythe Danner, and you, if you'll be so kind as to come. Blythe and Bobby are dying to meet you," he said.

"Bobby?" I repeated.

"Robert Duvall. That's what people call him," John Jr. explained.

"Got it. Well, John, I'm very touched and I can't thank you and Caroline enough. I'll see you this weekend, then."

"It'll be an honor to have you at Orange Grove," John said.

Though John Jr. and Caroline didn't really know me, they had been unfailingly kind to me from the time I was a young man until the present day. John carried himself like the well-educated gentleman he was, and Caroline was an exemplary representative of that fragrant-voiced, free-floating subspecies known as the Southern belle. Because I inherited my mother's hair-trigger sense of social insecurity, I thought of almost all the ways this invitation could go wrong, but I could come up with nothing to prevent me from attending. Going against my better self—which is my darker self—I decided to just go to the party and enjoy playing the big shot.

. . . .

Awaking early, I drove the five hours to my mother's house on Carteret Street in Beaufort. When I arrived, I found her sitting at her kitchen table drinking a cup of coffee. She was not looking happy when I walked over and gave her a kiss on the cheek.

"Can I ride with you and Dr. Egan over to the party at the Trask plantation?" I asked her.

My mother put her head down on the table and began her quiet weeping. I pulled up a chair beside her and waited for her to compose herself. When she sat up and began drying her tears with a napkin, I said, "Mom, what could it possibly be? You love parties. You always have. I hate them and always will. I only came down because I wanted to see you having a blast. People will make a big fuss over you."

"I wasn't invited," my mother sobbed. "Everyone else in town was, but *I* wasn't?"

"I'm sure it was an oversight," I said. "I'll call John Jr. and Caroline, and clear the matter up."

"I wouldn't go now if they sent that invitation in an armored car. It wasn't an oversight; it was an insult," she said, setting her jaw in that stubborn angle I knew so well.

"Instead of calling John Jr., I'll run over to Freddie Trask's house and see if I can solve this—or at least salvage it."

"You didn't hear me, son. The United States Marine Corps couldn't make me go to that party now."

"Don't make up your mind just yet," I urged. "Please."

Sprinting over to Freddie's house, I tried to form a logical plan that could bring some détente to this prickly social dilemma. I burst into Freddie's house, kissed his pretty wife, Louise, and went up to Freddie and said, out of breath, "Freddie, could you tell me why your goddamn brother didn't invite my *mother* to his party at the plantation tonight?"

Freddie looked at me as though I were teasing him in some mean-spirited way, his eyes going paranoid on me. "Party? What party?"

"Jesus Christ, Freddie! Doesn't your brother know we've been friends for years? I only know him because you and I are such good friends. He's having a party ten miles from here and he doesn't even invite his own brother? What kind of fucked-up family did you come from, Freddie? Louise, are you sure you didn't get an invitation?"

"Positive. It doesn't surprise me, however," Louise said.

"My family isn't as bad as yours, Conroy," Freddie insisted.

"I've always made it abundantly clear that mine is the most fucked-up family on earth. You've been far less forthcoming about yours," I said. "There's only one way to make this work. I'm not going to the goddamn party, either."

Freddie said, "I don't care what you do. I didn't even know there was a party."

I was born with a delusion in my soul that I've fought a rearguard battle with my entire life. Though I'm very much my mother's boy, it has pained me to admit the blood of Santini rushes hard and fast in my bloodstream. My mother gave me a poet's sensibility; my father's DNA assured me that I was always ready for a fight, and that I could ride into any fray as a field-tested lord of battle.

When I was a boy, I attuned myself to my mother's innumerable anxieties about her background. I remember visiting the house of a senior military officer, General Moore, where I saw my mother surveying the artwork on the walls. I knew that she was comparing it to the wretched artwork on our own walls. When General Moore's wife asked my mom where she had gone to college, I saw my mother's face burn with shame as she admitted she had not gone. My mother passed this incurable social mortification on to all her children. She went home from General Moore's house and went to an art supply store the very next day. When she returned, she got out her paints and her by-the-numbers canvases and took a girlish delight in painting ghastly paintings of Bozo the clown, the Virgin Mary, and others I don't remember. When my father got home from flying that day and saw the new paintings on the wall, he burst into mocking laughter and told Mom it was the ugliest shit he'd ever seen. Mom retreated into her bedroom upset, and I thought he was the cruelest person in the world.

My father was made of all the wrong stuff, but because I'm his son, so am I. In any social setting Dad found himself in, my father was comfortable in his own sense of presence and command. I never saw him intimidated by any socialite or celebrity he met. I don't think the thought crossed his mind. There was a fierce pridefulness in the Chicago Irish that fortified my dad's own image of himself. Unlike the poor whites of Appalachia, where my mother came from, the large family of Irishmen in Chicago were on their way up and they all knew it and all were proud of it. Though Dad's parents did not attend college, they sired nine children and eight of them got college degrees. Dad was part of a generation with grand ambitions and he always strutted in self-satisfied vanity down whatever street he walked. My mother's lust to be accepted at the highest levels of society contrasted with my dad's sheer indifference to it. Dad passed this indifference on to all his seven children. Mom seared us with her fear of being abandoned and valueless, but Dad taught us not to give a shit.

I don't like parties and I could sure miss one at Orange Grove plantation and never think of it again. I took Mom and John Egan to dinner at the Parris Island Officers' Club that night. Once more, Mom and I saved ourselves by retreating to the heart of the Marine Corps—our native land.

In the middle of dinner, my mother reached over and squeezed my hand, then said to her husband, "John, I told you I'd raised a son who'd always fight for his mother." She was looking at me with a sublime glance that suggested adoration. She had obviously forgiven me for not testifying in her divorce case.

The following morning Freddie was already drinking a cup of coffee in my mom's kitchen when I made my way downstairs.

"My father called me at seven o'clock in the morning," Freddie told me.

"What did you two lovebirds have to say to each other?" I asked.

"He's mad as hell at you and thinks you insulted our whole family," said Fred.

"Did you explain to your loving pa that you and your brother Charles were not even aware a party was going on?"

"No, I didn't tell him that," Freddie admitted.

"Why not?"

"He scares the shit out of me just like your old man scares you," Freddie said, and then added, "Pardon my French, Peg."

My mother was lapping up this conversation and gestured with her hand to let Freddie know there was no offense taken.

"Your son got me into some bad trouble last night, Peg, by not going to my brother's party," Freddie said. "Dad blames it all on me. He's demanding Pat meet him for drinks at his mansion on Bay Street."

"He demands?" I asked.

"Don't make this hard for me, Conroy," Freddie said. "I've got to produce you at his house at six. I may have to hog-tie you or handcuff you or put a gun to your head, but I've got to get you in his den."

My mother had a bemused, mischievous smile on her face and suggested to Freddie, "I know Pat better than you do, Freddie."

"Then how do I talk some sense into him? He's so goddamn stubborn," Freddie said.

"Yes, but he's also very nice," my mom said. "I suggest you ask Pat to help you get out of a tough position. Tell him you need his help—

that it would really help you with your relationship with your father, Big John."

"It'll really help me with my daddy, Conroy," he said to me.

"See you at six," I said to Freddie.

Ever since I had arrived in Beaufort in 1961, I had developed a curious attraction for the Trask family's domination of all aspects of small-town life. This type of powerful clan is well chronicled by Southern writers, with William Faulkner leading the way. The Trasks and the Snopeses seem interchangeable to me, and the rise of the Trasks took place out of a hardworking farming family from Wilmington, North Carolina. Big John and Beanie Trask led a migration south to Beaufort County, where they grew wealthy harvesting vast fields of cucumbers as well as the most admirable tomatoes grown in the South. The amazing success of those mouthwatering tomatoes put the whole family in mansions. To me, they've always been the most fascinating family in town. Like many such families, they seem to like everyone in town except one another.

At six o'clock sharp, I rang the front doorbell at the Trask mansion on Bay Street, and Freddie answered.

"You know we only use the back door," Freddie said.

"I wanted to see the Beaufort River at high tide," I explained.

"You already pissed him off," Freddie said. "You should've knocked in back."

We passed through the house to the well-appointed den in the back. Freddie's mother, Flora, was sitting with his wife, Louise, in straight-backed chairs against the wall. After I greeted and kissed them both, I looked up and saw Big John staring at me with curiosity.

He motioned for me to join him behind a fortlike embankment of leather sofas and chairs. I looked over my shoulder and poor Freddie had taken his position on a ladder-back chair against the wall next to his wife and mother.

Big John first chose the strategy of staring at me with a smirk, but after The Citadel, I could outstare any man who wished to test me. Then Big John pulled back, leaned over, and handed me a cigar.

"That's contraband, boy, but that's what Big John smokes." He handed me a bottle of bourbon and said, "This bottle is Rebel Yell. I got me a whole bottle of my own. It's the nectar of the South, boy. Pour you a glass and make yourself right at home. I always treat my guests like they were kings in my house."

As he took a puff from his Cuban cigar and a swallow of Rebel Yell, I got to study his face at my leisure. The handsomeness of Big John Trask was slowly undermined by the chalk quarries of age; signs of dissipation clustered around the dark folds near his eyes, and the skin around the jawline was sallow and sunburned at the same time. He had the eyes of a cottonmouth snake. He carried meanness in his eyes and menace in his ample frame.

"Do you know who I am in this town, Conroy?"

"Yes, sir, Mr. Trask. I think I do."

"You call me Big John like all my friends do," he boomed. "No, do you know how big I am in this town? How really big I am?"

"Yes, sir, I think I do, Big John," I replied.

"I'm the biggest thing in this town. The richest, the smartest, the meanest son of a bitch this town's ever seen. You hear that music coming from the speakers? I am the music of radio station WBEU. Russian sailors on the high seas listen to Big John's music when they piss off-shore. You don't believe that, Conroy? I'll prove to you I am this music."

He grabbed a phone like a six-gun and began dialing. When the phone was answered, he said, "Boy, this is Big John. Are you crazy? Big John Trask! I own this radio station. I own you. Oh, you're the new boy? Okay, that's all right. Right now, I want you to interrupt this program with an announcement: 'Mr. John Trask is entertaining the writer Pat Conroy over at Big John's Bay Street mansion. Mr. Conroy is the author of *The Great Santini*, which is being filmed in Beaufort.' Now go ahead, boy. Put it on air right now or I'll fire your sorry ass."

The disk jockey's voice immediately filled the room: "Mr. John Trask is entertaining the writer Pat Conroy over at Big John's Bay Street mansion."

When the deejay finished, Big John affixed me with his steady gaze again and said, "Does that prove to you I own that station?"

"No, that doesn't prove a thing," I teased. "You could've bribed that kid with a hundred bucks."

Again, the savage leap for the phone and Big John, agitated, said,

"Boy, Big John again. You play Big John's three favorite songs right now so Conroy'll believe I am WBEU."

In this surreal atmosphere I had the feeling I was a bit player in a Southern Gothic play written by Samuel Beckett. Big John's three favorite songs were played one after another without a disturbing word of interference from the flummoxed disk jockey. The first song was "Dixie."

Big John leaped to his feet, put his right hand over his heart, and tears came to his eyes as he listened to the anthem to the lost cause.

"You don't stand for 'Dixie,' boy?" Big John yelled at me.

"No, sir. I stand up for 'The Star-Spangled Banner.'"

"That's heresy, boy!"

"I was raised by a Marine, sir," I said.

But "Dixie" soon ended with a merciful flourish and was replaced by "I'm So Lonesome I Could Cry," which had a transformational effect on Big John Trask. He began crying at the first line and was sobbing by the time the song had ended.

"That's the way I feel, Conroy. I've been at the top of the heap so long that I don't even remember what the bottom looked like. I've been the top dog since I got to this town. But I'm lonely. Goddamn, a man as important as me gets lonely. It's me by myself—richer than shit, but lonesome."

"Must be agony, Big John," I said.

By then, the third song in Big John's sacred trilogy made its way over the airway and he went through another metamorphosis before my eyes. When he heard Jimmy Dean reciting "The Ballad of Big John," he straightened up, dried his tears, and assumed a hero's posture as he heard about the fictional Big John, powerful and mythic, saving a hundred miners by holding up a broken shaft after a cave-in at a coal mine.

"That's me, Conroy! That's who I am—a man so tough that he looks to save everyone but himself. I've always been the bravest son of a bitch in whatever room I've entered. What do you say about that?"

"Sounds good to me, Big John," I said.

The music stopped and Big John's mouth changed, sharpened into a grimace of cunning and meanness. His eyes took on a sneaky look, as though he were looking at me as some rodent who'd become his next meal. I took a sip of bourbon and awaited his strike. It came swift and certain.

"Conroy, I want to know why you insulted my son John and his wife by not showing up at their party last night. We had the whole movie crew out there, as well as the biggest movers and shakers in town. The party was for *you*, so why didn't you show up?" Big John demanded.

"I can give you two explanations. When you and Mrs. Trask were raising your sons, you should've taught them to have better manners. I came down for the party yesterday and found my mother crying at the kitchen table. It seems your son had forgotten to invite my mother or her husband to his party. I ran over to your son Freddie's house, and it seems like Junior also neglected to invite Freddie or Louise to his party. Fred and I've been friends for ten years, so it doesn't help my mood to find my mother crying and one of my best friends humiliated over a party at your son's house. So I skipped your son's party for his careless-ness. And I'll never think of it again."

"That true, Freddie?" Big John demanded.

"Yes, Daddy," Freddie admitted.

Turning back to me, Big John said, "You're just like Big John, Conroy—the spitting image of me. I'd'a done the same damn thing. And you've accomplished some things. You've made your way in the world. Freddie over there has never done shit and never will. You made your way in Hollywood. That's really something. I admire you, boy."

"Thanks, Big John," I said, springing to my feet. "I got to get back over to my mama's."

As we were filing out the back door, Big John grabbed my shoulder and pulled me back into the den.

"Conroy, before you go, you gotta tell me one thing. We're talking man-to-man here. I've made a ton of money, a millionaire many times over. But I hear Hollywood is a much bigger cat. I hear they dream in billions, not millions—so I'm dying to know. How much money are you making out of all this?"

I breathed deeply and told him, "I can't discuss exact figures here, Big John. But let me tell you this—I could buy you, could write you a check tonight that could make you the happiest man on earth."

He squealed with pleasure. "You're just like Big John, Conroy! Just like Big John. You've got my killer instinct."

. . .

I had learned much about the etiquette of a writer visiting the set of a movie being made from his or her book. The rule was a simple one—they don't want you there. They don't want your opinions aired on either their screenplays or the scenes you're allowed to watch them film. During the filming of *Conrack*, Jon Voight had avoided me as though I'd contracted a rare form of leprosy, and brought his discomfort to the set. It seemed odd to me then, but I learned the reason why when Christopher Dickey wrote a brilliant memoir about his father, James Dickey, in *Summer of Deliverance*. I was in Mr. Dickey's poetry workshop when *Deliverance* was filmed in the North Carolina mountains. James Dickey was a supernova among Southern literary personalities, and it seemed like he spent every moment on the set. Burt Reynolds and Jon Voight did not come away with grand-hearted memories of my favorite poet; therefore Voight reacted to me as though I were the second monstrous incarnation of a Southern writer in his life.

The set of *The Great Santini* seemed a happy one, however, and Lewis John Carlino ran a disciplined corps of actors and extras while Charles Pratt kept the production on time and on budget. The looming problem was one of diplomacy and infinite tact. My father still wanted to visit the set, and Mom was still adamantly opposed to the visit, no matter how artful or skillful our arguments were. Over a dinner at her house, I tried again to make her see the wisdom of generosity over bitterness and how it would be good for the well-being of all her children for some kind of truce to be signed. "Besides," I said to my mom, "it's Dad's story, too. He lived it as much as any of us did."

"And he was the man who ruined it all," she said.

"I agree, Mom. No one agrees more. But we're all getting older and we've got to figure out how to make something work out of this blown-up family. We've got to learn how to build something out of the ruins."

"I agree with you, Pat," John Egan said, a military set to his handsome face. "Peggy, it's time to put this behind us. There'll be more marriages and funerals coming up. Your family needs your help."

"I'll get Dad in and out of town, Mom," I said. "You won't even know he was here."

"I'll take Peg to Charleston instead," Dr. Egan said, sealing the deal. "We'll have dinner, then spend the night at the Mills Hyatt House." I shook John's hand, kissed Mom, and was out the door in a flash.

On the following day, Dad drove down from Atlanta as frisky as a parakeet that he was going to visit the set at long last. Charles Pratt embraced my father warmly and said that my dad embodied all the virtues he admired as a man. "My God," I whispered to Dad, "an American fascist."

"A real American, son," Dad whispered back. "You've always had a little trouble with the concept."

Duvall seemed to take real delight in meeting my father, and I could see in the scene I watched being filmed that he was closing in on a love affair with his character. The tension on the set was rising as some new disaster would overwhelm the discordant Meecham family.

As Bull grew more violent, Lewis John Carlino invited Dad and me to watch the scene between the furious father and the overwhelmed son. When I had first written this scene in the house on Hancock Street, I thought I had never written anything with such primal derangement—it seemed to emanate from an evil place inside me. In words and action, I tried to explain all the despair I brought to the hatred of my father during my long childhood. It took a single backyard basketball game, played on a makeshift court with the Beaufort River behind it, to have Bull Meecham ruin the small segment left of his son's unsuccessful boyhood. I had a hundred examples to choose from—Dad used to start games out when I was in ninth and tenth grade where he would slap my cheeks hard enough to bring tears spilling down my cheeks. But then I got stronger and faster and I wouldn't quit, so he developed the habit of throwing the ball into my forehead, then driving by me. Then I became really fast and my ball handing was as good as any in the state, so I wrote about challenging him to a duel in the backyard of the new house—a magnificent house that hid the family in residence there.

In the game I beat my father fair and square, and I began to walk off the court, but my father could never admit defeat in front of his wife, his family, or anyone. So he grabbed that basketball and he began bouncing it off the back of that boy's head—over and over again, taunting Ben that he'd always been his favorite little girl, his favorite little pussy, that he was going to buy him a Barbie doll for being such a good little girl. I could have used a thousand scenes from my childhood, but the theme was always humiliation and a shame that could never be removed or washed away. It's that indelible shame I feel today as I write some of the same words I wrote more than thirty-six years ago. The fear is the same—the self-loathing, the suicide wishes the same—the waking up screaming in the middle of the night will always be the same.

Then, in the yard of Tidalholm, in Beaufort, my father and I found ourselves seated in director's chairs in a place of high honor as we watched the actors perform their wizardry and magic. Robert Duvall and Michael O'Keefe came out as though they knew they were about to live through one of the best days of their lives. All the suppressed anger a father and a son could hide from each other in every excruciating moment of the basketball game with the taunting that was good-natured at first, but turned savage as the game built. The kids on the sideline tried to shout support for their brother, but they could feel the resentment of the father building up like steam in a kettle.

It was Blythe Danner who saw the danger waters about to break. When the game was over and she hugged her son after his first victory over Santini, it was she who spotted the incurable wreckage that had built up on the foundations of her family. She declared her son the winner and got a basketball in her face for her troubles. But the father refused to accept his loss. For his courage, his father bounced a basketball off his son's head in a long march from the court to his bedroom. In that courageous march Ben Meecham earned his wings in his father's squadron and began to prove himself a worthy son of his warriorlike elder.

I sat there breathless in that yard when that seminal scene was filmed. My father hadn't moved since the actors had gone to work. Everyone who had witnessed the coming apart of the Meecham family sat there drained and exhausted. Even the wisteria seemed capable of collapse. What was it? I kept asking. What was it I had just seen with my own eyes play out in a town that I had taken for a home?

Then I had it, and my soul filled with gratitude. It was art. I had watched art being created and made and honored. It was a dazzling thing to behold.

It was so powerful in its purity and its sheer honesty that it shook me, terrified me. But it changed me. That is what art always does. It always changes you and that change stays with you for a lifetime. The magnificent cast caught with rare perfection how quickly the Conroy family dynamic could explode, grow in anarchy and acuity, until all of us were lost in our own lunatic roles of trying to defuse the chaos that had swallowed us up in an abyss we couldn't avoid. These actors had captured the madness of our family and had done it by blending the powerful magic they carried with them in their belief in the genius of their own art. My father and I never spoke of watching that scene, but it did much to change our relationship as father and son.

CHAPTER 7

Two Premieres

My mother's humiliation at not being invited to the Trask party turned out to be nothing compared with what was to come, when the premiere of *The Great Santini* came to Beaufort.

Peg Conroy's most ardent desire was to have complete access to the crème de la crème of whatever society she found herself in, in whatever part of the country we were passing through. Her model for both imitation and inspiration was that cunning, treacherous beauty from the plantation South, Scarlett O'Hara. I think my mother saw her entire life as her becoming an amorous survivalist in a world dominated by men, a crucible of mysteriousness the only weapon at the disposal of a woman who was both desirable and unreadable at the same time. Miss Scarlett gave Mom the white-throated image of the ivory-skinned woman who lived in immaculate cameos throughout the South. My mother willed herself to be one of those pampered women of the cameos.

She also dressed for the part with chicness and finesse. Her embittered daughters still talk with envy about my mother's lavish wardrobe and they both insist my mother was the only woman on base who had her own personal dressmaker. All I know for sure is that Mom looked scrumptious whenever she went out of the house and that she made Dad a handsomer man than he actually was. She dressed her children as though we were foundlings—with the girls, it was particularly cruel, and she seemed to go out of her way to make my two pretty sisters as unattractive as possible. They were given eyeglasses that looked like they were made from fins of Chryslers. The boys didn't count when it came to what we wore, and the siblings still get together and howl with laughter when we look at albums of our growing-up years. In some photographs, I see Tim and Tom wearing shirts I wore ten years before they were even born. But our mother was always ready to step out onto the veranda at Tara toward her fateful deliverance at the party at Twelve Oaks. Through an act of homage and will, she lived the life of Scarlett O'Hara. Everyone we met referred to her as a Southern belle and she did nothing to disabuse them of that notion. Beauty was her letter of transit out of the mean Appalachia.

Though my mother's imitation of the Southern belle was well rehearsed, it lacked authenticity. She lacked the quiet confidence that comes from the leisure and gracefulness of coming up right. Social ease issues out from the accumulated weight of generations of high achievers. Fashion and style were not tests you could study for—they were endowments passed down by families with the weight of culture behind them and the emotional dowries to back them up. Mom would wear the hills of Piedmont into whatever ballroom she entered, and her children would wear these same hills plus the wounds of slipshod, madcap Ireland wherever we roamed. Your birthplace is your destiny and it hunts you down in whatever cotillion you've run to hide in—it is a bad tattoo that is defining, accurate, and irremovable. My poor mother thought she had fooled everyone, but in the end, she barely fooled anyone, and especially not her children.

It began to come apart for my mother after her divorce from Dad. Overnight, my mother became a desperate, nearly hopeless woman. Though Mom had never drunk in her life, I heard rumors that she was now drinking heavily and even sleeping around. The kids were worried about her, and I think my brother Jim was simply disgusted with her. Then I heard a story that truly alarmed me and set me on the road to Beaufort at full speed.

When I got to Mom's house, we drove out to the beach on Hunting Island and we walked to the south end of the beach talking about everything. Mom told me, "I think I'm going crazy, Pat. I really do. I've lost all status and respect in this town. I used to be asked to serve on boards and was invited to the biggest parties. That's over for me. Some of these bitches won't even talk to me now."

"Have you been smoking dope with their kids, Mom? That's what I'd heard in Atlanta."

"Of course not! I've never even seen marijuana. I don't know what it looks like," she said. "How dare you believe those lies they're talking about me?"

"I was just asking. That seems like a big response from an innocent woman."

"Beaufort is making me paranoid. I can feel the people talking about me. Watching me from behind their window shades. Everyone's waiting for me to make a mistake. When I first came here I was the most popular woman in town. Now they act like I should be put out with the morning trash."

"I've got a suggestion, Mom. Let me send you to college."

"That offends the very core of my being," she said. "So even my son doesn't think I'm smart enough. Even you've betrayed me while I've lost my way temporarily. Son, I was like a prisoner in your father's house for thirty years, saddled with all those kids and no life of my own. I'm having some fun, Pat, just a little fun. Maybe I'm sowing a few wild oats. Kicking my heels up before I have to get married again. Besides, I graduated from Agnes Scott with honors."

"Just be careful, Mom. Beaufort can turn mean in a heartbeat."

"I think my redneck roots are showing through, and the mountain girl is finally up in arms. I come from bootleggers and murderers and they don't want to mess with pistol-packing Mountain Peg."

"Oh? When did Miss Scarlett die?" I asked, and my mother ran into the ocean laughing.

On one of my visits to Beaufort during the filming of the movie, I went to a bar above Harry's Restaurant to meet with Mom and Dr. John Egan. Mom had gotten together a cordial group of ten to twelve neighbors from Beaufort. Many were pals of Dr. Egan's, and had spent their lives on bases around the world. They were sophisticated and comfortable with themselves, and told great stories.

Toward the end of the evening my mother struck a wineglass with a teaspoon to get everybody in the restaurant's attention. She took well to the limelight and glowed with a peculiar shine of pleasure surrounded by her friends and her oldest son. I remember being proud of the fact that she was so pretty and liked to be around old boys who appreciated that beauty.

"I've got an announcement to make and I wanted Pat to be here when I made it. Last night, I got a phone call from Charles Pratt, who is the producer of *The Great Santini*. Mr. Pratt said he and the studio had thought about the opening of the film being in Hollywood. Some wanted it to open in Toronto, others in New York. 'But then it hit us all,' he said. 'Let's open the movie in Beaufort, where Pat lived the life and wrote the book that brought us all to that beautiful part of the world.'"

A cheer went up from the patrons in the restaurant, and the rumor hit the streets.

"Charles Pratt promised me that this premiere is going to be one of the biggest blowouts this town has ever seen. He said it would be the hottest ticket in town. I want to invite all of you to come to help me celebrate what I know will be one of the most joyous nights of my life," my mother said as friends came up to hug and congratulate us.

When I left the next morning for the long drive back to Atlanta, I gave my mother a cautionary warning: "Mom, I would tone down your triumphalism about the premiere coming to town. Ease up on the pedal when you start bragging about me."

"I'll brag about you all I want. Don't think those women who have a lawyer or a doctor in their family don't run their mouths every time they see me. One of the pleasures of being a mother is bragging about your kids."

"Then brag about the other ones. I'm afraid this will get back to the kids and hurt their feelings."

"No, no, this is your negativity again. You're trying to squelch my fun when I'm just starting to have some, and I won't let you do it. You never enjoy any of the good things that've happened to you. Not one thing. You see the dark side of everything."

"I don't trust the world. I'm cautious about it. I don't know how it will come, but there's always trouble lying ahead."

"You watch for the trouble all you want," she said. "I plan to enjoy the ride."

I went back to writing and editing *The Lords of Discipline* and I realized that I could finally make a sentence sound exactly how I wanted it to sound. Under my editor Jonathan Galassi's watchful eye, I wrote scenes and tightened others and have rarely enjoyed working on a book with such passion and ardor—I looked at what I did for a living and adored making the English language sing and strut on a sheet of yellow legal paper where I wrote it down in my own handwriting. The book would be published by Houghton Mifflin on the fall list, about the same time the *Santini* movie was being released around the country.

But there were storms passing through in my own life that I could not ignore. I had fallen in love with a fetching woman named Lenore Fleischer, who in the next ten years would ruin my life and lead me into a suicidal spiral that I thought I could never recover from. She failed to tell me she had gone off birth control three months before our wedding, then surprised me by getting immediately pregnant, maybe even on our wedding night. Her rodentlike, morally repugnant ex-husband was suing me so often in the Atlanta courts that I would end up taking the whole family off to live in Rome, Italy, for three years in the eighties, mostly to get away from him. In Rome, I finalized two hundred and fifty pages of *The Prince of Tides*, but Jonathan Galassi had stunned me by taking a job with Random House and wanted me to make the move with him. When I visited the new office of Jonathan at Random House, it soon became apparent that the editors and publishers at that august publishing house had no interest in my writing career and almost none in Jonathan's either. We were insulted in every office to which he took me. I never felt like more of a Southern hick, toothless and feckless with holes in my shoes, than I did for those two shameful hours wandering the halls of that gutless company. Jason Epstein has no idea how close I was to breaking his bigmouthed jaw when he mortified a crestfallen Jonathan in front of me and refused to raise his eyes to meet mine, nor his hand to shake mine in friendship. He was a braying, overbearing man, not a lonesome dove among his discourteous colleagues. I sprinted out of Jonathan Galassi's life and Random House went on to fire him in 1986. He went to Farrar, Straus, and Giroux and succeeded in becoming one of the most successful and distinguished publishers in New York history. I ran back to the warm embrace of Houghton Mifflin and fell under the sway of the glorious Nan Talese. Nan would later receive the first Maxwell E. Perkins Award for lifetime achievement in editing. Two years later Jonathan Galassi won the third Maxwell E. Perkins Award. My life as a writer has been a well-cobbled one; I was lucky to work with editors of supernatural gifts. At times, I made a ham-fisted unruly guest in their stable of writers, but we did some good things together that I'll always be proud of.

Then *The Great Santini* premiere made a full-fledged charge at my mother's poor artless heart. The strategy caught the whole family by surprise, but it was admirable in its cunning and its blitzkrieg swiftness.

Every morning, Dad would join me for coffee in my living room in Atlanta, where we'd dissect the *Atlanta Constitution* and talk about the news of the day. At the beginning of the summer, I could tell that Dad's excitement about the premiere was rising as he began talking about how many of his brothers and sisters he could sneak in the back door. He talked about the Conroy kids and their families all sitting in a group and then said, "In the best seats in the house, of course."

"Dad," I warned, "I don't know where the premiere's going to be. The theaters in Beaufort are the size of kayaks."

"Hey, you and I are the whole show, son," he said. "They can't do it without us. Your mother's right, Mr. Negative. Sheesh."

The news came to my mother on a Monday afternoon. Dr. Egan reported that Mom cried out when she received the devastating news of how many premiere tickets were allotted to the Conroy family. She went to argue her case the next day with the same result and the insistency that the allocation of the tickets was irreversible and nonnegotiable. Dad came over to my place on a rare nightly visit and his look was distraught.

"Your mother needs you, son. She needs you bad," he said.

"How in the hell would you know she needs me? You two haven't talked in years," I asked.

"Her husband, John Egan, called me. He asked that we keep his call secret from your mother. But he says that she needs you more than she ever did. Beaufort got her again. But this time, it really got her."

In what was becoming another great circle in my life, I pushed off for Beaufort the next morning, even though I lacked any clue of what had mortified Mom this time. Though I'd called her after talking to Dad, she was far too hysterical to talk to me on the phone. As I drove along the forested borders of I-20, I went over every single thing that could've gone wrong, but I could come up with no scenario that could've sent my mother into this paroxysm of rage and shame. She could handle her rage just fine, but shame always brought her to her knees. The way an Inuit knows a thousand forms that snow can take, I knew all the separate registers and cries that mother's lifelong vocation of twisting the claws of her shame could take.

Dr. Egan was downstairs when I came in the back door. The tide was high and there was a soft breeze that seemed to carry a little of the river with it, while the sun shone off the bay giving it a milky, opaque light. The doctor pointed upstairs and I headed to the bedroom.

I knocked softly on the door and heard Mom's frailest voice asking me to enter.

"I heard they've been messing with my mama again," I said.

It did not have the calmative effect on my mother I was hoping for. Instead, she put her face into a very wet pillowcase and sobbed to the point of screaming. Massaging her shoulders, I tried to get her to tell me what was wrong, but she began saying things like, "I told John that we were moving out of this goddamn hypocritical town—maybe move to Lake Lure, where Stanny had a home, or to Asheville, where I've always wanted to live. But it's farewell to Beaufort. Goddamn little crapola of a town! I can never walk down its streets again—ever. I'd have to wear a Halloween mask or a bag over my head."

"Just tell me what happened, okay?"

"I got a call from the head of the *Great Santini* premiere committee," she said.

"I didn't know there was such a committee."

"Neither did I, until I got the call," Mom said.

"Who is the chairman of it?" I asked.

"Col. Paul Sigmund," she said. "He flew with your father in the Marine Corps. I met with him at his office and he told me that all the plans have been solidified for the premiere."

"It's his job," I said. "No harm in that."

"I asked him how many seats my family was allotted," she said, and I could tell by her voice that she was lining up to place the sword into the bull's spine.

"Do tell," I said.

"Three," she said.

"Three?" I echoed, realizing that the skimpiness of the number had taken me by surprise.

"One for me. One for your father. And one for you," she said.

"It seems I have business with Colonel Sigmund this morning," I said.

"He's expecting you," Mom said. "He told me you've no chance to change his mind, and no matter what you say it will not affect the decisions of the great premiere committee."

I looked at my mother. "Wanna bet?"

The committee worked out of a simple office in downtown Beaufort. My mother was right: Colonel Sigmund was waiting for me with I thought a little too much emphasis on being confrontational and not enough on being conciliatory. After we exchanged pleasantries about the Marine Corps, Colonel Sigmund got right down to business.

"I know why you're here, Pat. Your mother has gotten hysterical in this office several times. But the committee has taken a very disciplined approach to this. We are having the premiere at the local cineplex, where seating is extremely limited. Your mother has made this most difficult and frankly hasn't done her cause any good."

"May I see the list of the committee?" I asked. He handed me two pages of names in a double-spaced list. "How many members of the *Great Santini* premiere committee are there?"

"There are ninety, Pat," Colonel Sigmund said.

"How many tickets do members of the committee receive?" I asked.

"Each receives two."

"Ah, one hundred eighty tickets for the *Great Santini* premiere committee. Three for the Great Santini's family. Do you know my mother remarried, Colonel Sigmund?"

"I know Dr. Egan well, but he'll not be coming," Colonel Sigmund said. "I already made that perfectly clear to your mother."

"This list. It's all white people," I said.

"I believe it is," the colonel said.

"Anybody read my books in this town?" I said. "And they're going to give me a segregated premiere? Are you aware that Don and Peg had six other children besides me?"

"And they won't be coming either, Pat," he said.

"You don't seem in the mood to solve this with any sense of diplomacy."

"I've nothing to deal with. These rules were carved in stone."

"Anyone think of putting my mother on the committee?"

"I wasn't privy to any discussion like that," the colonel said. "Well, I told you I was sticking by my guns and I've done it."

"Yes, you have, and now I'd like to present you with my own commands and wishes."

"You're not in a place to issue commands," Colonel Sigmund said. "Didn't you learn anything about the chain of command at The Citadel?"

"I learned everything about the chain of command at The Citadel," I said. "And here is what you didn't learn about the chain of command in the Marine Corps."

"And what is that?" he asked.

"You ain't in command. And if you don't do something about making my mother happy before this premiere, I promise my father and I will not show up."

At that point, Colonel Sigmund made one of those mistakes that people who don't know me always do when he said, "I bet wild horses couldn't keep you and your father away."

"You're going to learn about me and my dad before this is over. And because you made that snotty remark, neither of us will be at the *Great Santini* premiere."

"I have my doubts," he said. "Your dad's got quite an ego, and I'm betting that you do, too."

Colonel Sigmund and I shook hands and said farewell to each other forever.

I was no stranger to the city-states of colonels, and I knew a great deal more about Paul Sigmund when I walked into his office than he would ever learn about me. First, he possessed an elegance and sophistication that I found a rarity in the Marine officers I'd grown up with. His polish and sense of self-possession made me surprised he'd never made general, and in his smoothness of manner and pleasantness of speech he exposed my father for the happy vulgarian he always was proud to be. Yet I liked Colonel Sigmund a lot and I thought we could've become good friends if circumstances had been different between us. But by becoming an agent in my mother's humiliation, he made me draw up the most explosive card I carried in my deck and flip it at him to give him ample time to think over what the committee had done.

When I returned to the house on Carteret Street, Mom was still in bed and still weeping. When I tried to lift her head to change her pillowcase, she wouldn't allow me to touch it. Though she did not say it, it appeared that she wanted some accurate measurement of how much grief the town had caused her.

"How did the meeting go with Colonel Sigmund?" she asked me.

"Exactly like you said it would," I reported.

"He gave you nothing. Not a single ticket," she said.

"Not a one," I said. "But don't worry; that's all about to change."

"How can you be so sure?" she asked.

"Because I told him the Great Santini and I were not going to the premiere."

"But it's your big night. And Don's," she said.

"Not anymore," I said.

"How will you talk your father into this?"

"I'll tell him what the committee did to you. I know Dad. He won't come near the joint."

"What if it doesn't work?"

"It'll work. But don't you jump at the first offer. Let it play out, Mom. Have fun with it," I said. "Make 'em squirm."

"That's a promise, Pat," she said.

The next night I took my father to Petite Auberge, a nice French restaurant in the Toco Hills Shopping Center. Though he rarely let me take him to restaurants where the food cost more than three dollars a pound, I told him I needed to have a serious talk with him in a muted, convivial atmosphere.

As Dad looked over the menu, I watched the old sneer cross his eyes as he said, "Frog food. This place doesn't have anything but frog food."

I said, "It's called a French restaurant. French restaurants kind of specialize in frog food. Shall I order for you?"

"Yeah, you've lived in France," he said.

With great mischievous intent, I ordered him a meal of escargot, frog legs, a salad, and a crème brûlée. With his Chicago obstinacy, he ordered himself a Budweiser, scoffing when I offered to buy a bottle of wine.

"I'm a beer drinker—wine is for pussies."

When his escargot came, Dad stared at it as if I'd ordered him a plate full of roaches. The escargot was not served in snail shells, but in those indented metal plates that held the escargot swimming in that ineluctable butter and garlic and parsley sauce.

Dad stared hard at the first snail he held at the end of his fork. "Now, what in the hell might this thing be?"

"It's from a very rare French cow, bred near the Alps. They cut precious bits from near the tenderloin and a master butcher makes sure the cuts all look the same. Put some sauce on it, Dad. Then sit back and enjoy."

Dad ate the first one and said, "That's the shittiest beef I've ever eaten, but damn, that sauce is terrific."

When the frog legs came, I informed Dad that these were the legs of Bresse chickens, the most prized hens in a French kitchen. The salad he approved of, and he moaned with happiness over his crème brûlée. Then we came to the business of the evening.

Starting from the beginning, I told about Mom's first meeting with Paul Sigmund.

"Hey, I flew with Paul. He's a great guy. I'll give him a call and straighten this out."

"Listen to the rest of the story," I said. I told of finding Mom in bed, where she had been lying for several days crying with a sense of morbid disgrace she could neither hide nor deny. When I told him about the three tickets they promised the entire Conroy family, my father's face darkened with fury.

"Three fucking tickets!" my father exploded. "That's an outrage."

"To get Mom the tickets, I cut a deal with Colonel Sigmund," I said.

"But you said you walked out of his office with only three tickets."

"I told him that if he didn't make Mom happy, then the Great Santini and I would not attend the premiere. Colonel Sigmund went too far with me by saying, 'I bet wild horses couldn't keep you away from that premiere.'"

"God, he doesn't know your oversensitive ass, son," Dad said.

"And he doesn't know about your loyal one."

"We won't go, son. We'll do it for Peg," he said.

"I knew you'd say that," I said.

"How'd you know that?" Dad asked.

"Because you're an Irish Catholic from Chicago. I think your people are the biggest pains in the ass in the world, but they're also the most loyal. I remember your family coming after me after *The Great Santini* came out. I didn't like it much, but I sure could admire it."

"How do you know your little trick's going to work?" Dad asked me.

"I don't. We'll just have to wait and see."

"You could be making a damn fool of yourself, Pat."

"There's always that possibility—in everything we do," I agreed.

It was a luminous, green summer in the section of Ansley Park where I was living in Atlanta. I was still jogging during that time of my life, and there was not a more beautiful place in the city to run. It was a cutoff enclosed hermitage with shapely, eccentric houses shoulder to shoulder with one another, streets that harbored well-tended gardens, and the smell of jasmine always hovering in the air. The oak trees lorded over the lesser species in the park and offered the entire neighborhood the cool silages of darkness and the peacefulness of shade.

My mother heard nothing back from the *Great Santini* premiere committee until late September. Colonel Sigmund was charming and conciliatory this time, and invited Mom up to his office again. This time, John Egan accompanied my mother so that she would not be bullied or overwhelmed once more.

"Colonel Sigmund upped the ante, Pat," my mother said. "The Conroy family now gets five tickets—five big ones. But it comes with a catch. You and Dad have to attend."

"None of the kids can go," I said. "Not interested."

"I think Hollywood found out that you and Don were boycotting the event. There's a lot of pressure to see this problem settled."

The next week Mom had ten tickets, and the following week she scored fifteen. As time for the premiere to occur loomed as a large lunar force on the political and social forces of Beaufort, the complimentary tickets began taking to the airwaves over Mother's place like homing pigeons.

"Fifty tickets," my mother said one night, her voice flushed with victory that I found unfortunate.

"Mom, drop that tone out of your voice. You don't want your neighbors to see you gloating over their embarrassment."

"I don't mind gloating and I certainly don't care if they see it."

"Mom, be gracious, be thankful, and be classy. You've always gotten through your worst times by showing great class," I advised.

"The class comes with the whole package. I thought you knew that, son," she said.

"But I also know the killer Peg who comes in that same package. Keep the killer Peg under wraps," I said.

"I'd like to strangle every member of that committee and run them down on the street."

"Tell me that, Mom. Don't tell them," I said.

During the week of the premiere, Mom received her final tally from Colonel Sigmund. She called me with complete exhilaration and cried out, "Paul said I could have all the tickets I wanted. Every one of them. I told Paul that I'd try my best to get you and Don down here for the big night."

"Sorry, Mom; that's why this worked. It wasn't a threat—it was a promise. Who're you inviting?"

"Everybody I'm related to. You've got cousins coming whom you've never even heard of. I'd like to empty the jailhouse and invite all the inmates," she said.

"Easy, Mom. You won. No victory laps, please," I suggested.

"Pat, I can't thank you enough. What other son would do this for his mother? And please thank Don for me. It's going to be hard for your egomaniac father to miss his own show."

But my father did not miss his own show. Unbeknownst to me, he had been plotting with the producer Charles Pratt to have an early showing of *The Great Santini* at the Omni theater in Atlanta. Dad and I called everyone we knew and loved in Atlanta. The whole Atlanta writing community showed up—Anne Rivers Siddons in her luscious, sexiest prime came with her dapper husband, Heyward, at her side. Terry and Tommie Kay arrived, followed by Marshal and Gudrun Frady, Larry and Dee Woods, Joe and Emily Cummings, Vern Smith, Paul and Susan Hemphill—my college girlfriend Terry Leite, armed with her radiant beauty, walked in with Cliff Graubart and Bernie and Martha Schein. It was a sweet gathering on an auspicious evening.

Dad had another great surprise as the theater filled to capacity. A bagpiper team with fife and drums entered from the lobby. The men were a Marine contingent who were sharp as the wings of falcons as they stopped and played "The Star-Spangled Banner" as the whole theater rose in an unrehearsed corps de ballet. Then the bagpipers marched in fine order as they played the Marine Corps hymn and the crowd let out an exultant roar of approval. For five minutes they put on a marching display that was mesmerizing. The ovation they received as they marched back into the lobby was immense.

Then the theater darkened and the movie began. Before the movie started, my father reached over and squeezed my wrist.

"Semper Fi, Pat," he said.

"Semper Fi, Santini," I answered.

The movie was superb, as perfect as anything I could imagine. Robert Duvall, Blythe Danner, Michael O'Keefe, and Lisa Jane Persky taught me what it was like to be brought home to the tabernacle where art is turned into an essential thing that a human soul can feast on. Each of these actors exuded a power that seemed otherworldly, far beyond the realms of anything I thought possible. They fit together as a wounded family with both a naturalness and grandeur. Lewis John Carlino's direction was seamless to me, and I was moved to see the town of Beaufort filmed with such a loving eye of a camera crew that had taken in the comeliness of my river-shaped town. They filmed a French class in Gene Norris's English classroom I attended at Beaufort High School. They filmed a basketball game in a gym on the air station where I used to play against Marines who served under my father. They filmed the grueling scene of the father and son's two-step dance on the Green exactly where it happened in real life.

But my favorite scene by far took place at the end of the movie, when they're burying the Great Santini and the "missing man" formation soars over the cemetery in a salute to a lost aviator.

I glanced over, and to my delight my father had tears running down his cheeks as the colonel watched the burial of his fictitious self.

"Oh, Dad, give me a break," I said. "Santini crying at his own funeral. Over the top, Colonel."

"Fuck you," Dad said lovingly.

My book did much to tear my family apart, but more than anything, the harrowing story of the Conroy family found a form of mysterious healing when the movie *The Great Santini* was loosed to the world.

In the bar in the Atlanta Omni we drank with our great friends in rowdy boisterousness and the knowledge that all of us had just experienced a signatory time in our lives.

At the real premiere the following evening in Beaufort, my mother took to her queenship of the night with graciousness and flair. She held center stage like a consort in Balmoral Castle as she accepted compliments and bouquets from a town that had neared a point of no return with her. During the first showing of the film, all the Conroy family sat in the front row in a place of high honor. The town watched in fascination as the film began to spread out the breakdown of a single military family embattled with one another while the Cold War played out around them. In a visceral scene, Robert Duvall comes home drunk from happy hour and becomes engaged in a pitched battle with his family that leaves his tribe lying all over the kitchen. Beaufort was shocked by the ruthlessness of the encounter, and the audience held its breath as the Conroy family watched from the front row.

Finally my brother Jim, who sat in the last seat of the aisle, went down on one knee and whispered to his mother and siblings: "Bambi. Duvall is like Bambi beating up on his family. Dad should've shown him how to take a family apart. This guy's Bambi."

The Conroy family, as odd and imbalanced as any group who had ever entered the Beaufort city limits, fell apart laughing. The town watched us with a noncommittal gaze, and much pity.

PART TWO

. . . .

CHAPTER 8 ·

Stanny

Every family produces one unconventional, breakout member whose sheer willfulness and obstinacy will change the course of that family's history. When my grandmother Margaret Nolen Peek deserted her four children and husband in the middle of the Depression and hitchhiked a ride on a mule wagon heading for Atlanta, where she got a job in the notions department at Rich's department store, then married a Greek salesman of adding machines who also ran the numbers racket in the city, she transformed everything about how her children looked at themselves in the world. My mother's family pulled out of impoverished but honorable bondage to subsistence farming in the mountains of Alabama. In her flight, my grandmother proved she was not a big fan of starvation, country living, or a future that seemed desperate and hopeless to her. By marrying Jack Stanton, she shifted her social status overnight. When I was learning to talk as an infant, I gave her the nickname "Stanny" because I could not handle the "Mama Stanton" she wanted me to call her. Her pridefulness was a clear spring inside her, so no grandchild ever dared call her "Grandma." She reveled in her flamboyance, earthy beauty, acquired sophistication, stylish attraction to expensive clothes, and her passion for traveling to exotic nations. She once told me that she had a third-grade education and married my grandfather Jasper Catlett Peek when she was eleven. "Before I was even a woman," she whispered in her gravelly voice. I was horrified even though I didn't have a clue what she was talking about. If you want to find yourself completely lost in the mysteries of either God or sex, have a Roman Catholic education even though you were raised in a family who came out of the primitive Baptist tradition of the mountain South. I sometimes feel that my faith issued forth from a mustachioed nun who spoke in tongues. Stanny never belonged to a church that I'm aware of, but my grandfather spoke to Jesus of Nazareth, out loud, every day of his life. After Stanny deserted him and her children during the Depression, Jasper Peek never dated or looked at another woman. Stanny was married six or seven times, maybe more. In her house on Rosedale Road, I once walked into her living room and encountered a complete stranger lying on the couch listening to an Atlanta Crackers baseball game on the radio. Openmouthed, I stared at the man, who seemed very much at home. When Stanny rounded the corner and sensed my discomfort, she said in a cheery voice, "Pat, aren't you going to kiss your new granddad?" I walked up and kissed the man on the cheek. I never saw the man again or learned his name. But my mother later corroborated that I had met one of Stanny's many husbands. Mom dismissed Stanny's collection of husbands as a bad habit, but it was a habit she continued until her late seventies. Stanny considered her addictions to bourbon, high-rolling men, and matrimony as venial sins and "nothing to write home about." In her simple, lucid theology, she claimed that she had never committed a crime serious enough for any loving god to burn her in the lake of fire for all eternity. There was much wrong about my childhood, but Stanny will always remain one of its shining glories.

On March 10, 1947, my mother went into labor in Manassas, Virginia. My father drove her to Annapolis, Maryland, where he was a member of the Navy Olympic basketball team. Stanny had ridden up on a train to take care of me during my mother's two weeks of convalescence in the hospital. (I always have to explain this anomaly to my own daughters, whose nurses forced them to do wind sprints up and down the hall about fifteen minutes after they gave birth to my grandchildren. Or so it seemed to me.) With great gentleness Stanny tried to prepare me for the surprise entry of a sister and rival into my one-child kingdom. She later reported the news to me and I seemed less than thrilled. Though I was two years old, I seemed satisfied with a single-child household. For the rest of my life, Stanny would file reports about my inconsolable jealousy over the new arrival in my family. On day three I struck back: When Stanny went out to pick some flowers in the yard, I locked the front door behind her. I was blond when I was a little boy, and I was looking out the window standing on the couch when she realized the trick played on her by a mischievous grandchild. At first, she tried sweet talk and flattery to coo me into unlocking the door. Laughing, I shook my head, a defiant no. For an hour, Stanny remained good-natured about it. Then she grew irritated and began to threaten me with a spanking. She tore a switch off a bush and stripped it of leaves and small branches. If I didn't unlock the door, she would switch my bottom till the cows came home. When she changed tactics, so did I, and now I refused to unlock the door because she was going to spank me.

More time passed, and Stanny finally blew up and screamed, "Now I'm not going to just switch you, Pat—now I'm gonna kill you."

I stuck out my tongue at her. She would swear, many years later, that she almost picked up a brick and threw it through the window. Instead, she walked to a horse stable across the highway and bought two Popsicles, the orange ones I preferred. Back at her window, she began to lick her Popsicle and, moaning with pleasure, said, "It's so good, Pat. So sweet. It's the best Popsicle I've ever had. I'd sure like to give you yours, but I can't with the door locked. I guess I'll have to give it to that nice little girl Susie, next door."

I opened the door and Stanny charged in waving that switch like a wand of battle. I sprinted into my parents' bedroom and hid under their bed. Later, she'd swear I was the fastest toddler she'd ever laid eyes on. Stanny began laughing hysterically as she lured me out from under the bed by dangling the Popsicle before my eyes. She hugged me and tickled me and told me stories for the rest of the night. She had made a friend for life.

. . .

Stanny grew up in a lowborn, remorseless South that is nearly impossible to exaggerate. My mother's mordant shame about her Alabama mountain family produced a sense of impermeable social inferiority that would mark all her waking hours and disfigure the edges of her own mother's life—a girl from Piedmont, Alabama, dropping out of school in the third grade with a future dominated by despair and by the prospect of nothingness. Stanny spent her whole life sprinting away from those Alabama hills. My mother ran even faster.

There was great hurt in Stanny's unannounced departure from her children's lives in the middle of the Depression. At the time of Stanny's leaving, my grandfather owned and operated his own barbershop in downtown Rome, Georgia. But Grandpa Peek had an extraordinary and intimate relationship with the son of God, and he received a summons from Jesus himself to renounce all worldly goods and take to a soapbox to preach the news of the apocalypse and the Second Coming of Christ. He shuttered the barbershop and took to the streets of Rome, to announce the harsh prophecy of the living God. His family began to starve, and my aunt Helen answered a call from the principal's office after my mother fainted from hunger in her first-grade class. My mother carried the dark wound of this alarming event for the rest of her life. A few days later, Stanny stuck out her thumb and caught a ride on a mule wagon going to Atlanta. She revealed her secret flight to no one, and her children woke up motherless in a desperate home where their father had gone insane over his love of God. None of Stanny's four children ever recovered from her sudden abandonment of them for the uncertainties and the bright excesses of Atlanta. But the story had power, and room for growth. My youngest cousins grew up hearing that a rich man picked Stanny up in a white Cadillac.

Before their summons to Atlanta, my mother and her siblings had to endure a few years' worth of misery as Grandpa Peek lost himself in the deep ecstasy of his street preaching. All during her life, my mother could barely bring herself to talk about her bewildering childhood in the small town of Rome, Georgia. A childless black couple who lived on a sharecropper's farm down the dirt road from them heard about their frantic situation and began bringing eggs and fruits and vegetables to their house. Occasionally, they would kill a hen and the farmer's wife would come up to the house to fry it. Eventually, she would teach my mother and her sisters how to fry the best chicken in the world. My mother told me that this black family had saved the lives of the impoverished white family who lived down the road. It helps explain a great anomaly in my mother's life: She and Stanny were the only white women I knew who were raised in the cruel-eyed South without a racist bone in their bodies. When I was four years old, I said the word "nigger" and my mother slapped me to the ground. She had never hit me in my life, and the ferocity of the attack shocked me as she started screaming, "I was raised colored. That's how poor we were. A colored farm family saved my family's life. They were as poor as we were and saved us for no reason except their kindness. No child of mine is ever going to use that horrible word or I'll beat their faces clean off their heads. The whole world hates poor people, but I'll be damned if my kids will."

My mother was born a cracker, a redneck if you will, poor white trash if you must, and she never believed in that night-riding, lynching South, that apartheid, Jim Crow South. Years later, she would sit in front of our TV set to watch with steely resolve those intrepid black walkers who made such a success out of the Montgomery bus boycott. I would find her weeping at the eloquence of Martin Luther King, and she fell in love with the black children of Birmingham for their indomitable courage and irresistible enthusiasm as they ran out of churches and into the mean streets of Alabama to face dogs, fire hoses, and an out-of-control police force. My mother hated the inglorious, indefensible racism of the South she was born into, and so did Stanny. It makes no sense except for that nameless black sharecropper and his wife, who heard about four white kids abandoned by their mother in the middle of the worst Depression in history and saved these children with the fruit of their labors and the unforgettable kindness of their hearts. Because my mother and Stanny both loathed the apartheid South, I consider myself the luckiest white boy who ever grew up beneath the burning sun of Dixie.

After Stanny's defection from her family, my pretty aunt Helen took over as a substitute mother at the ripe age of fourteen. She cooked, cleaned, put clothes on the line, and got her three siblings to school each morning. In early-morning darkness, she led them two miles to where they caught a ride to their school. According to family tradition, Jasper Catlett Peek began his lifelong career traveling the back roads selling Bibles, cutting hair, and trying to convert every stranger he met. For many long weeks, Aunt Helen would be raising her siblings alone, and all four would develop a fear of abandonment that would haunt them until the end of their days. The following year Aunt Helen convinced her father to rent a house on Euclid Street in Rome, near the school they all attended.

When I was five years old, we were living at Stanny's house on Rosedale Road in Atlanta during the time my father was flying sorties in the Korean War, and my mother and Stanny got into a terrible fight. The sound of their voices awakened me.

My mother shouted, "You abandoned your own children. You placed a gun against your own family's head and pulled the trigger, Mother."

"I couldn't bear to watch my children starve," Stanny said.

"You didn't watch your children starve. You deserted us. Daddy deserted us. We were terrified."

"I did what I thought was best at the time," Stanny said, "in the long run."

Tears were running down my face as I entered the living room, and both women rushed to comfort me. Those women knew how to love a crying boy, and Stanny soon walked me back to my bed. Even today I take the most charitable view of Stanny's flight from bondage, her break from the manacles that had indentured her to the hard traditions of a mountain South she had been born into in 1899. She set forth toward the rumors of a vast world and found it in Atlanta. Her defection enabled her daughters to marry military officers and her son to become a military man himself. All of Stanny's grandchildren attended college because of her unpraised boldness. That ride in the mule wagon became a trail of tears to her mortified children, and was passed on to their children as some kind of indelible stain on the family honor. I saw her escape into the future as a mythological trek that carried her family out of a cureless poverty that was both her heirloom and destiny. For me, Stanny came to symbolize the irreproachable standard-bearer of voyage in my family pantheon.

Not that she did not make some mistakes along the way. Stanny got a job the first week in Atlanta at Rich's department store downtown. She ran the notions department, but soon moved into lady's fashions selling dresses. She ended up selling fur coats to the wealthiest and most well-heeled women in Atlanta. She began to dress with considerable style and flair, and I remember pressing my face into her own full-length fur coat whenever she and Papa Jack, her husband at the time, went out to a party. They were a glittering couple around town and I thought they were rich as pirates when I was living in their Rosedale Road home.

My mother received the beckoning call to Atlanta when she was in the second grade. Of the four children, she was the only one whom Stanny would claim as her own child. Helen, James, and Evelyn were introduced as cousins and had to carry out that scurrilous charade until they left Papa Jack's house to jump-start their own lives. None of them ever recovered from this injured aggrievement that cut out the heart of their childhoods.

Stanny's Greek husband, Jack Stanton, was a storytelling wizard who entertained Carol Ann and me for hours with stories out of Greek mythology—war stories about the skirmish among the gods and the envy of goddesses too beautiful to imagine. He was an adding machine salesman who kept his efficient machines neatly arranged in the attic. But it was after his death that Stanny revealed how Papa Jack had run the numbers racket in Atlanta and had left my mountain-born grandmother a large fortune. This information caused much social embarrassment to my mother and she forbade me from sharing this story with anyone. She admitted to me later in life that one morning she woke up to get ready for school, then looked out her window to discover the entire house surrounded by well-dressed men in hats. When she ran upstairs to warn Papa Jack and Stanny, she found Papa Jack eating lots of small paper chits and Stanny in the bathroom flushing the toilet over and over again.

"Why are you eating paper, Papa Jack?" Mother asked.

"A bad habit I got into in the old country," Papa Jack said. "Greeks believe eating paper helps the digestive system."

"Is that why Mother's flushing the toilet so much?"

"Just stomach problems," he told her.

"Why are all these men around the house?"

"Just old friends," he said. "It's nice of them to drop by, don't you think?"

"They don't look very friendly to me," Mother reported saying.

"You just got to get to know them," Jack answered, chewing faster.

When Papa Jack died, Carol Ann and I did not take his passing with much grace or stoicism. When they lifted Carol Ann up to kiss Papa Jack's embalmed face, she flipped around in Stanny's arms like a freshly caught trout. My own grief rushed in on me as I went down to kiss the sweet face of a man I'd come to adore, but when my lips touched his cheek, the coldness was my undoing. That night, Carol Ann crawled into bed with me and we fell asleep talking about how much we missed Papa Jack. Already, I was having intimations that I was growing up beside the most brilliant little girl in the country. That Carol Ann was precocious was already conventional wisdom among the adults in the family. But her use of language, which she used to make butterflies dance in the fragrant blooms of lantana, was an early gift she brought to the dinner table. I first heard about lantanas from her, and when I asked what kind of flower a lantana resembled, she showed no interest at all—it was the sound of the word she loved. About Papa Jack, she added this valedictory note: "Who's going to tell us stories about Zeus now?"

. . .

The wild child in Stanny spread its wings and took to glamorous flight in the years after Papa Jack's death. Her grandchildren whom I interviewed don't quite know how many times she embarked on around-the-world cruises, but most think it was five. She would write illegible postcards from Hawaii, Bali, Hong Kong, Capetown, Genoa, Israel, Lebanon, and Tanganyika. Carol Ann and I pounced on that last word, and she thought it was the most romantic, exotic place that she had ever encountered. My mom would decipher Stanny's preposterous handwriting that looked like a mouse had its tiny feet painted with blue ink and had run back and forth on a blank page. Stanny would send back news of encountering tigers as she rode on the back of an elephant in a Bengali jungle, and of watching elephants working hard labor for their masters in a Thai village. She made brief notations about the men she met aboard ships, and her family believes she might have married a small colony of them. She told me once, "Men come to me like bees going to a rose."

After Stanny's death in 1989, the family photographer, Uncle Joe Gillespie, sent me a film he had made of Stanny and his family at the beach during the seventies. Uncle Joe produced more film than Cecil B. DeMille, and I personally believe that this loving father shot the entire waking life of my cousin Johnny and much of his sleeping life too. But we had just buried Stanny, so I was missing her when I watched the latest documentary in Uncle Joe's vast oeuvre. Assuming the role of narrator, Uncle Joe opened up with the shot of the infant Johnny waddling down toward the ocean with Aunt Evelyn in hot pursuit. Uncle Joe describes the scene: "Here we are, the entire Gillespie family. Locals in Jacksonville call this 'the beach.' In fact, people in the know call it Jacksonville Beach. It's where people in Jacksonville come to swim."

Then he shifts to Stanny and a much younger man who are walking toward the waves hand in hand. I screamed, "What?"

Uncle Joe's narrative continued: "That's Margaret Stanton, Evelyn's mother. She lives with us and is quite the character. That's her husband, Ralph. Yes, there is a big age difference, but they seem to get along pretty well."

I laughed for a long time and was grateful that I had a grandmother who could delight, amaze, and surprise me even after her death.

Her long cruises left Stanny exhausted, almost broke, and seriously addicted to alcohol. In a last flourish of wealth, she bought the Hotel Monroe, which is now a parking lot in Monroe, Georgia. It was an impressive brick building in great need of a face-lift. We stayed there several times, and Carol Ann and I would roam through the derelict kitchen and disused dining room for hours. Mom would send me up to the attic to throw a baseball at the rats. Stanny's days as a hotelier were short-lived and she sold the hotel at a loss. During my childhood

I looked upon my grandmother as a rich, sophisticated woman, but she also taught me that life was full of heartbreak and reversals. After she sold the hotel, I looked on her as a very poor and unfortunate woman.

In 1973, after I became a controversial figure when *The Water Is Wide* stirred up racial tensions in the town, I moved Barbara and our family to Atlanta, into a pretty home on Briarcliff Road, less than two miles from Stanny's old house on Rosedale Road. It was both a homecoming and a betrayal of home, since I would miss Beaufort all the years I lived in Atlanta.

In the month after we moved into our new home, I received a phone call from Stanny, who informed me she was moving to Atlanta to be close to her favorite grandchild.

"Since when did I become your favorite?"

"Since you became famous. I always wanted to be famous. I want to be near you to soak up some of the reflected glory."

"Do me a favor, Stanny. Don't tell the other grandkids."

"I already have," she said.

Three months later I moved Stanny and her meager possessions into the Lutheran Towers on Juniper Street. The building was a high-rise of undistinguished architecture and that soulless ambience where old Lutherans found themselves stacked up like cords of hickory until they left the building feet-first to endure the embalmer's art at Patterson's Funeral Home a couple of blocks away. I had met the annoying manager of the building when I signed Stanny up for what I thought would be her final residence. As soon as the man opened his mouth I knew he hated old people with every cell in his body.

His voice was hostile and acerbic when he asked, "What is your grandmother's religion?"

"Stanny's been a devout Lutheran her whole life," I lied.

"That's what they all say." He snorted. "Does your grandmother drink?"

"She's been a teetotaler her entire life," I said. "As far as I know liquor never passed between her lips."

"Is your grandmother sexually active?"

"How in the hell would I know?"

"How many times was she married?"

"Once. She never looked at another man after my grandfather died."

Stanny really liked the Lutheran Towers, and I thought she would be a member of that gentle community for the rest of her life. But she found herself in the crosshairs of that dyspeptic manager from the beginning of her time there. He began to call me with dozens of complaints concerning Stanny's behavior.

"Mr. Conroy, I have it from a good source that your grandmother has slept with five members from the Lutheran community."

"Yeah, she'd probably do the same thing in the Presbyterian community."

"She is breaking one of our bylaws," he said.

"I'll talk to her about it."

When I confronted Stanny about the accusation, she laughed her husky-throated Stanny laugh. "It's a complete and total lie. I swear to you, Pat, on my word of honor: I never slept with five men. There were at least twelve or thirteen."

I hollered and Stanny laughed until she was leaning against the wall to maintain her balance. Her nemesis at the Lutheran Towers, however, bided his time and waited for Stanny to stumble over the trip wire of some other bylaw. A month later the manager telephoned me that my grandmother was a hopeless alcoholic, and they had found her passed out in the hallway, in the TV room, and on the elevator.

"We're evicting Mrs. Stanton today. If her furniture is not removed by four o'clock this afternoon, I'm personally going to put her out on Juniper Street along with her furniture."

"If you put Stanny out on the street, pal, you'd better reserve yourself a bed at Grady hospital," I said.

"Is that a threat?"

"Sounds like one to me."

So I moved Stanny into our new home on Briarcliff Road, where she stayed for three months before moving into a decrepit mansion in Ansley Park run by a hunchbacked giant and his mother. Stanny and her landlord became simpatico and she regaled him with stories of safaris and high teas while he told her heartbreaking stories of his childhood solitude as a freakish, misshapen boy. My father went to visit Stanny every day.

CHAPTER 9 ·

Piedmont

S tanny was mountain-born and broken by the eclipsed imaginings parceled out to the Southern girls of her time. Few women escaped the lunar pull of those hard mountains in Alabama, where she was born to a family that had gone off half-cocked, thumbing their noses at the law, and already famous for being infamous in a town that didn't have much use for any of them. But the Wife of Bath can make her presence felt in any family. Stanny walked through her childhood with a bruised but valiant heart. My meek and God-fearing grandfather Jasper Peek had hitched his fate to the wings of a firebird, and Stanny left her talon tracks everywhere she took flight. No one in her family lay untouched by her flaunting of the boldest form that womanhood could assume in her day and time. She was born to a mountain range not large enough to stifle an insurrectionary spirit. In her misshapen youth, Stanny found herself in full possession of woman's sorrowful complaint against the fate she was born to burn down in her leisure. Even though Piedmont, Alabama, had locked her away in the prison of its town limits, the cutoff geography of her birth had created a girl who lit freedom's torch for herself and anyone who cared to go along with her on the ride. When she first abandoned her four children and husband to their tearful lives in west Georgia, she was lighting hill fires for the gathering tempest of feminism that would soon move through the land, as well as planting her own flag of liberation in downtown Atlanta as she began to arrange the brand-new words she would need to fashion herself for all time as an American original.

My grandmother was passionate and radical, and she helped to bring the New South screaming against its will into the twentieth century. I'd have it no other way. I wouldn't change a thing about Stanny. Instead, I thrilled to see her work her sorcerer's gift on my family and friends.

Stanny developed a deep and affectionate friendship with Bernie Schein, one of the necessary friends of my life, whom I met my junior year at Beaufort High School. Bernie struck me as hilarious, profane, openhearted, curious, mischievous, and again, a very strong emphasis on the word "profane." When I first introduced my grandmother to Bernie, he shocked me by saying, "Hello, Mrs. Conroy. It's such a pleasure to meet you. I guess Pat told you that I've got the biggest dick in Beaufort."

I was stepping forward to break Bernie's jaw when my grandmother answered: "No, Bernie. Pat told me just the opposite."

Whenever I threw a party or went out to some new Atlanta restaurant, I would issue a Bernie proviso, a small caution sign to men and women whose tender sensibilities were easily offended. With Bernie anything can happen, and something always does. My grandmother was putty in his hands, and Bernie was a devotee and an adopted grandson to her for the rest of her life. The more profane he became, the more Stanny snickered and urged him to even lower depths of the unspeakable. One could not appeal to Bernie's sense of decency, because he never considered decency to be a praiseworthy goal.

Even so, I tried to incorporate Stanny into the lives and times of my Atlanta friends. Anne Rivers Siddons had her over for dinner at her house on Vermont Road on several occasions. I took her to parties at friends' homes all over Atlanta, where Stanny would sit back with a cocktail that Bernie always rushed to fix her when she flashed some arcane signal they'd developed between them. Stanny would coo with pleasure at what she called "high-class discussion among the literati," although I can't remember her having a single discussion with the literati or anyone else. Jim Townsend, the founder of *Atlanta* magazine, fell hard for Stanny and would entertain her with lewd jokes from his endless repertoire. Other friends, like Terry Kay, Frank Smith, and Clifford Graubart, invited Stanny into their lives and fussed and joked and flirted with her. I think my grandmother thought she was traveling on a world cruise, with hostesses and suitors bringing her hors d'oeuvres and filling up her dance card in her role of a lifetime as belle of the ball restored to her once and future glory. But her friendship with Bernie Schein eventually brought about Stanny's exile from Atlanta to her daughters' homes in Florida.

My mother's family is passionate about visiting and cleaning the graves of their deceased. Once a year, the Peeks and the Nolens would gather to clean the tombstones and plant flowers at the grave sites of their people. Once, in Piedmont, when I was a little boy, I was helping to clean a grave of an ancestor of my grandfather named Jerry Mire Peek. When I asked my cousin Clyde whom this unknown relation was named after, he said, "He was named after the prophet—Jerry Mire."

Stanny was the most fanatical grave visitor I ever encountered, and I drove her out to the Greenlawn Cemetery three times the first week she was living in Atlanta. In the center of the cemetery sat a mausoleum where we visited the vault that contained the mortal remains of Papa Jack. We would lower our heads and pray for the repose of his good Greek soul. Then Stanny would begin a long, free-flowing monologue with Papa Jack that went on for long, excruciating minutes. "We miss you, Jack. You remember Pat here. He's Don and Peg's oldest. He and Carol Ann used to love to hear you tell stories. I had to sell the house on Rosedale Road a while back. It was getting too much for me to handle. But I'm living in Atlanta again, and my grandson Pat has promised to bring me out here to visit you every week."

"I'll be damned if that's so, Papa Jack," I said.

"Please, Pat, I'm praying."

"You ain't praying. You're talking to a dead man."

"I'm communing with the soul of my husband."

"You've had eight husbands."

"Not eight. I never had eight. I don't think," she said, then giggled. "The number's in dispute."

"Let's clear it up. How many were there?"

"You know I'll be buried here when I go to be with Jack," she said, "The worms'll never feed on this flesh. Eight's a workable figure."

During the following years, relatives from the Alabama mountains began drifting down to Atlanta to pay their respects to the matriarch, especially after she suffered a heart attack when her only son, James, died. Distant cousins, all of them carrying worn copies of their family Bibles to read passages of uplifting quotations, came to speed along the salvation of Stanny's immortal soul. I used to call this noncontact sparring "dueling Bibles." My aunt Helen and cousin Carolyn could play it with the best of them. But these second- and third-string cousins were also adept at quoting citations from both the Old and New Testaments. The fact that they were wielding their Bibles against the most notorious sinner our family had produced stimulated them into an ecstatic zone of sanctimony. In a wheelchair, with her head bent against her chest, Stanny endured the incoming fire of scripture with admirable forbearance. But the lichen of boredom made her eyes filmy and fogged in.

A Nolen cousin from Piedmont read, "You've got to get right with the Lord, Margaret. It says here in Deuteronomy 32:22, 'For a fire is kindled in my anger, and shall burn into the lowest hell, and shall consume the earth with her increase and set on fire the foundations of the mountains.'"

In a fierce turning of pages, another older cousin said, "You must turn your ear toward God's words, Margaret. It says right here in Psalms 16:50, 'For thou wilt not leave my soul in hell; neither wilt thou suffer this Holy One to see corruption.'"

An uncle on Stanny's mother's side trumped the first two. "Margaret, raise your arms and pray for Jesus's divine forgiveness, for it says in Revelations 1:18, 'I am he that liveth . . . and was dead: and behold, I am alive forevermore. Amen; and I have the keys of hell and death.'"

Through my living room window, I watched horrified as Bernie Schein made his way up my driveway from Briarcliff Road. I sprang to my feet and met him halfway up the drive and put both my hands around his throat. I said, "I don't have time to explain it to you. But my Alabama relatives are visiting Stanny. They're country people and they never met a profane, foulmouthed Jew who spends most of his time making fun of the baby Jesus. If you say one word that pisses me off, I will cut your pecker off and feed it to the rottweiler next door. You understand me?"

Bernie grinned and said, "Pat, if you can't trust your best friend on earth, then who can you trust?"

When my wife, Barbara, saw Bernie, she removed herself from the room like a plume of smoke. Bernie went over to greet Stanny. He kissed Stanny gently on the lips—then he kissed her with exaggerated passion and much moaning.

"Stanny," Bernie said, his voice loud and boisterous, "I've been so worried since I learned about your heart attack. But here's the good news—I still get horny when I see you."

"Thorny!" I shouted. "Bernie and Stanny have a very thorny relationship."

"I know just the thing that can make you better, Stanny," Bernie said. "I've got just what the doctor ordered."

In her weakened, feeble voice, Stanny said. "What is it, Bernie?"

Bernie Schein then became infamous in the history of my Southern family by telling my wheelchair-bound grandmother, "Stanny, let's me and you go out and fuck."

I have a vague memory of Bibles slamming shut all around me, but the room started to empty with none of the small courtesies usually observed in leavetaking. Stanny said, "Where we going to do it, Bernie?" And both of them collapsed in laughter.

From the kitchen, I watched the flight of primitive Baptists hurrying toward their cars and away from my ungodly house. My reputation among my mother's family took a solid hit after Stanny and Bernie's mating ritual was disseminated into another sordid family legend.

A few years earlier, when my uncle Cicero died, I had driven Stanny to Piedmont for the funeral. Uncle Cicero was the brother of my grandfather Jasper Catlett, and he was as God-possessed as my granddad. Once, he sent us a photograph of himself carrying a wooden cross on his shoulders on Good Friday to atone for the sins of backsliding Christians. (Eventually, I stole this story and handed it over to Grandpa Wingo in *The Prince of Tides*.) After an extraordinary Southern feast served by the churchwomen, I went home with my cousins Clyde and Pluma Baker, whom I'd adored since childhood because they comforted me with stories. Clyde rode me around the county in his pickup truck showing me the last shack Grandpa Peek lived in before dementia struck him, and his children had to put him away in a nursing home. He drove me to Aunt Ruby and Uncle Howard's farm, where I had stayed overnight with my mother and Carol Ann during our two visits to Piedmont as kids. Then he took me riding through the countryside. I'd never realized that the land around the town was marvelous in its lushness, in the profligacy of its own contained beauty. I could see how people could become enchanted with such a landscape, numerous with creeks and the patient feeding of herds. Though my grandfather Peek was known as "Jasper-blooded" because of his restlessness and the sheer scale of his wandering about the South, I noticed he always returned to the place of his birth and talked of little else during the duration of his visits with us.

Passing a hill not far from Howard's farm, Clyde pulled the truck to a stop and walked over to a creek that looked as if its banks were covered by an evergreen prayer rug. Leaning over, he cut off a large portion of greenery with his pocketknife and handed me my share. It was watercress so cool and fresh, it was like eating the plant for the first time. The watercress felt like something growing new in the Garden of Eden.

"Best patch of watercress in the county," Clyde said. "Your grandfather Jasper told me about this place."

"I never tasted anything so good."

"You know what they call that hill in front of us, Pat?" he asked. "It's named Nolen Hill—in honor of your family."

"Stanny's family?"

"The same one," Clyde said, and I could see a mischievous glint to his eye. "You're a Nolen, Pat. Up here that means you're gonna die with your boots on."

"Please explain that, Clyde."

"Nolens don't hurt other folks," Clyde said. "They just got a bad habit of killing each other."

As Clyde began to tell his history of the Nolens, I realized that I had never heard Stanny say a word about her own parents. I didn't even know their names. According to Clyde, both her mother and father were famous for their explosive tempers and foul mouths. One night a terrible argument broke out between Stanny's parents in their upstairs bedroom, he told me. Old Man Nolen was keeping his wife from running downstairs by blocking the stairway with his wheelchair. Both were slapping each other and cursing with profanity-laden vigor. The argument ended when their oldest son ran out of his upstairs bedroom with a shotgun and blew his father down the stairs, sending the man and his wheelchair airborne in a long tumble toward the entryway. The son was arrested for murdering his father and sent to prison to serve hard time.

"My uncle killed Stanny's father?" I said, aghast.

"No," Clyde said. "He didn't have anything to do with it."

"You just told me he went to prison."

"He did, but he didn't kill the old man," Clyde said, and like all good storytellers he was playing this out.

"Who killed him?"

"His wife, your great-grandmother. Her son took the rap for it. He went to jail for his mama. Every good ol' boy in the mountains would've done the same thing."

I said, "I wouldn't do it."

"You tell me your mama kill your daddy, you wouldn't take the heat for her?" Clyde said.

In a brief reverie, my childhood passed in review before my eyes. "Yeah, I'd've been happy to do it for Mom."

"You just like us, son," Clyde said. "You can do all the college you want, but Nolen blood don't change. You know your uncle Joe, Stanny's brother?"

"I used to visit him in the Atlanta penitentiary when I first got to the city."

"He tell you why he was in the big house?"

"Said it had to do with shoplifting," I said. "Uncle Joe said it was a bad habit."

Clyde laughed out loud. "He shot and killed one of Stanny's other brothers."

"Why?" I asked.

"I think he got pissed off," Clyde said. "You Nolens got a short fuse."

"Stanny's a sweetheart. So are Aunt Faye and Aunt Nellie."

"Good mountain girls. Strong girls. Course, Stanny's got quite a reputation up here. You ever hear about her putting on her track shoes during the middle of the Depression and hauling ass to Atlanta? Left her kids and everything."

"Yeah, I heard that one, Clyde," I said.

"Didn't set too well with the people up here."

"Didn't set real well with her kids, either," I answered.

"Your uncle Joe wants to see you," Clyde said. "He lives in a school bus with twenty-six dogs."

"Why?"

"He likes dogs, I reckon," said Clyde, "or school buses."

On the way back to Atlanta, I tried to engage Stanny in some accurate recounting of her family's history. Her relationship with truth was scant and fugitive—her talent for subterfuge inventive and slippery by nature. Her parents were people of the finest type, pillars of their church community life. Her brothers were the handsomest boys who ever lived—a little on the wild side, but men of high breeding and quality. When she admitted that her brother had dabbled in moonshining, it was an act of rebellion against the revenuers and federal agents who interfered with the stern code of the hills. Their land was sovereign property, and not even the king of England or the U.S. president could cross their threshold to tell them how to use their God-given land. Besides, the Nolen boys were artists in the moonshine they made in their copper-kettled stills around Piedmont. Stanny had brought a mason jar full of it on a world cruise, and the ship captain himself declared it the equal of French cognac.

"Did Uncle Joe kill his own brother?" I asked Stanny. "Everyone in Piedmont says he did."

"You're talking to the Peeks. They're nothing but religious fanatics," Stanny said.

"Did Joe do it?"

"He was framed," Stanny said.

"Who framed him?"

"The Mafia."

"I didn't know they had branches in Piedmont, Alabama. There isn't even a pizza parlor in town."

"The Peeks love running my family name into the ground."

"Let's tell them about the Mafia."

"That'd only make it worse," Stanny said. "Then they'd spread the word that the Nolens were associating with Eye-talians and Roman Catholics."

"Roman Catholics?" I said. "A fate worse than death."

"They think it is. Those lying, no-'count, mouthy Peeks! They can't stand it that I've always been a good ol' Southern girl, but one with style and class."

What I was looking for, Stanny couldn't tell me. In both my mother and Stanny, Piedmont was a branding iron of shame, a starry-blooded omen, an underbelly of the Deep South, and a place to fly away from. Piedmont lit fires of the deepest shame in their bloodstreams.

Because she was dressed in her funeral best, I took Stanny to dinner at Gene and Gabe's restaurant when we returned to Atlanta. Gene and Gabe's was a Northern Italian restaurant that represented the elegance, sophistication, and refinement of the big city to me. Its clientele was urbane and its decor was muted and made larger by an interplay of artwork and long mirrors on its crimson-washed walls. It was the anti-Piedmont to me and the anti-Piedmont to my grandmother.

"It's like the stateroom on a cruise ship," Stanny said the first time I brought her there. "You know you've made it . . . just walking in the door."

"The sky's the limit, Stanny," I said as the waiter handed us menus.

"First a cocktail," Stanny said. "I want to make a toast. I'll never go back to Piedmont again. I don't care if Jesus Christ dies there."

I carried Stanny drunk into her boardinghouse and put her to bed that night. I did that on many occasions, but I was young and strong and was one of those boys who had grown up head over heels in love with his grandmother. As a young writer, I was trying to learn what kind of man I was becoming and what I wanted myself to become in the future. I wanted to ripen into a man I could be proud of—one I could present to the altar of God without shame or hesitancy. I was trying to open myself up to the full experiences of life—not to be judgmental or harsh, but to be curious and always on the alert and ready for every encounter, no matter how bizarre or exotic, I found on the road. I was following the path of the third-grader Margaret Nolen, who married as a young mountain girl, deserted her children when they began to starve, lit out for Atlanta and a new life and found one. Stanny and my mother raised Carol Ann and me to be Southern writers before we knew what one was. We spent our childhoods listening to Stanny describe meeting Masai warriors tending their cattle on the plains of Kenya, watching a school of sharks following the ships she circumnavigated the globe on, visiting a gorilla colony in Rwanda, having an audience with the pope in the Vatican, and always, always her morbid sadness when her ship glided into New York Harbor and her dread of return at the sighting of the Statue of Liberty, proof she would never escape the cloistered margins and limitations of Piedmont. Stanny always had to return and it was always to the same place—just as it is for all the rest of us.

In the late seventies, the forces of Piedmont began a strategic campaign of collusion to draw Stanny back into its adhesive and killing webs. I missed the moment when my mother and her sisters grew tired of me hauling Stanny to one Atlanta party after another. The Peek sisters scolded me for introducing their mother to a Gomorrah-like Atlanta that emphasized sin, happy hour, and ungodly goings-on. After the novelist Terry Kay took me around to various strip shows he covered for the *Atlanta Journal*'s entertainment section, I took Stanny on the same tour the following month. Some of the strippers remembered my name and made a big fuss over Stanny, who was courtly and attentive to them. We ended the night at a huge gay bar on Monroe Drive, where we watched an elaborate dance of the drag queens. Stanny and I danced the night away until we could barely stand. I consider that night among the drag queens as one of the finest nights my grandmother and I spent in our rich and unusual life together. But I will always believe Bernie Schein was the one who provided the catalyst and produced the dangerous chemical reaction that drove Stanny into exile from her Atlanta life.

. . .

No matter how hard Stanny tried to guilt-trip or cajole me, I never took her to Greenlawn Cemetery to communicate with the dead again.

I told her I wouldn't take her back there if every dead person she knew had undergone a resurrection and all were ready to receive Stanny and chant heavenly songs and any daily gossip they might have picked up from their vantage point on Jesus's knee. Bernie Schein overheard this skirmish with delight and said, "What a no-good white-trash grandson Pat turned out to be, Stanny. What kind of Southern boy is it who won't even take his beloved grandmother to the cemetery to visit her loved ones? You deserve a much finer grandson. Someone just like Bernie Schein—sensitive, caring, loving, dutiful, and handsome. Not like that Irish lout, that uptight ingrate who doesn't know how to worship a wonderful woman like you."

"Shut up, Bernie," I suggested.

"Will you take me to the cemetery tomorrow, Bernie?" Stanny asked, sealing the deal.

"Of course I will, Stanny. It'll be an honor. It makes me sick to my stomach that you produced such a sorry grandson. You deserved one just like me . . . a true hero, a gentleman, a Jew."

Bernie and Stanny took off the next day with the enthusiasm of big-game hunters setting off to intercept the migrating hordes of the African bush. Their ill-conceived safari among the Southern dead became the stuff of family legend, and both of them would tell their different versions of the story for the rest of their lives. Since Bernie was a small-town boy, I knew that the only cemetery he was familiar with was the diminutive Jewish cemetery on Bladen Street in Beaufort. Later, he admitted that the sheer size of Greenlawn Cemetery had unnerved him as he entered its gates and saw the vast acreage of the tombstones reveal itself to him in all its green, well-ordered silence.

"I didn't know there were that many dead people in the world," Bernie declared. "It never occurred to me that more people have died in Atlanta than at Auschwitz."

From past experience, I knew that Bernie's problems were only in the beginning stages. Stanny's eyesight had deteriorated in recent years so that her eyes bulged in geckolike protrusions. She had a heroic incapacity for navigation and as little sense of direction as anyone I ever met. Like most men I know, she would never admit that she was lost or had no idea where she was going. Twice, Bernie had circumnavigated the cemetery, waiting for Stanny to tell him where to park the car.

"Stop right here, Bernie," Stanny said, pointing to a hill covered with marble stones.

"Is this where your folks are buried?"

"Yes," Stanny said, "I can feel it, and I can hear my son, James, calling out to me."

"What's he saying?"

"He's not saying nothing, Bernie," she explained. "He's just telling me he's right over there."

For the first hour they wandered about in a fruitless search for some poor lost Nolen or Peek. Bernie read the names of a hundred tombstones as Stanny moved in her tortoiselike gait to other pastures of stone. Then Stanny announced she could not walk another inch. When Bernie observed that they were half a mile from his car, Stanny shrugged her shoulders with indifference and said, "Just call Pat and tell him where you deserted me and he'll come pick me up."

"That son of a bitch would never let me forget it," Bernie said. "Get on my back, Stanny. I'll carry you up that hill. Just like Jesus carried that cross up the hill. Holy God, you're heavier than that cross. You feel like you weigh a thousand pounds."

"I've always been considered petite, Bernie. You make me feel like a pig."

When Bernie filed his report on the afternoon, he spent the next hour as a pack animal bearing Stanny's weight from grassy hill to grassy hill. She would issue orders to bear right or left as she kept hearing her son calling out to her again and again. She kept telling Bernie they were getting closer and she had started hearing her dead relatives cheering on their efforts to find them in the great jigsaw puzzle that had enclosed them in a dazzle of names. Coming to the point of breakdown himself, Bernie finally had an idea to extricate himself from his excruciating ordeal.

"We found it, Stanny. We finally found it. James Peek. How wonderful," Bernie lied.

Stanny mentioned the names of five relatives buried near James, and Bernie shrieked, "Hallelujah, we found them all, Stanny. It's the prettiest spot in the cemetery, and goddamn, darling, we've seen every one of them. Now, you pray your ass off to James right here; then we'll make like horseshit and hit the trail."

Stanny dismounted and Bernie claims he fell face-forward into the grass and lay there for several minutes, his body cramping in muscles he wasn't aware of having.

The light was too bright for Stanny and sweat was pouring down her face as she began her long soliloquy with her son, James. I had endured a few of these long-winded conversations with the lost soul of my uncle and had memorized every portion of the drill.

Stanny began, "Hey, James, it's me again, your mother. But you know that. You're in heaven now and I guess know everything. I talked to your wife, Chris, the other day and she told me what your boys were all doing. Steve's got a good job for himself and Paul got himself married the other day. She seemed like a nice girl, but the marriage was annulled after twenty hours, so I'm guessing they didn't get along that well. Don Conroy took me to a Braves game the other night, but the other team won. It was a pretty night, and the stars were all out. You forget that stars still shine on Atlanta."

Bernie raised his head from the grass, curious about this strange aspect of Christian faith that he had never imagined. He listened as Stanny went over each and every family member who would hold interest for Uncle James, then took it to higher and more personal realms.

"Enough about me and the family. I hope you are doing well, James, and that Jesus is taking good care of you and that the angels are serving you breakfast in bed every morning."

"Jesus is the nicest guy I ever met, Mother," said Bernie, answering for my uncle James. "In fact, he reminds me of that great, great American Bernie Schein."

This interference in her train of prayer stopped Stanny in her tracks for a few seconds; then she continued her conversation with her son. "Do you get to see Jesus very often? Do you have long talks? Do you tell him about the family? Does he know about me?"

"Mother, I talk to Jesus all the time. Hell, to tell you the truth I get sick of him every once in a while. That boy runs his mouth way too much. I think he got the big head, you know, being God and all that stuff. But he tells good stories. I've got to hand him that."

"Does Jesus ever talk about me, James?" Stanny asked.

"All the time, Mother. Hey, he's right here. Jesus, would you say hello to my mother? They call her Stanny."

"Jesus?" my grandmother said.

"Hey, Stanny. How you getting along, cupcake? You sure got a great set of jugs for an older woman, if you know what I mean, hon." Bernie, whose perversity was limitless as far as I knew, realized he had gone a bit far in his sacrilegious imitation of Christ, and said, "No, Stanny, James and I pray for you every night. He can't wait for you to get up here so we can get to know each other better. You know, go out for a few drinks, tell a few lies, relax and kick back."

"So I'm going to heaven, Jesus?" she asked.

"You're going to be in my lap the second you die. And I'm not just whistling 'Dixie,' sweetheart. All your friends and relatives are coming up to live with me in heaven. Especially that fabulous guy that I love more than any other creature on earth, that king of personality, that pure delight—who else but Bernie Schein. Of course, his friend Pat's gonna burn forever in hellfire. I'm going to smite his sorry ass for all eternity. His screaming, moaning, and wailing gonna be music to my ears."

From the front window of my house on Briarcliff Road, I watched as Bernie and Stanny drove up the driveway. It was seven in the evening when they arrived home, and they'd been gone for more than five hours. Bent double, Bernie staggered out of his car and, with movements resembling a hurt beetle, he went and retrieved Stanny, letting out an audible cry of distress when he lifted her onto his back and walked her up the stairs leading to the front door. When I lifted Stanny off his back, Bernie crumpled to his knees, his whines both pitiful and aggrieved. Though Bernie had never suffered from back problems in his life, Stanny presented him the gift of sciatica for his generous offer to take her to visit Uncle James at Greenlawn Cemetery. When I helped Bernie inside, he told in profane detail what had occurred on his field trip with Stanny. When he finished, Stanny told her own fanciful, sanitized version of the day's events. As they talked, the story began to build and change, as all great stories do.

. . .

After my separation from Barbara, I moved to an apartment in Ansley Park, where I had yet another breakdown following the publication of *The Great Santini*. I loved Barbara's explanation to our families about the failure of our marriage: "When I said my wedding vows, I said 'richer or poorer.' I didn't say a damn thing about crazy." It was the third breakdown I'd suffered, and there would be three more before I finished with them or they finished with me. Though I had written my novel as a way of trying to save myself, the screams of the hurt boy I had been still echoed in the deep well he fell in when I became a man. The stories I hadn't told or was afraid to tell were the ones that were killing me. My course and my history as a writer were now set in granite—my work would be father-haunted and emotional enough to ward off these exhausting bouts of madness.

But there was much more to my divorce from Barbara than I ever admitted to either Barbara or myself. It had never occurred to me that when I started writing books it would make me more attractive to smart and pretty women, or that they would want to sleep with me. That I would cheerfully agree to do so came as one of the great surprises of my young manhood. I thought I'd be a much finer man than I turned out to be. But I brought a real sense of endangerment to these affairs and couldn't sleep with a woman unless I fell somewhat in love with her. Though I tried discretion and restraint, in the end my marriage with Barbara failed because I was an asshole. I hurt a fine woman and cast an intricate web of grief over the lives of my three daughters. The marriage came apart because I fell in love with a flashy, dark-eyed woman from the Dominican Republic named Maria Margarita Jimenez-Grullon. She was intellectual, hilarious, and politically situated somewhere between Mao Tse-tung and Pol Pot. Conversation was a runaway train in her presence, so much so that she would stamp her foot to make a point. Barbara overheard a conversation I had with Maria Margarita and wisely declared the end of our marriage. By then, I had gone to the dark place that more and more seemed like home to me. I lost Barbara and I lost Maria Margarita; and on a devastating, inexplicable rebound, I married Lenore Fleischer, who would teach me everything about life and love that I did not want to know.

When I told Stanny that Barbara and I were getting a divorce, she surprised me by saying, "I just don't believe in divorce. Never have."

"You?" I said. "Stanny, I thought you invented divorce."

"I admit I did it a few times," she said. "But I never believed in it."

Stanny's second life in Atlanta proved to be stormy and short-lived. My aunts Helen and Evelyn disapproved of the sinful, Bohemian life I was subjecting Stanny to as I tried to entertain her in the increasing solitude of her old age. But events began to conspire against my old girl and she was kicked out of two more boardinghouses for drinking. By 1980, my aunts had managed to move Stanny back to Jacksonville, Florida, where she lived out most of the rest of her life with Uncle Joe and Aunt Evelyn. When she could no longer care for herself, they exiled her to a nursing home in Orlando, where Aunt Helen visited her every day. When I stopped by to see her on a book tour, she screamed at me, "If you love me enough, Pat, you'll get me out of this goddamn hellhole!"

I didn't love her enough. It is a final, unbearable judgment I pass against myself. I should have moved Stanny into my house and taken care of her forever. Because of my intemperate youth, my selfish spirit, my wildness and years of breakdown, I failed to do the right thing. Stanny's long-ago flight to Atlanta amidst the suffering of the Depression was the great blow of her liberation from my mother's entire family. There was boldness and madness in her escape from a poverty she found ruthless to her children and humiliating to her. Heedlessly, she abandoned her children at the most desperate moment of their lives and tore out for the big city to find a radiant life, full of possibility and hope and danger, for all the rest of us.

Hey, Stanny—you'll always be my girl.

CHAPTER 10

Peg Conroy Egan

I don't believe in happy families. A family is too frail a vessel to contain the risks of all the warring impulses expressed when such a group meets on common ground. If a family gathers in harmony for a reunion, everyone in attendance will know the entry-ways and exits have been mined with improvised explosive devices. The crimes of a father or the carelessness of a mother can defile the taste of oyster dressing and giblet gravy on the brightest Thanksgiving Day. Birthday parties are an abomination. I hated them even when I was a child, especially mine. Long ago, I decided I liked funerals far more than I did weddings. The pretense of being festive at these events is both crushing and debilitating to me. Feigned happiness and forced bonhomie take a toll on my spirit that deflates me for a week. My parents taught me many things, but they never taught me a thing about faking joy.

Since the melancholy of families has remained a constant theme of my books, I often encounter readers and friends who strive at great lengths to convince me that they emerged from homes of stalwart happiness and unbreakable harmony. Taking care, I always congratulate them on their great good fortune and tell them how lucky and how rare they are in this troublesome world.

The happy family is one of the treasured romances of the American epic, something akin to the opening of the West. All who reveal this truth about their family do so with a conviction and resolution that are always touching to me. Many of my readers have moved me by their recollections and myths of their childhoods, making it seem to me that their families tried as hard as they could to be well rounded and not fragmented, happy and not bereft. Their families always did as well as they could, and that seemed like quite enough for me. I admired these families and their messengers for carrying on the necessary work of making these impossible unions less a curse and more a virtue. A good country springs from these families.

In 1986, I was signing copies of *The Prince of Tides* in the book section of Rich's department store on Lenox Road in Atlanta. A large contingent of Peeks and Nolens had driven down from Piedmont for the signing, delighting me with their presence. It was one of the last times I would see any of my mother's people until Stanny's funeral. In the middle of the signing, I spotted Dad and invited him to join me as he'd done on other occasions.

Soon after my father took his place beside me, a charming young couple approached the table, a young woman with palomino hair and an opaline complexion, her husband with a face that looked more designed than born into. Their beauty was a celebration of each other, and they bore the look of a young governor and his first lady. We began to talk as Dad took his avuncular time oversigning each book as his own line began to gather.

The couple had graduated from the University of Georgia more than a decade before, and yes, he had been president of his fraternity and she had been president of her sorority. Both looked poised to lift off in the launch zone of their pure potential. The young man leaned down and said, "We both read your new book and loved it. But I've got to tell you, Pat, your family is really fucked-up."

"Yes, they are," I said. "There's the main reason over there." And I introduced them both to my father.

"I can't believe he's still talking to you after *The Great Santini*," the man said.

"It was touch-and-go for a while," I admitted.

"Was your family really that fucked-up, or did you make a lot of it up?" he whispered.

"They were very screwed up," I said. "What about your family, pal? How do they stack up?"

"Oh, my family," he replied, "they're just wonderful. I'd say almost perfect."

"Then let's go deeper. How far do I have to go in your family before I hit the first crazy? Dad. Mom. Brother. Sister. Aunt. Uncle?"

His pretty wife broke under the pressure and spit out the words, "His mother's nuts!"

Not a single family finds itself exempt from that one haunted casualty who suffered irreparable damage in the crucible they entered at birth. Where some children can emerge from conditions of soul-killing abuse and manage to make their lives into something of worth and value, others can't limp away from the hurts and gleanings time decanted for them in flawed beakers of memory. They carry the family cross up the hill toward Calvary and don't mind letting every other member of their aggrieved tribe in on the source of their suffering. There is one crazy that belongs to each of us: the brother who kills the spirit of any room he enters; the sister who's a drug addict in her teens and marries a series of psychopaths, always making sure she bears their children, who carry their genes of madness to the grave. There's the neurotic mother who's so demanding that the sound of her voice over the phone can cause instant nausea in her daughters. The variations are endless and fascinating. I've never attended a family reunion where I was not warned of a Venus flytrap holding court among the older women, or a pitcher plant glistening with drops of sweet poison trying to sell his version of the family maelstrom to his young male cousins. When the stories begin rolling out, as they always do, one learns of feuds that seem unbrokerable, or sexual abuse that darkens each tale with its intimation of ruin. That uncle hates that aunt and that cousin hates your mother and your sister won't talk to your brother because of something he said to a date she later married and then divorced. In every room I enter I can sniff out unhappiness and rancor like a snake smelling the nest of a wren with its tongue. Without even realizing it, I pick up associations of distemper and aggravation. As far as I can tell, every family produces its solitary misfit, its psychotic mirror image of all the ghosts summoned out of the small or large hells of childhood, the spiller of the apple cart, the jack of spades, the black-hearted knight, the shit stirrer, the sibling with the uncontrollable tongue, the father brutal by habit, the uncle who tried to feel up his nieces, the aunt too neurotic ever to leave home. Talk to me all you want about happy families, but let me loose at a wedding or a funeral and I'll bring you back the family crazy. They're that easy to find.

In my novels, I've often written about the immense and mysterious powers I associate with the perfect shape of a circle. When my past circles back on me and completes itself in my present life, it often seems both covert and ominous, acting as both a herald and a sign. In the first years of my marriage to Barbara, I bolted up in bed one night when I realized I had married the wife of a Marine Corps fighter pilot. The circle almost always takes me by surprise, leaving me breathless and in awe.

In 1984, I was living in Rome, Italy, with my second wife when I received a phone call from my brother Mike. I stood overlooking the two fountains of the incomparable Piazza Farnese and a changing of the guard at the gates of the French embassy.

"Pat, you've got to get on the next plane out of Rome," Mike said. "Mom's in a coma. She may not even last the night."

"Mom's dying," I said to Lenore and the kids as they hovered near the phone.

"What's she dying of?" I asked Mike.

"Cancer. She looks terrible, Pat. Just come."

"What kind of cancer?" I asked.

"I'm not going to tell you. Just get your fat ass here," Mike demanded.

"I can't fly a thousand miles without knowing what's wrong," I said. "Be reasonable, Mike."

"Okay. I'll tell you. Mom's dying of leukemia." And as he spoke the words, I laughed loudly and explosively. I had to sit down on a chair; I was roaring with such amusement that it took me a minute to regain control of my voice. My family was staring at me as though I were the most heartless son imaginable.

"Even God doesn't have that good a sense of humor," I said, and then heard something. "Mike, Mike—is that you? Are you crying?"

"Yeah, I'm crying. So what? My mother's dying. Yet every one of the kids reacted the same way you did, Pat. Exactly the same way. What a fucked-up family we come from."

"I'll be at the Savannah airport tomorrow afternoon," I said to Mike.

On the way over the Atlantic the next evening, I thought that my mother had just learned of the immensity of a circle's power. The reason all my siblings and I had started laughing at the terrible news of my mother's leukemia was because of a priest named Father Dave, who had befriended my parents when Dad was CO of the Marine Air Division in Pensacola, Florida.

Mom and Dad had always taken great pleasure in the company of Roman Catholic priests and loved nothing better than to treat those priests to dinner at the officers' club. Whenever these men visited our house, my parents were fawning and unctuous, with Dad laughing too loud at the priests' jokes and Mom cooing with pleasure when these interchangeable priests would spout some thought she took in as wisdom brightly dispensed. Mom saw genius and a depthless spirituality whenever she spotted a man in a white collar. I think my mountain mother, with her upbringing in the primitive Baptist church, believed that converting to Roman Catholicism was a step upward in the social order. Of course she was wrong; when I grew up in the South, a Roman Catholic was the weirdest thing you could be. There was no second place until the Hare Krishnas showed up with their tambourines and saffron robes in the Atlanta airport. The only thing my mother understood about the Catholic Church was its teaching on birth control.

Father Dave was a handsome but forbidding man, one of those taciturn priests who treated children as though they were houseplants. I had met him one Christmas when I was still a cadet, on a visit to the family in Pensacola. Father Dave's personality was unglittering and severe. His Christmas sermon could have put an insomniac to sleep, but he would end up playing a larger part in my family's sad history than I could ever have dreamed.

My mother had taken up golf as a hobby and played almost every day with Father Dave, who had bought her an expensive set of clubs. Something about that made me worry. All during my visit, my family seemed like a vessel of pure madness to me, with hopelessness our daily bread. I became concerned my mother was having an affair with Father

Dave, whom I had come to hate in a very short time. One day Mom had asked me to meet her at the golf course to watch her on the driving range. She wanted me to witness firsthand the joy the sport of golf had brought into her life. It was a pleasure standing by my car to watch my mother select a three wood and drive a golf ball a hundred yards with a swing that was surprisingly fluid. Also, I noticed from a distance the raw power of my mother's physical beauty, her full-breasted figure, and the coquettish pleasure she took in just being pretty.

Then I saw a man move toward her, talking to her with great intimacy, and recognized Father Dave, who began giving her tips to correct her swing. He moved behind her and folded his arms around her. Through five practice swings, Father Dave kept his arms around my mother. I could have been watching a golfer taking the time to correct the imperfections of an amateur's swing, but there was a carnality and intimacy in the embrace that disturbed me in the extreme. I drove back home conflicted about how I was supposed to react to such a scene, which could be explained away in a dozen innocent scenarios. Returning to my parents' house, I was met by my sister Carol Ann, who asked me if I'd been out to the golf course. I told her Mom had given me bad directions and I couldn't find it.

"She golfs with Father Dave almost every day," Carol Ann said in a conspiratorial voice. "There is something sicko-sexual in their relationship. Mom's always been weird about these misfit priests."

"I think she feels safe with them," I said.

A few years later, after my father's departure for Vietnam in 1970, the creepy and reptilian Father Dave arrived at my mother's house in Beaufort for a two-week stay. His presence alarmed my brothers and sisters so much that the house was seething with anxiety every time I came over for a visit. My mother had sent my sister Kathy out of her downstairs bedroom and up to the guest room on the top floor. Father Dave took possession of Kathy's bedroom, which had a door connected to my mother's room. My mother kept that door locked when Kathy was staying in the room, but Carol Ann found it unlocked the day of the priest's arrival.

Every morning, they would golf on the course on Parris Island and often go out for drinks and dinner at the air station officers' club. Mom would dress as though she were going to a party after the Oscars, and Father Dave would wear his dapper navy uniform. It was the first time I noticed that my mother had simply stopped raising her children, and already, I thought, she had caused irreparable harm to my youngest brothers, Tim and Tom.

I confronted Mom about her children's unanimous disapproval of the presence of Father Dave. It was one of the most disagreeable conversations we ever had. Though I knew she would be defensive, I didn't have the slightest notion that I would be caught out in the open field trying to bell a tigress.

"Father Dave, Mom?" I said to her as she was gardening in the late afternoon.

"What about him?" Mom said, her hackles aroused.

"The kids don't like him."

"Which ones?"

"All seven of us."

"What don't you like?"

"We think he's an asshole," I said. "And the whole thing feels odd. Him living in your home."

"Are you brats accusing me of having an affair with a Catholic priest, a man as good and holy as Father Dave?" she asked, her voice biting.

"That's a pretty good summarization of how we feel," I said, growing more uncomfortable in my role of her inquisitor.

"I'll not dignify that with an answer. So all of my children have turned on me? *Et tu, Brute?*" Her eyes flashed with rage and mortification. Mom adored peppering her speech with literary allusions that long before had become clichés.

"Yeah, ol' Brute feels pretty strong about this one."

"It's none of your goddamn business!" she shouted.

"That's true, Mom. So why don't you just deny it and I'll get the word back to the kids."

"That my own children would turn on me. I rue the day I brought any of you bastards into the world."

"You can rue the day all you want. But you got seven kids who love you, Mom, and every one of us is worried as hell about you."

"Get the hell out of my yard," she said. "You're on private property."

I laughed and said, "Ditch the creep, Mom. Good advice from a son who adores you."

I bided my time and finally caught Father Dave off guard when I found him reading *Golf* magazine on the back porch of my mother's house. He looked up, nodded to me, then went back to reading his magazine—we had noticed before that he never spoke to the Conroy kids, so his silence was rude, but not unexpected. Finally, he put the magazine down and said in an aggravated tone, "Do you want something from me?"

"Hey, priest," I said, "are you fucking my mom?"

"No, of course not," he said, outraged.

"My brothers and sisters think you are."

"They're wrong, and you're a horse's ass to even ask the question," said the bristling Father Dave.

"I ever find out they're right, then you'll have a very bad day."

"I'm a priest. The church will excommunicate you if you lay a hand on a priest."

"Be still, my heart," I said.

"Your mother and I are very good friends. I'm her spiritual counselor." His voice was chilling.

"The spirit's fine. The body ain't," I said, walking out of the house.

After the priest described this inelegant encounter to my mother, she entered my house suffused with an ungoverned fury. Her rage spread in crimson blotches across her face in a way I had once seen, when she stabbed my father.

"How dare you insult a guest in my house," she spit.

"We had a discussion," I said.

"He said you threatened to beat him up."

"I implied it, with great delicacy."

"We're not sleeping together," she said, and then, in her frustration, burst into tears. I was rendered helpless when my mother's tears entered the playing field.

"Fine, Mom. I'll tell the kids," I said.

"None of you believe me."

"I'll tell them anyway," I said.

The off-duty priest began to bedevil our lives as he moved through the rooms of my mother's house with a slither rather than a pace. The whole house felt unholy, haunted by some unclean spirit who answered only to the archfiend. Though he was a handsome man, his demeanor appeared scorched by an unclean spirit rather than an angel of light. The house on East Street, which had seemed like a hermitage of great serenity when my family first moved there, suddenly seemed in dire need of an exorcism.

At night, Father Dave and Mom dressed up with great style and went out to one of the base clubs to dinner. They would come in after midnight and often even later. The reason I knew this was because the family spymaster, Carol Ann, was in residence that summer. From the time she was a little girl, Carol Ann displayed a prodigious talent for espionage. When I was seven and Carol Ann five, she showed me the hiding place for all our Christmas presents and said that belief in Santa Claus was bull. I cried in the attic because I still believed in Santa Claus. Mom and Dad's bedroom was an area of supreme interest to Carol Ann, and she would make periodic sweeps through their room, searching out incriminating evidence that our parents were having sex.

In her clandestine surveillance of every nook of our mother's house in Beaufort, my sister finally hit pay dirt. With her spy-in-training sister, Kathy, Carol Ann had discovered something so shocking and disgusting that it would transform the history of our family. Even though Carol Ann had always been a drama queen of prodigious skills, she sounded more a harlequin and fool with this announcement than she did a leading lady. Her joy was at her discovery of some undisclosable documents she had found while reconnoitering my mother's dressing table. She phoned me, with Kathy, usually scrupulous in her anonymity, backing her sister up this time.

"It is irrefutable proof of our mother's perfidy," Carol Ann said. "You must come over here quickly, Pat; I've called a family council to confront Mom."

"Hold your horses," I cautioned. "Remember Tim and Tom are still little boys."

"They're old enough to learn about perfidy," she said.

When I arrived at the East Street house, the tension was almost unbearable. Mom sat in her chair looking murderous as Carol Ann and Kathy formed a witch's tribunal, with the Conroy kids as the only witnesses. Carol Ann stood up to assume her role as lead prosecutor as I sat on the couch with Tim and Tom. Carol Ann began her inquiry with her remarkable gift for subtlety. "I have conclusive proof that you are having a sordid affair with Father Dave. Do you admit it, Mother?"

I put my hands over my face and groaned and heard my mother spit the words, "I most certainly do not."

"Kathy and I were conducting surreptitious operations in your bedroom. We discovered a secret compartment in your jewelry box that we'd never known was there. Naturally, we inspected it."

"You sneaky little bitches!" my mother cried.

"We discovered two plane tickets to Washington, D.C. One was in your name and one was in Father Dave's name. You'll be staying in a little love nest for a week before you come back to Beaufort."

The announcement stunned me into a withdrawn silence. My jaw felt like a dentist had just anesthetized it with Novocain. My mother's eyes had turned into hornets' nests as she stared my sisters down with an unconcealed hatred. Then Peg Conroy took a deep breath, brought herself under perfect control, and delivered a soliloquy that—in its shocking content—would hand back her two daughters' heads on a plate.

"I didn't want to upset my children. Your father was horrible this summer. You kids had to put up with a lot. I certainly wanted to protect you from bad news about my health."

"What does Father Dave have to do with your health?" Carol Ann demanded.

"I asked Father Dave up here and he came as a personal favor to me. He's taken me several times to the Naval Hospital in Charleston and once to the Eisenhower Medical Center in Augusta. Next week we are flying to Washington so I can check into Bethesda Naval Hospital to be treated for my disease."

"What disease?" We screamed it in one voice.

My mother paused with chilling effect, then said, "I've come down with the deadliest form of leukemia. I'll probably be dead in two weeks."

Each of us burst into tears, which streamed down our faces as we ran toward our mother, begging her forgiveness for our puritanical doubts against her. Carol Ann and Kathy were on their knees with their arms around her legs, trying to find ways to correct their apostasy concerning her moral character. They recanted their tainted evidence, and as they did, Mom said with a steel-edged voice, "Give me my goddamn tickets back."

So my mother traveled north to Bethesda and disappeared among the oncologists of the navy and returned a week later and never mentioned her cancer to any of her children again. A couple of months after she returned I was driving my brother Tim to school one morning when he began weeping at a stoplight.

"What's wrong, Timmy?" I asked, hugging his neck, his sobs out of control.

When he started breathing normally again, Tim looked at me and said, "Why isn't she dead?"

"I don't know, but I'm sure glad she isn't," I told my brother.

Now, fourteen years after Peg Conroy told her kids that she would be dead in two weeks from leukemia, she had leukemia.

. . .

The Conroy clan had begun to gather in earnest as I was flying across the Atlantic the next evening. When I saw my mother in a coma, I burst into tears. I sat on her bed and kissed her face and hands. From my point of view she looked as though she might die in the next minute. Empurpled from bruises all over her body, she resembled the survivor of a terrible car crash. I prayed as hard as I could and even found myself whispering the confiteor in Latin from my years as an altar boy. I spent the rest of that week in a state of shock, but the week proved fruitful, because the only subject on anyone's lips was the life and hard times of Peg Conroy.

My brothers and sisters had all assembled, and my two aunts had shown up with Stanny a little before my own arrival—the cousinry would not disembark until the weekend. The entire family was shaken hard by Mom's catastrophic condition. The Conroy humor, which could range from savage to boisterous, was nowhere to be found. My mother's husband, John Egan, busied himself making phone calls to his own seven children, giving them twice-daily reports on my mother's prognosis. He motioned for me to accompany him out to the hall. We embraced and he began weeping against my shoulder. Though it embarrassed him, it took several moments for him to compose himself.

"I need to ask you a question, Pat," John said. "Could I have your permission to call your father? He was married to Peg for thirty-three years and I think he should be here."

"That's as nice a thing as I've ever heard," I said.

"Do you think the other kids will mind?" he asked.

"I think they're gonna love your ass forever," I said, "Just like I will."

Slowly and over time, the glacier that formed between my parents had begun to thaw as the years of their separation added up. Their children delivered reports from the front lines about both of them. Mom was particularly interested in the number of women my father was dating. Grandchildren were born to Jim and Janice, who lived then in Atlanta, as well as Kathy and her husband, Bobby Joe, who were still in Beaufort. Time passing has a soothing, ameliorative effect, and memory softens as its tides flow out to sea. And to the amazement of all his children, Dad was turning into a man of decency and self-control.

The news lifted us when once it would have dropped us into a lightless abyss. Dad's rehabilitation of himself as a father was still a work in progress, but had inched along with such tortoiselike persistence that he had already established his reliability and steadfastness to his younger children. Unlike my penny-pinching mother, Dad was always generous with money where his kids and grandkids were concerned. In his retirement years, Dad had surprised himself and shocked his children by developing a terrific sense of humor. Of all the shameful things he did to us when we were kids, he never once made us laugh. When he entered the hospital waiting room, a cheer went up from the family and the Great Santini strolled into his element, shouting, "Stand by for a fighter pilot." Our spirits soared as we moved to embrace our dad.

It was during that long vigil that I learned most of the stories of my mother's early life—a subject I knew next to nothing about. I'd sit across from my aunts Helen and Evelyn, along with Stanny, as they talked about the early years in Rome, Georgia, and Piedmont, Alabama. All three of these women doctored their stories and memories with a flattering infusion of nostalgia and intentional blackouts when it came to the occasional murders, bootlegging, convictions, or out-of-wedlock babies.

Sister Kathy asked, "How did the family get to Atlanta? I've never heard that story."

Since I knew Kathy had never heard "the creation myth" of our own family history, she didn't understand the immediate emotional shutdown that made the three older women in the room voiceless as stones. Evelyn's eyes flashed hatred at Stanny—Helen's eyes moistened with hurt.

"Our mother abandoned us right in the middle of the Depression. She left four helpless children to fend for ourselves. There wasn't no pie in the window when she left either," Evelyn explained.

"I couldn't throw a penny at a june bug 'cause I didn't own one," Stanny shot back. "I did what I thought I had to do, Evelyn. You'd have done the same thing if you were in my place."

"I'd never leave my kids to starve to death," Helen said. "Never. Those were terrible times."

"It turned out well," Stanny said to her grandchildren. "My girls all married military officers. My daughter had a movie made about her and the actress Blythe Danner played her. My son-in-law Don was played by Robert Duvall. My grandson Pat wrote the book *The Great Santini*. I became a world traveler and a hotelier of note in Monroe, Georgia. I've had a pretty good Southern life, if you ask me."

Carol Ann said, "You had the heart of a giantess, Stanny. You were like the huntress Diana who went out tracking down her one true life. You were Odysseus trying to get back to your home after witnessing the unspeakable atrocities of war. You are the woman who freed my muse from the chains that the patriarchy enslaved women with for all these long centuries."

"We get it, Carol," Jim said.

"Message read loud and clear," Tim said.

"It's a wrap," Mike added.

"Ah, the voice of the patriarchy!" Carol Ann mocked. "They try to silence me, but my voice can never be stilled because of your glorious break for freedom, Stanny."

"It hurt our feelings, Carol Ann," Helen said.

"It scared us to death. And I think it ruined your mother's whole life. I really do," Evelyn added.

With those dark words hanging in the air, I took my father down the long hallway to my mother's room. As I opened the door, I said, "Hey, Dad, I'll wait outside while you see Mom. Prepare yourself—she looks bad."

"I'd like you to go in with me, Pat." And so I did.

Dad gasped when he saw the graveness of her condition, then bent over and kissed her cheeks and forehead. He broke out his rosary blessed by the pope and we said a rosary for my mother's recovery. As we returned to the waiting room, my father seemed to be in a state of unbearable shock.

"How's Frances doing, Don?" Aunt Helen asked, reverting back to the name they called my mother as a child.

Mute as a streetlight, my father raised his right hand and put his arm straight out, his palm parallel to the floor. Then he slowly turned his hand over, simulating a jet plane going into a right-turning roll before going into a stall and falling out of the air on its way to a fiery crash when it met the earth. I used to see my father repeat that hand gesture whenever he described the fate of some fighter pilot who died in Korea. There were tears in Dad's eyes that he tried to hide from the rest of us, but he was deeply shaken by the condition of my suffering mother.

As I sat in the hospital, I tried to figure out why we'd been to Piedmont only twice in all of my growing up. Except for her sisters and their children, no one with any Piedmont connection was present in the waiting room. Then it occurred to me that not a single relative of my father's had arrived from Chicago to help my father in his grief, either.

Again, I returned to memory, and I thought hard about the visits I had made to the Conroy family seat in the heart of Irish Chicago on the South Side in St. Brendan's Parish. The first unfortunate visit was when I was a toddler. I was a photogenic kid as an infant, and I'm sure my mother expected to present her blond, smiling first grandchild born to the clan. Also, I have a strong belief that this was the first time my mother had met my grandparents or any of my aunts and uncles on the Chicago side. Most all of Dad's siblings were still living at home in this cramped, wretched apartment house on Bishop Street.

I remember the attack on my mother with a strange vividness that still has the power to unsettle me.

I think it was Uncle Willie who said this first, but I can't be sure: "Hey, Peggy, y'all want some grits for dinner? Lawdy, lawdy, they sho' do love their grits, don't they, girl-lee."

A woman's voice rang out: "Was yo' raised by a mammy on a big plantation with yo' slaves working in a cotton field?" That was my grandmother's voice.

All this phony Southern slang unhinged my mother, and her discomfort level kept rising as the raucous, horse-laughing Irish pack closed in for the kill.

"We got you some Aunt Jemima pancake mix so y'all won't feel homesick in the big city."

Then rough hands reached out to tickle me and hurt me instead. In less than thirty seconds, Mom and I were both seeking comfort in each other's arms. The city of Chicago, that brutish spitfire of a city, was lost to me forever that day, and I have met no one who has a stronger and more troubled relationship with being Irish than me. When I sign books in Chicago, the city's Irish are open-armed and affectionate when they meet me and buy my books. They know my intimate ties to Chicago through my father, and always they ask me when I'm going to write a book about the Chicago Irish. It pains me to tell them I can't, that I don't know a single thing about the Irish Catholic in Chicago or my father's people. I would have loved to write that novel, but the opportunity was stolen from me by a family that was hostile to strangers. I went back to the great city when I signed my book *The Water Is Wide* at the bookstore at Marshall Field's, and realized what an incomparable loss the city of Chicago was for me.

As I sat there with my mother fighting for her life beside me, I thought about the uniqueness that shapes the destinies of all families. I visited the family seats of my two families only twice in my childhood, and both before I reached the first grade.

"I did not have a family," I said to myself, startled I'd never noticed it before.

By the weekend, the cousins started to arrive. My cousin Carolyn was deeply inculcated with the religious fanaticism of my grandfather. In fact, Carolyn might be the holiest of holy rollers I've ever encountered in my circuits around the planet. Once at a book signing in Jacksonville, she was mumbling something in the stacks when the distraught owner came over and whispered to me, "Pat, we think there might be an assassin in the store." He pointed to my cousin.

"No, sir. That's my first cousin."

"What's she saying?" he asked.

"She's speaking in glossolalia. You know, the unknown tongue," I said.

"What the hell is that?" he asked.

"Don't ask. Hey, Carolyn, how you doing?" I shouted out to her, and Carolyn answered back, "Hey, Conroy!"

A small line had formed at the table, and I was talking to several of my readers when I felt Carolyn's hands enclosing my poor head. In her unknown tongue, Carolyn tried to remove the legion of demons who had taken possession of my immortal soul.

"Get your hands off my head, Carolyn," I said.

"I've got amazing new powers you don't know about. God has blessed me with the power to heal."

Later, after she visited my mother at the hospital, Cousin Carolyn, who is always capable of spiritual surprises, took me aside and whispered to me about my mother's condition.

"Lo and behold, I bring tidings of great hope," Carolyn said. "Christ, the lord, has blessed me with new powers. Last week I raised a turtle from the dead."

With the evangelicals of my mother's family, I always found it problematic to enter into a comfort zone of conversation without it deteriorating into some form of shouting and testifying in a tent revival of the absurd. I considered the lucky turtle, then turned to my cousin and said, "Why?"

"To test these powers the almighty God has granted to me and to heal my fellow man," Carolyn explained. "They've come just in time for me to raise your mama from the dead."

"It couldn't have come at a better time," I assured her. "I'll let the brothers and sisters know. They'll be so relieved."

An elegiac sweetness touched our vigil as the days drifted by and all the cousins gathered. We listened to the cautious reports issued by

Mom's doctor, Steve Madden, a handsome and exceptional oncologist who made us all feel confident that Mom was in good hands. He thought that Mom had a fair chance of surviving her coma, though he added that she could also die at any time. He recommended that we adopt an attitude of restrained hopefulness, and that if we were religious people, we should pray hard for her recovery. He need not have mentioned prayer, since there was more praying rolling out of that room than sweet iced tea from a local truck stop. Bible-thumping of a very high order was drumming the airways above the ten stories where we looked down to the parking lot below.

"Do you know that neither Mom nor Dad attended my graduation from college?" Jim said during one of our vigils. "What kind of family is that?" I think Jim was trying to cleanse the room of the roiling vapors of prayer and turn the subject back to his favorite topic—his contemptuous scorn for Mom and Dad as parents.

"Sounds like our family, Jim," Mike said. "They missed my graduation too."

"Same for me," Tim said.

"Mom and the kids were at my Citadel graduation," I said. "I think Dad was there."

"No, Uncle Jim was there. That other flaming asshole from Chicago," Mike said. "Dad took a rain check."

"Hey, Carol," Jim said, "did Dad go to your graduation?"

"No one went to my graduation," Carol Ann said. "Not even my asshole brothers. Because I'm only a woman. The morning trash to the patriarchy. I grew up in the racist, unspeakable South, where women are just dirt."

"I agree with her a hundred percent," Tim's new girlfriend, Terrye, chimed in. "From the things Tim has told me, I hate everything about a Conroy male," she added.

Carol Ann answered by saying, "Five boys and two girls, Terrye. It made for a monstrous girlhood. Kathy and I were chattel slaves, devalued by our mother, unnoticed by our father, bullied to tears every night by the odious brother overlords."

"Oh, yeah, Carol," Mike said, "the only bully we produced was you, and the kid you bullied was me."

"Amen," said Jim.

"You were a jerk, Carol," Tim added.

Carol Ann said to Terrye, "The rewriting of history is the true enemy of feminism. The male power structure selects a male with his jackboots on to write a text that makes women powerless or invisible. Even worse, it makes us witches or she-devils or banshees who need to be burned at the stake. I've played the role of Joan of Arc since the day I was born. My mother was always my greatest enemy. One day, I'll write a poem describing this scene—my shallow, messed-up brothers trying to feign sadness when they've felt nothing of substance their whole lives."

"Jim, you're up next to stay an hour with Mom," I said as I saw John Egan enter the room and walk over to my father to give him a report on Mom's condition.

Over the ten days my family spent in Eisenhower, arguments and old grudges would flare; disappointments and hurts would take center stage, then retreat into alleyways of exhaustion as the different groups began to coalesce and join one another in the evening talks, where stories of Peg and Don were related by eyewitnesses like Aunt Evelyn, Stanny, our cousins, the Harper boys, and their mother, Aunt Helen. It was the first time the Conroy kids had ever heard the full rendition of Stanny's mythic flight out of Egypt toward the bright lights of Atlanta, and the irreparable damage she had done to her children. But her defense of herself was rigorous as she pleaded for mercy from her two judgmental daughters. Aunt Evelyn said my mother's departure frightened her so badly that she'd been afraid of everything for the rest of her life. She looked shaken as her children, nieces, and nephews heard her recitation of the story for the first time. I believe it was also the first time I saw Evelyn as a tragedy of a desperate white South, where the simple act of learning to read was revolutionary in nature. This was an ugly, morbid, unflattering South that my mother kept hidden from her children, just as she had refused to expose her kids to the rough-hewn Chicago where the grotesque Irish world of my father filled her with dread.

One day when Dr. Steve Madden came into the waiting room for his 11:00 p.m. consultation, he walked in with a springier step and then gave his hand away with a smile.

"I'm pleased to announce that Peg Egan is out of her coma and in remission. She passed her first great test of chemotherapy with flying colors."

The shout that went up in that room would have awakened the entire hospital had it occurred at the midnight hour. We hugged one another and screamed out with relief. Even Carol Ann and I found ourselves hugging and me carrying her around the room.

Then Dr. Madden spoke again when the pandemonium eased up a bit. "I've given Peg something that will let her rest a couple of hours. Then I think she'll be strong enough to entertain some short visits."

Because I was heading back to Italy the next day, I was one of the first to visit Mom in her conscious state. It thrilled me to see her smile when I entered the room, and it pleased me that she had applied makeup and lipstick before she agreed to entertain visitors. When Mom wanted to be pretty for the world, it meant my girl was fighting back to her old self. Leaning down, I kissed her on both cheeks and began crying softly on her shoulder. She joined me in crying, and we held each other hard and long.

"Welcome back, kid," I said fondly.

"It makes a mom feel good when her boy flies thousands of miles to sit by his mother's sickbed as soon as he gets the word. I dreamed you were reading me poetry."

"I was actually reading you poetry," I said.

"I had a terrible nightmare. One night, I dreamed your father came into my room and I felt his huge head hovering over me. That nearly brought me out of my coma."

"He's out in the waiting room, Mom," I said. "John Egan's been great to everybody. He invited Dad down. He's been here every moment."

"John's my sweetie pie," Mom said.

"I've got to get back to Rome," I said. "We're thinking about moving back to Atlanta to be closer to you, Mom. You fought hard. You were incredible."

"Never forget that your mama is a mountain girl, and there's nothing tougher on earth than a mountain girl," Mom said. Then: "By the way, what's the name of your new book?"

"*The Prince of Tides*," I said.

CHAPTER 11

Trip to Rome, Georgia

By the sad winter of 1984, I would find myself once again in my mother's hospital room, at Fort Gordon, Georgia. My stepfather, Dr. John Egan, sat on the other side of the bed. Mom's chemotherapy treatments were agonizing. This round of treatments had moved like a whirlwind through her weakening body again.

I didn't enjoy watching people hurting in general, and found it all but unbearable to be the eyewitness of my mother's morbid suffering. Even then, I couldn't bring myself to believe that the person I loved most in the world was dying. As she regained her strength she'd begin to tell me stories of her childhood, repeating the ones she knew I loved, then going deeper into stories I had never heard. When Dr. Egan arrived, the nature of her reminiscences would pivot and change in a revolutionary way. In telling her history to me, she was a poor mountain girl who almost starved to death in the Depression, but in John's presence, she turned herself into a privileged belle of the old South, who knew well the languor of mansions and the smell of wax from candelabras after a ball. Transfixed, I sat in complete, awkward silence as my mother lied with convincing sincerity to the man she had wed after her storm-tossed marriage to my father. In one preposterous tale of taking a train to Atlanta (after the cotton crop was brought in by worshipful sharecroppers), her parents took their three daughters to Atlanta to shop at Rich's department store for their new trousseaus.

"Daddy wanted his girls to be beautiful," Mom said. "He only bought us the very best."

My stepfather, who was wide-eyed in love with my mother, said to me, "It's a miracle that a poor Irish kid from New York would grow up to marry a Southern aristocrat."

"Aristocrat?" I echoed.

Mom interrupted. "I may never have told you, son, but my family once owned more plantations than any of the other first families of Alabama. They stretched from the Chattahoochee to the Mississippi."

"What happened to that fabulous race, Mom?" I asked. "I've met their descendants. Something bad happened."

Looking infinitely sad, my mother said, "the Woe."

"The Woe?" I asked.

"The Civil Woe," my mother said, exaggerating her Southern accent, which needed no extra frills. "They lost everything. Their land. Their money—but not their pride."

My mother had never lost her capacity to make me feel like I was living inside a badly lit, moss-draped Southern movie.

"Okay. The war was bad. Then what happened? Something bad had to happen to those Piedmont people up in Alabama," I said.

"The Depression," my mother replied. "One day they're owners of banks and insurance agencies. The next day, they're penniless and without hope."

"But they kept their pride," I said.

"Oh, hush," my mother said. "No, both you gentlemen go to the waiting room. I need my beauty rest."

John left immediately, but it took some time for me to gather up my books and journals. "Mom," I said, "I've met these people. Okay, the war was bad. The Depression was bad. But when did they reach the point that none of them could read or write?"

She threw a pillow at me, but I saw her laugh.

The following day, Aunt Helen Harper arrived from Orlando for a visit with her youngest sister. From the time I can remember, I was crazy about Aunt Helen. She was lovely and poised and delicate, and as religious as any human being I'd ever met. A field of disturbance always existed between Aunt Helen and my mother, yet I never understood its origins. In the first half hour of her visit I could tell that Aunt Helen was getting on my mother's nerves. My aunt had the temperament of a Carmelite nun, while my mother descended from a showier, flashier breed. Throughout her lifetime, my mother grew accustomed to being the prettiest girl in the room. When my aunt Helen pulled out her well-used Bible and began reading from the Gospel of Luke, I saw my mother roll her eyeballs in despair. Knowing that Aunt Helen's stamina for Bible reading bordered on the supernatural, I let her read for ten minutes before I stood up, clapped my hands, and said, "We've stayed too long, Aunt Helen. Doctor's orders."

My mother surprised me by asking, "I'd like the two of you to do me a favor."

"I'd do anything for you, Frances," Aunt Helen said, using my mother's childhood name that always irked her.

"I've never seen the house I was born in," my mother said. "I've never been back to Rome, Georgia, since we left there. I'd like Pat to drive you there, Helen, and let him take a picture of it. It had charms. Not a mansion, but close to being one."

"It was a nice house," my aunt agreed.

"We'll leave tomorrow morning and we'll be back for dinner," I said.

"Have you ever been to Rome, Pat?" Aunt Helen asked.

"It's strange. I lived in Rome, Italy, for two years, but I have never seen the town where you and my mother were born."

Taking the back roads, I passed over the lush blue highways of a rural Georgia I was unfamiliar with as Aunt Helen filled me in on the news about my far-flung family. I was happy that I was relieved of hospital duty, as I had come to hate the cancer ward of the Eisenhower hospital almost as much as my mother had. Aunt Helen updated me on my relatives in Piedmont, whom I barely knew. As we drove I listened to my aunt's soft Southern drawl as she filled me in on the details of a large group of relatives my mother had written out of my life.

When she finished she asked me about my own family, and I invited her to visit us in Atlanta, where we had recently moved. Then she asked me about the new book I was writing, a subject she always brought up and one that caused me great discomfort.

"It's about a shrimper's family in Beaufort," I said. "I'm calling it *The Prince of Tides*."

"Is it filth like your other books have been?"

"Yes, according to your harsh standards, it's trashy beyond human belief."

"You know, I think you have talent, Pat. I've told friends of mine at church that one day you'll write a book that even a Christian can read."

"Oh, happy day," I said.

Halfway through the trip, we stopped at a country store, and a slouching local boy came out to fill my car with gas. I went inside the store and purchased some snacks for the journey and an icy bottled Coke for my aunt Helen. When I returned to the car, Aunt Helen was talking to the boy as he finished filling the tank.

"There he is," my aunt said. "That's my nephew Pat Conroy. He wrote the book *The Water Is Wide*, which became the movie *Conrack*. Jon Voight was the star. He wrote *The Great Santini*, about my sister and her husband, and also *The Lords of Discipline*. You should remember this day forever."

The boy looked at me and displayed the same amount of interest as if my aunt had introduced him to a highway underpass.

"Be quiet. Don't do that again," I said to Aunt Helen, as we got back into the car.

"I'm very proud of you," she said. "Even when all you write is pure trash."

When we pulled into the pretty hill town of Rome, Georgia, it surprised me in its modest comeliness and pretty streets, stately architecture and well-tended yards. My mother had spoken of her hometown very few times in my life, and she cadenced these stories with a narrow-gauged layer of pain. There was not a single day of the Depression that my mother liked. It pollinated every corner of her personality with the dark ash of insecurity she would take to her death. In the rare times she mentioned Rome, her whole face darkened with memories she found all but unbearable to retell. It puzzled me that my mother never mentioned the uncommon prettiness of her native town.

"Let's go see the house all of you were born in," I said to Aunt Helen.

"I can't. I don't know where it is."

"What? Didn't you grow up there? You went to high school here," I said.

"It was all so long ago," Helen said. "So much has changed."

In the next block we passed the Carnegie Library, and I pulled into the parking lot and told my aunt I would sift through old records of the town. She and I entered the front door and I went to the main desk and asked the librarian on duty where they stored the microfilm of old newspapers, and where they kept the census records, tax records, anything that might help me complete our assigned task. The lady delivered good advice and soon I was going through census records of the 1930s. I was looking for the name of Jasper Catlett Peek, my grandfather, and could not find mention of him in the few documents I checked, when my search was interrupted.

Looking up when I heard a swoosh of footsteps bearing down on me, I saw my aunt Helen leading the charge of a covey of librarians as they bore down on my desk armed with folders. I laid my head down on the library table and moaned out of frustration. I should have known that if my aunt bragged about me to boys pumping gas out in the country, she would have a field day with librarians.

We introduced ourselves all around, and the librarians opened their folders, all of which contained stories and articles about me.

"Ladies, I'm sorry my aunt has a big mouth. Before this trip I always thought she was a pious, demure woman," I said.

"They have a right to know," my aunt replied. "Remember, Pat, they're librarians."

The woman I took to be the head librarian said, "Mr. Conroy, we've been on your trail for a long time. This is serendipity. We've heard you have roots here?"

"Call me Pat. This is the first time I've ever been to your town. You need to ask my perfidious aunt any questions about my family's ties to Rome," I told her.

The second librarian said, "Aunt Helen, we've done a lot of research on this and we can't find anybody in town who even remembers your family living here. We studied church records, club records, and tax records—you don't seem to exist."

Embarrassed, my aunt blushed deeply and said, "We were poor. But we were very clean."

"But surely you remember the names of friends, or the church you attended, or the names of the preachers, or where your father worked?"

"My father had a barbershop on your main street," Helen said. "But he was touched by the Lord when the Depression hit, and he closed the shop and started to street-preach about the end of the world. We were poor but very clean," she added.

"Where did you live?" a librarian asked.

"I don't remember," my aunt said. "We were poor but very clean."

By this time, I realized they were accidentally humiliating my aunt Helen. I jumped in. "Would you quit saying you were poor but very clean? Tell them you belong to the family they're dying to know about."

"It's not a sin to be poor," Aunt Helen said to me.

"It's certainly not," I said, then looking at the librarians, who were good-natured women, "but Helen and her family were filthy as pigs."

"He's kidding!" Helen said. "He's just like his father."

"I get suicidal when someone tells me that," I said, then saw a television crew sprinting down an aisle of books.

"Congrats, Aunt Helen," I said. "You just got yourself on the evening news."

"I confess," the head librarian said, "I called them."

The news crew was skilled and professional, but before the interview started, my aunt was paralyzed with fright. Her hands trembled noticeably.

"I've never been on TV," she said, "in my whole life."

"Except for that booger coming out of your nose, you'll do fine," I said.

Her compact snapped open and she said, "I look all right, don't I?"

"You've always been a doll," I said, and the reporter started the interview by asking what business had brought us to Rome. I explained about my mother's leukemia and her burning need to see a photograph of the home she was born in. The problem, so far, was that we didn't even know where to begin looking, but the librarians were proving invaluable in helping us.

"We were very poor, but very clean," my aunt said, repeating her mantra three or four times during the interview.

But the librarians hit pay dirt when they found my aunt's high school yearbook and located her photograph in the senior section. There she was, her beauty a form of homage to delicacy itself.

"What a babe, Aunt Helen," I said.

She pointed to a young man and said, "He used to court me."

A librarian said, "He still has a law practice in Rome. Let me try to get him at his office."

In less than five minutes a dapper, well-dressed man walked in the front door of the library and moved toward the crowd of us. Coming to Aunt Helen in a beeline, he shook her hand and said, "You're as lovely as you were in high school, Helen Peek."

"I wish that were true," she said.

I shook hands with this very nice lawyer and promptly forgot his name, as I did the names of all those helpful librarians who were so good-natured about assisting us in our quest. Uncharacteristically, I had left my journals and notebooks back in Augusta, and I recorded none of the facts that we discovered that day.

The lawyer drove his own car out into the country, reminiscing about high school with my aunt Helen beside him. I followed in my car as we passed farmhouses and small run-down churches on the way to my mother's mythical childhood home. Turning onto a dirt road, we made our way past modest houses and parked in the dirt yard of an exceedingly unprepossessing white farmhouse. A black family poured out of the house, and I got out to introduce myself to the grandmother, who was watching over five of her daughter's babies. I explained our mission and that my mother had been born here fifty-nine years before. A tall, craggy white man made his way up the road and into the gathering, listening to me asking whether I could be allowed to visit inside the house.

Finally, he said in a friendly voice, "You a Peek, son?"

"Yes, sir, I'm a Peek on my mother's side," I said. "This is my mother's sister Helen Peek."

"Helen, I grew up down the road in that brick farmhouse. I was a little fella myself the night your sister was born. I came up to sit in the living room. I heard your mother's first cry, son."

"Do you remember the room she was born in?" I asked.

"Sure do. Maggie, you mind if these folks look around your house? I can vouch that they lived here."

"The boy wants to see where his mama was born," Maggie said. "Let me get you some iced tea."

"My mother's dying," I said to the black woman, and I realized it was the first time I'd uttered this terrible phrase, even to myself.

"You close to your mama, son?" Maggie asked me.

I found myself wordless, afraid that if I even spoke I would fall apart. Grateful, I heard my aunt behind me: "Pat worships his mother. Always has."

"That's the way it's s'posed to be," the woman said as she led us through her front doorway. The house was small, but neat and well cared for. The white man put his hand on my shoulder and led me to the front bedroom.

"Your mama was born in this room," he said, "in a bed that sat exactly where that bed is today."

So it began here in this bedroom, the woman who would become my mother, born in a rush of blood and fluid. She now lay in a hospital room and would soon be buried in South Carolina earth. The secret of her great irreparable social shame had also found its conception in this same house. I would bet my life that my mother's embarrassment over her roots had originated in the shades of this dreary house and the inhospitable fields around it. But that girl had done all right. She became an officer's wife, danced at a ball at the White House, shared a stage and gave a speech beside President Jimmy Carter, was the commanding officer's wife on a base in Hawaii, had traveled the world, and saw her fictional self played by the magnificent Blythe Danner. My mother had risen from this bed and turned her life into something glamorous as well as something ruined and sad. But she and her children were the only ones to know of that sadness. That baby girl born here so long ago had produced two writers, a novelist and a poet, because of her insatiable love of reading and the majesty of words strung together in a way that tried to make magic in a hard world.

The girl born in this room had gotten up and done some things. After making our farewells, taking a few snapshots of the house, I drove back to Rome. Then I stopped off at a drugstore. I went into the store and looked at a rack of postcards. I chose one of a historical home in Rome, a proper Southern mansion of suitable grandeur.

That night when I went up to the Eisenhower hospital to say good night to my mother and stepfather, I handed the postcard to my mother.

"This is it? My house?" my mother asked. "Are you sure?"

"Five librarians helped me and Helen find this house," I said. "They found some old records, and the residents of this house were Jasper Catlett Peek and his wife, Margaret. They listed the names of the kids. That's the place. You were born in the upstairs bedroom. We got a tour of the house today."

"John, it's even more beautiful than I remember," my mother said, handing it to her husband. "Promise me we'll go there when I beat this thing."

"A Southern mansion," John said. "Where else would a woman like you be born? We'll go there. That's a promise."

It was a trip they would never make.

CHAPTER 12

Gnome

Time caught up with me in the years leading up to my mother's death, and pulled me to the ground in its merciless grip. The truth is, I couldn't tell you anything about time and what it did to me that year, except that it manhandled and defeated and horse-collared me. On November 17, 1984, it broke my heart with an ax blow of destiny. Time did not even take notice. Its eyeless immensity passed over me without pause or recognition.

Augusta is now a fearful word to me, and so is Eisenhower. Both city and hospital have retained the power to cause inflammation and distress when I hear those words in a sentence. Although my mother had held her own since her last remission, finally the word came. She had gone out of remission, and was back in the hospital. In the waiting room I embraced John Egan yet again and could tell sadness had overcome him long before I got there. It was the fall of 1982, and I had driven over from my home in Atlanta.

"It's bad this time, Pat," he said. "It's really going to hit Peg hard."

"Dr. Madden said it would get worse each time the cancer went out of remission," I reminded him. "So far, he hasn't been wrong."

Dr. Madden came into the waiting room shortly after I arrived there. He and I had become friends by that time, and he knew I had implicit trust in his decisions about Mom's health. But he was not optimistic about my mother's chances.

"Pat, the leukemia might kill her this time. Or *I* might kill her with the treatment," he said. "She went out of remission and the leukemia moved in fast. So I put her on the strongest chemotherapy possible, but it's a balancing act in this stage of her cancer."

"How's she taking it?" I asked.

"She's a fighter, Pat. But tomorrow she's going to have to use every ounce of that fighting spirit. It's about to get ugly."

And ugly it got. On the second night, with me sleeping on a cot beside my mother's bed, I woke up as she was projectile-vomiting off a far wall. In a flash I was out of bed and brought her a wastebasket she could vomit in, which she practically filled until she stopped long enough for me to rush it to the bathroom to empty and wash it out. When I returned to her bed, the diarrhea had started, and it was far worse than anything I could imagine. I leaned down to pick her up, and during a brief pause in her falling apart, I grasped her and placed her on my shoulder and made another run to the bathroom and deposited her on the toilet seat. I undressed her completely and left her with the waste-basket and listened as her entire body collapsed in on itself. I washed my hands as carefully as I could but realized I was covered in excrement and vomit, and my mother's room had the feel and smell of an abattoir. As I looked at her sheets and pillowcases, I realized that time had started to kill my mother with a callousness it had not shown before. Into laundry bags I threw all her sheets and towels and defiled clothing and hurled them out into the hallway, where the night workers would pick them up at five the next morning and have them back in her room by five in the evening. I scrubbed down the bed with ammonia and water and cleaned every wall and floor where my mother had spewed those poisons fleeing from her body. I made her bed with sweet-smelling sheets the way they taught me to do it at The Citadel. Going across the hall to an empty bedroom, I stole all the fresh pillowcases on its bed and placed them on her bed. Then I waited outside the bathroom for her.

Since I used all of our towels cleaning the mess around her bed, I went across the hall on another scavenger hunt, where I lifted bars of soap and shampoo and towels. After another fifteen minutes, I heard a weak tapping on the bathroom door, and I opened it to find a bathroom where it looked and smelled like a murder had taken place.

"You okay, Mom?" I asked stupidly, and she answered me with laughter.

"I think I've seen better days, Pat," she said, and we both started giggling.

"I've got to bathe us to get us clean again, Mom."

"I'll never be clean again," she said.

"I'll be damned if that's so," I said.

I turned on the shower, then picked Mom up and we stepped into a stall where the water fell in a hot steaming rush of cleansing. I emptied small bottles of shampoo on our heads. Soapy washcloths cut through the dried vomit and diarrhea as I worked up and down Mom's feverish body. My mother was squeaky clean, but she noticed the nature of our human predicament long before I did. As I washed the soap off her body, she leaned against the shower stall and said, "You shouldn't be doing this, Pat. It's not natural."

"It's the most natural thing in the world, Mom. You did it for me."

Somehow I got her out of that shower, dried her off, got her into a clean nightgown, doused her with White Shoulders, and got her back in bed. For the next half hour, I was cleaning up the bathroom, which smelled like an outhouse. Eventually, I would fill two bags with laundry and throw them out into the hallway. With infinite relief, I put myself on my cot, as exhausted as a Channel swimmer. As I turned toward Mom to wish her good night, she surprised me by being awake, and the moonlight was coming in the window, lighting up her face. Her wig was lying on the bedside table, and I went to retrieve it and helped her place it back in position. She spoke to me first. "Are you writing about me in your new book?"

"No, Mama, I'm not," I answered.

"You're lying," she said. "I can always tell when my children are lying."

"You might not like what I'm writing about you."

"I'd like you to promise me one thing," she said.

I went to her bedside and said, "You're in a great position to bargain, Mama."

She turned toward me, turned the pretty blue eyes that not even the cancer could touch and said, "Don't write about me like this. Make me beautiful."

"Oh, Mama, oh, mother of mine," I said that night, "you who opened up the universe for me with all the stuff of language, I'll make you so beautiful. Because you made me a writer and presented me the tongues and a passion for language, I can lift you off that bed, banish the cancer from your cells forever. When they speak of beauty in the South, my mother, they'll talk about you, mention you by name, praising you to the sky."

Although I swore to my mother I would not write about her in this condition, I knew I was lying as I tendered the promise, because she had never appeared so beautiful to me as she fought against the forces determined to kill her.

After I made this pretty speech, my mother reached up and squeezed my hand. "I'd like Meryl Streep to play the role."

When my mother got released from Eisenhower, everyone who loved her knew that we were losing her. She had suffered through the chemotherapy for more than a week, and I took her by wheelchair out to my car, where I started down the long, lush drive that would take us through the pretty towns of Allendale, Fairfax, Varnville, and Hampton before the countryside began to open, revealing the bright green marshes like mile-long prayer rugs along the creeks. Mom was surprisingly talkative on the trip east through the comely railroad towns. She talked a lot about her reconciliation with my father, and how she had once planned never to speak to him after their trashy divorce. Dad had come down for the whole time Mom was in the hospital this time, and a real friendship was forming between John Egan and my father. Mom was proud that her two husbands were in attendance in her time of greatest need. Two such different Irishmen never met on such a desperate stage. Dr. Egan with his great gentlemanly reserve and my barnstorming peasant father were complete opposites, but the love of my mother presented them with the most fragile linkage to a friendship that would last both of their lives.

When we neared Beaufort, my mother stunned me by asking, "Where are we going to lunch today?"

I had not considered lunch because of the delicacy of her condition, and I tried my hardest to talk her out of it. But she refused to be deterred by my lack of enthusiasm.

"It's a tradition between us. My girlfriends at Fripp love to hear me tell about the expensive meals you order me, even when you know I can't eat a single thing," she said.

"Did you tell them I start with a little champagne?" I asked.

"The most expensive bottle they've got, and you always ask them to ice it down by the table. They've invited me golfing next week. And I plan to play in that golf match," she said.

"My girl's a tough girl," I said.

"Damn right," she said. "I haven't given up yet, and you can say that to anyone, Pat."

"Good to know," I said. "I'll spread the word."

A new restaurant with a good reputation had just opened on Lady's Island, with splendid views of the Beaufort River and the magical town built on its bluff. Though I heard the food was good, restaurants in Beaufort had always proven to be much more mediocre than the approval of the street indicated. I struggled to get Mom out of the car and into the restaurant, which was large and airy. The menu was nice by Atlanta standards and spectacular by Beaufort ones. I ordered the most expensive things they had, then had them boxed up and ready to carry home. At that point disaster struck. A ladies' club that my mother had once tried to join, over her son's strong objections, walked into the restaurant, singly and in groups, and filed in silent review past the table where my mother and I sat. It was a commonplace club in the small towns of the South and, perhaps, small towns everywhere. On a regular basis one member of the club would read a scholarly paper that she had written for that particular meeting. They were formidable wives of powerful men in Beaufort, and all of them had been members of the infamous Great Santini premiere committee. They formed the intellectual underpinning of this small town, and their fingerprints were all over every cultural event that took place in the city limits. The club put out a fragrance of respectability my mother couldn't resist, and she'd turned in an application for membership. One of the club's ironclad rules was that its women be college graduates. Naturally, my mother claimed she had graduated, cum laude, from Agnes Scott College, and just as naturally, the club turned down her application. When the club proved the falsity of the college degree, it stung my mother's deepest sense of herself.

But now the society ladies passed my mother and none of them spoke to her. She was sobbing by the time I got her out of the parking lot, and made a right turn on the road to Fripp Island. Language failed me, and I couldn't think of a single word to assuage my mother's complete social humiliation. Her sobs cut through me like slivers of glass. For five miles they continued and grew even louder and more despairing, until I finally broke and said, "Hey, Mama, do you want me to turn around, drive back to that restaurant, and throw every one of those women through a plate-glass window?"

My mother tried to gain some control of herself, because she knew that she'd unleashed a fury inside of me. In the weakest, most timid voice, she said, "You're just like your father. A beast. Nothing but a beast of the field."

"That may be so, Mama. And by the way, I never got to thank you for mixing my gene pool with that guy. But since you did, this is what you get. Hey, Mom, do you know that those women back there are all in my new book, *The Prince of Tides*?"

I felt a reawakening in my mother, a return to vibrant, ecstatic life as she asked, "Did you get 'em, son?"

"I got the living shit out of them." And my mother giggled.

"Will they know who they are?"

"Tour guide operators moving their horses down Bay Street will be able to point them out to tourists as they come out of stores."

Again my mother giggled, but more of a cackle this time, and said, "Son, you're just like me."

. . .

My mother's two-year battle with cancer provided a new entryway into the lunatic center of the Conroy family. Furthermore, it provided a wick of time where we could measure her diminishment as she went in and out of remission during several harrowing years when the grotesque gnome "leukemia" came to rule all of our hours. I got to the point where I couldn't mention either the word "cancer" or "leukemia" to anyone—and would say only that my mother was a very sick woman. The language itself seemed to have turned on us.

The rules of engagement became very clear to all of us. Since moving back to Atlanta from Italy, I had been a full participant in Mom's recovery from the devastating results of her chemotherapy, when her body would react as if the doctors were overdosing her on arsenic. My duties were clear and my siblings gave me my marching orders.

Mike said to me during my first week back, "Pat, you've got to come and stay with Mom at the hospital whenever she goes out of remission. That may take a week or even two weeks. The rest of us will come down on the weekends to help you."

My first call to arms came six months after I returned to Atlanta. Dr. Egan called me from his and Mom's new house on Fripp Island, and he sounded distraught and confused on the phone. "Doesn't look good, Pat. Though I've been a medical doctor my whole career, I can't stand to see Peg suffer like this."

"Just get Mom up to Eisenhower, John. I'll be there as soon as I can."

Yet again I arrived in Augusta to find Mom already hooked up to the poisons that eventually would kill her. Dr. Steve Madden had given her a sedative that would put her to sleep through the following day. I found Dr. Egan in the waiting room that now contained just the two of us. I noticed his hands were trembling.

He said, "Peg was doing so well. She was jogging a mile on the beach every day, walking another four miles, eating the right stuff. Your mother thinks she is going to beat this thing. She really thinks this cancer won't kill her . . . that it can't kill her. She is terrified, though."

"So am I," I said. "Look, John, this has been very tough on you. Why don't you go back to Fripp Island and rest for the next ten days? You know that Mom's going to be out of it for the next week, and it'll give you some time off from being her caretaker. I'll be up here every day. I'll stay on a cot beside her bed. I'll make sure she's comfortable and well taken care of."

"But she'll need me," he said.

"She's going to need you to be strong and fresh, Doc," I said. "Not like this. You're exhausted. Let me walk you to the parking lot. When she wakes up and starts speaking coherently, I'll call you back up for duty."

"Will you promise to do that?" he asked. "She was so frightened last night. Just terrified."

"Mom's a warrior, John. That's the first thing you need to know about her. She'll have some setbacks, but she'll come out of it, and you'll know you married Athena before she dies."

"Peg and I are already sick of this trip from our house on Fripp Island to Augusta."

"You'll be a lot sicker of it before all this is over, Doc."

I sent Dr. Egan down the road toward Fripp Island; then I went down to fetch my overnight bag and the six paperbacks I had brought up to read to Mom on those occasions when she could tolerate the sound of another voice. The chemotherapy devastated her, as though a plague had entered her bloodstream. I learned there was nothing more painful for a worshipful son than watching his mother lie in her bed of anguish and being unable to do a single thing for her. Before Dr. Madden left for home that night, he made a correction in Mom's medicine that brought her fever down and let her sleep through the night, at least.

When we looked back at my mother's futile rearguard battle against her cancer, she and I both agreed that the first rounds of her treatment were halcyon compared to the last fierce and killing encounters. This time, she had two days of grievous symptoms, until her compact, agile body enabled her to gather reinforcements for a counterattack. Her body was hard and game for battle. The leukemia was not a worthy opponent in those early days of siege, but it would grow into unseen power as though it were a tsunami, gaining monstrous strengths undetectable to the human eye.

She would often ask me to read to her, and I would always start out with *Dunkirk*, by Robert Nathan, a poem I had taught in a sophomore class at Beaufort High School and that I had loved with a passion I brought to all things British. The entire history of England seemed contained in that remarkable poem. Then I would switch over to Dylan Thomas, and James Dickey, and Carol Ann's book of poetry *The Jewish Furrier*. When she was ready for bed, I'd read the books I had brought up for her pleasure. I read her *The Greengage Summer*, by Rumer Godden, and *The Lords of Discipline*, because she insisted I read it to her aloud. As I was reading through it, Mom would pepper me with questions.

"Did that really happen?" she would ask.

"Not to me, but to a boy I knew," I'd answer.

"That couldn't've happened, could it?"

"That did happen," I'd say.

"It sounds preposterous."

"It is preposterous. Welcome to The Citadel."

She would go into a sweet, purring repose when she got too tired to stay awake for another moment. I would mark the book and go to sleep on my cot beside her. I felt lucky I could do this for my mother. I could feel the old resentments between us melting like wax, like altar candles reducing themselves in the name of light and heat. My resistance to Mom disappeared as her dependence on me increased disproportionately every day she woke up.

Each day Mom would lose more and more of her hair, and it alarmed her to see her visage in the mirror as her hair was calving off in huge chunks. On Friday before the kids began their arrivals, I went down to Augusta's lovely but neglected main street to shop for some wigs or a turban for Mom. It tickled me that Augusta had the tallest Confederate memorial I've ever seen anywhere. The lone soldier atop the monument is invisible to the citizenry who pass it each day; one would have to check it out as a skydiver even to catch a glimpse of this lonely soul.

The wig shops were all owned and operated by black women who showed a great flair for commerce. They were earthy, funny women who hovered about me as they shouted back and forth.

"We got any wigs for white girls?" a large woman shouted to a colleague in the back.

"Why would we? A white girl's never walked into this store," the woman in the back said.

"I got just the thing for you. Follow me, gentleman." She opened up a large drawer and began drawing out such beautiful turbans that some of them sucked the breath out of me.

Frances ("Peg") Peek
and Donald Patrick Conroy,
just married, 1945.
....

Don Conroy at the time he
was selected for the
Navy Olympic basketball
team, 1947.
....

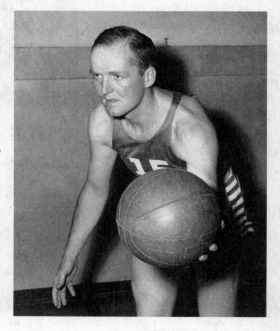

Peg Conroy holding her
firstborn son, Pat.

Just a small family at the
time: Pat; his mother, Peg;
and his sister Carol.

The boys with Peg.
Left to right: Jim, Tom, Tim,
Mike, Pat.

The South Carolina All-Star Team in 1963.
Pat is kneeling on the left.

The whole family together in 1965.
Back row: Jim, Carol, Pat, Kathy, Mike.
Front row: Peg, Tim, Tom, Don.

To: Cadet D. P. Conroy. Congratulations on the high honor bestowed on you by your fellow cadets when they elected you to the Honor Committee.

Hugh P. Harris

(Above) Pat finally goes to college and attends The Citadel.

(Left) A commendation.

(Below) Pat graduates from The Citadel in 1967.

Pat and Barbara's wedding,
October 10, 1969.
....

A family picture taken
in 1970 to send to Don,
who was overseas.
....

Pat's thirtieth birthday
in 1975. With him are
Marion O'Neill; Cliff
Graubart, who owned
the Old New York
Bookshop; and his
sister Carol, the poet.
....

VENIA PEEK CORA PEEK DEE HOLTZCLAW (PEEK) HOLTZCLAW PEEK PEEK

GARDY ROBERT DORA JASPER PEEK JERMIAH PEEK FATHER ALFRED PEEK TELITHA (MENSHEW) PEEK BABY CICERO PEEK VRSTIE PEEK
MOTHER: SUSAN HOLTZCLAW

The Peek family of Alabama. Jasper is Pat's grandfather.

The Conroy family of Chicago.

Pat at the Old New York Bookshop in 1976.
He had just published *The Great Santini*.

Pat talking with Royce Bemis, a sales rep from
Houghton Mifflin, the publisher of his first four books.

Don signing books at the Old New York Bookshop in 1976.

Pat playing one-on-one with Michael O'Keefe during the filming of *The Great Santini* in 1979.

Pat, Don, and Col. Thomas Courvoise, also known as "The Boo."

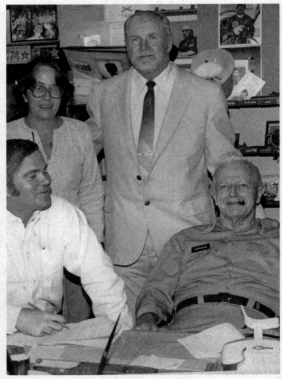

Don, Cliff Graubart, and Pat.

Barbara, Jessica, Megan, and Melissa
with Pat during a summer in Minnesota.

The Conroys move to Rome from 1982 to 1984
and live on the Piazza Farnese.

Peg, her granddaughter Susannah, and Pat in Rome, 1982.

Shannon Faulkner and Pat autograph books after speaking at a St. Helena Island art gallery in 1995.

The trip to Ireland, 1996.
Kathleen Kennedy Townsend
is in the foreground at left.

Pat with his favorite teacher
from childhood, Gene Norris.

Don's last birthday with Pat, Carol, Kathy, Jim, Mike, and Tim on April 4, 1998.

A drawing by Doug Marlette in honor of Don after his death.

" STAND BY FOR A *FIGHTER PILOT!* "

Pat and Cassandra's wedding in May 1998.

"They come from Istanbul. That's in Turkey—I went there early this year with my business partner and lo', hon, what a city! Those Turk women wear these things with style and class."

I chose two of them and took them to the cash register.

"Those are my two most expensive turbans," she said. "Well over a hundred dollars apiece."

"A bargain," I said. "Wrap them up. My mom's going bald, but no one's going to witness her humiliation now. I'm going to turn Mama into a Turk."

In her two new turbans, my mother looked like a million dollars. The colors rainbowed over her paleness. She took an hour to apply makeup. The nurses made a fuss over her, Dr. Madden praised her beauty, and when I saw her I bowed deeply, like a servant in waiting. My pretty girl was back.

"Pat, I love you for the turbans. I wouldn't have ever thought of that. It gives me a confidence I thought I'd never recover, but look at me now. Just look at me. And I promise you something, son: I'm going to beat this cancer. I'm going to beat it like a dead snake!"

When the weekend came, Mom found her room besieged by children and relatives who came to pay her homage. There was a general feeling that the cancer had dissolved the tissues of Mom's insecurities and turned loose a much finer woman. Though she could exhaust herself quickly with the incoming wave of visitation that would surge into Augusta each weekend, she adored the attention her family flooded her with.

On the other hand, Mom had been controversial enough as a mother to make many of the encounters with her children into force fields. My mother had never been affectionate with her children; she was the kind of woman you had to learn to love through interpretation, osmosis, or guesswork. As far as I know, none of us ever sat in our mother's lap or watched TV with her arm around our shoulders. She had not been able to breast-feed any of us, and she would kiss us in the most gossamer fashion, as likely to stir the air around our cheeks as to actually touch us with her lips to our faces.

Until John Egan arrived, I served guard duty at the entrance to her room, directing people in and out, watching Mom for signs of exhaustion, hustling people down the hall when she put a finger on the tip of her nose, indicating it was time for a nap. Dad arrived on Saturday, and it amazed me how much spirit he brought to the room. He always entered the waiting room saying, "Stand by for a fighter pilot!"

Dad's visitations became my mother's favorite part of the weekend ceremonial. He brought laughter, a chatterbox sensibility, and a complete denial that his ex-wife was dying twenty yards down the hall.

The confrontation I feared the most was my mother's devastating phone calls from my sister, Carol Ann. Carol Ann had a precise genius for calling my mother when I was out of Mom's room or when I was watching a baseball game with Dr. Egan. Always I took a seat by the doorway so I could see down the hall clear to my mother's room and keep one eye on the Braves game. I saw a pretty blond nurse with horn-rimmed glasses running full speed toward me, and that gave me my signal that Carol Ann's timing had been perfect again.

I entered the room on the fly and took in the scene immediately. Mom was crying as hard as a woman could cry. When I grabbed the phone from her hand, she offered no resistance.

"Hello, Carol Ann, you may not remember, but I'm your brother Pat, the firstborn, the favorite by far," I said into the phone.

"Oh, humor boy. The Conroy male spirit rises up to mock the only serious writer this family will ever produce. Go ahead, trickster. I'll find a way of talking to my mother. Don't think I won't. We need to get some things straightened out between us before she dies."

"Yeah, that'll really lift her spirits. Especially in the condition she now finds herself. Why don't you write her long letters full of gossip and makeup tips, and the new fashions you see on the streets of New York?"

"I live in serious New York, among serious literary people," Carol Ann said. "I decided not to bury myself in the racist, unintellectual South, which has empty space where its greatest minds should be producing serious poems and novels. You've thrown your life away in the South, Pat. You know that, but don't have the guts to admit it. Put my mother back on the phone or I'm going to file a federal complaint."

"My heart will dance like a tequila worm when I hang up this phone."

"Mom and Dad have got to let me explain the crimes against humanity I endured through them," she said. "Only then can they understand why my life's been such a disaster."

"Why don't you write a book about this?" I suggested, hanging up the phone.

.   .   .

When Mom was released from Eisenhower after two short weeks and I drove her to her house on Fripp Island, John was waiting for her, and their reunion was tender. I unloaded the car and brought her luggage upstairs to her bedroom. Then I went downstairs and joined John and Mom in their recitation of the rosary in gratitude for Mom's safe return.

I then heated up a magnificent meal for me, Mom, and Dr. John. In the middle of the meal, I looked up and saw my brother Tom, in his twenties now, try to sneak into his bedroom without anyone noticing his passage—he had a hunched, disconnected walk and a face as troubled as a fallen angel.

"Tom, come get something to eat," I called out.

He said, "I hate that foreign shit you fix."

"Try it, Tom," I suggested.

"I've always hated you!" he screamed. "You act like you're such a big-shot son of a bitch, when all you are is a fucking asshole just like the rest of us."

As he left the field of battle, he slammed his bedroom door.

I was as shaken as I had been for a long while. Mom and John had not uttered a word. Finally, I said, "Tom, Mom?"

My mother looked up and nodded her head. "Tom—it's not going to be pretty."

CHAPTER 13

Tom's Breakdown

I never got to know my brother Tom. I was fifteen when he was born while Dad was stationed at Quantico. My father woke me in the middle of the night, brought me downstairs to sleep with my two-year-old brother, Tim, who could not sleep unless he held on to someone's ear. Unless he had access to an ear, Tim would stay awake all night long, crying inconsolably. I eased into my parents' bed and Tim latched onto my ear with a naturalness that surprised me. I blew Mom a kiss and wished her all the luck in the world. It was Mom's twelfth and final pregnancy, and Tom would become the Conroy family's last "baby."

Tom was the best-looking of the Conroys, by far, but his handsomeness never seemed to grant him much pleasure or confidence. When I'd come home from college, he seemed to avoid me, would not even try to make eye contact with me or engage me in conversation. His face contained a quiver full of brimming emotions, but he was quiet as a whelk. Anything I asked him, he would respond with a monosyllabic answer without a molecule of substance to back it up.

Now, I look back and see I could've done a lot more to shore up my relationship with my youngest brother, but I failed to do so. I found him tedious to be around and his diffidence bored me. On the other hand, I had felt close to my baby brother Tim the moment he took up residence in our house, even though he was only two years older than

Tom. Because birth order and the gap in our ages betrayed us, Tom and I could never recover what time had stolen from us. We were strangers to each other our entire lives.

The movie *The Great Santini* bestowed many acute gifts upon the Conroy family. The film itself did much to restore the hazardous equilibrium of a family badly shattered by our parents' divorce. Though the movie held up a mirror for the world to glimpse a family in extreme breakdown, by God, it was a family where great love and loyalty could grow even in such a disastrous garden of souls.

But there is a gift the Hollywood people gave us that seemed happenstance at the time. When I finally got a tape of the movie many years after its release, I went straight to a scene where Ben Meecham is hurt during a basketball game, with his parents watching from the stands. Directly behind Blythe Danner, Lewis John Carlino has generously seated my real mother, who looks as happy as I've ever seen her, and as pretty as a boy could ever want his mother to be. She follows the game as it races up and down the court; my brother Tom, the boy wearing black horn-rimmed glasses, is playing on the same team with Michael O'Keefe. The camera goes from court to Robert Duvall and Blythe Danner, back to action on the court, where Tom is running a play with Michael O'Keefe, back to Mom, back to Tom, back to the court, then my mother again. Then my brother once more. Then I turned the movie off because I couldn't bear to watch another frame.

The Conroys were never a picture-taking family, and when the Marine Corps movers of 1954 lost both of my mother's two huge albums that bulged with photographs telling the history of her family, she splintered into a grief that had no restorative or cure. As she wept, she kept saying in what sounded to be true bitterness, "They lost our history. All of it. We don't have a history now, no record for the future. Everything's lost."

Before this incident, I remember Mom constantly taking pictures with a cheap Kodak. After the loss of the albums, we took photos in a haphazard and unserious way. As a family we were spectacular failures as photographers. There are pictures of Conroys without legs, Conroys with their eyes closed, Conroys in too much shade or obliterated by sunlight. We seem to have been born with a low-grade incompetence whenever a camera is in our hands. Our scrapbooks and archives are frightful in their ineptness. But Mom always claimed that those lost picture books were storehouses of irreplaceable treasures to her, brilliantly done and professionally preserved.

It was 1995 when I first found the strength to watch *The Great Santini* again. I had returned to Fripp Island and my isolated life on a sea island to heal myself in silence. The nineties had turned into a ghastly decade for me, and I'd suffered some grievous setbacks on the way. But I'd survived the greatest suicidal episodes of my life with the help of the superb therapist Marion O'Neill, and was putting my shattered psyche back together again. Part of her therapy was to have me watch the movie *The Great Santini* once more.

I put in the cassette and watched Robert Duvall and his Marine pilots outfly the navy pilots. In the life I was raised in, the Marines never let the navy beat them at anything, and I knew all the steps in that military dance. Soon there was a scene of Blythe Danner and her children waiting at a deserted airport for the arrival of the plane bringing the Great Santini home from a cruise. I had waited for at least twenty of these arriving planes in the span of my childhood. All the excitement and the anxiety of the soldier's return hums through the family as Blythe Danner straightens up and checks the appearance of her children before the actual inspection begins. The father walks off the plane and the booming cry goes up: "Stand by for a fighter pilot!"

Realizing I was approaching the emotional wreckage I'd barely dealt with in more than ten years, I continued to watch the movie, admiring its perfection, its low-budget daringness, the exceptional quality of the performances. I watched as David Keith made his powerful entry onto the Hollywood stage, playing Red Petus (David Keith would later play the part of Will McLean in *The Lords of Discipline*). Stan Shaw brought a perfect touch to the role of a black flower salesman named Toomer. The film has a sense of solidity and it gains in confidence as it moves along at a well-timed pace. But then there are basketballs beating a familiar tattoo on a wooden court, and I returned as an eighteen-year-old boy to the most joyous part of my unhappy childhood.

Then I lost it completely when I saw my poor, unlucky mother smiling and enjoying herself behind Blythe Danner. My sloppy sentimentality went into wilder, more hysterical territory when I saw my brother Tom throwing a pass to Michael O'Keefe. This is the only place where I can come and see my mother and brother, alive and breathing and moving through the certain motions of their foreclosed days. Mom, the mother I failed. Tom, the brother I never stood up for as a brother, the brother I failed, and possibly even the brother I helped kill.

It all began for me when I observed Tom on the set of *The Great Santini*, and he seemed exempted from the action going on around him. He looked aloof, unreachable, and always slightly confused. He did not fraternize with the boys who'd been hired to play on his basketball team. He was wordless whenever he was with either his mother or father. A teenage golden girl played the role of my sister Kathy, a delightful, beautiful girl who took to hanging around me when she wasn't on the set. Once, she asked me if my brother Tom was dating anyone and I told her I didn't think so. She seemed pleased by that answer and asked if I would get Tom to call her for a date. She had developed a crush on him during her time on the set.

That night I informed Tom that a young movie star wanted to go out on a date with him and that I thought it was a swell idea.

"You've got no right to interfere with my life," Tom said, his anger immediate and obvious. "I don't try to interfere with your big-shit life."

I turned to my mother. "Mom, what's going on with your youngest kid? He seems detached from the whole world," I said. "He barely says a word to me."

"He's shy, just like you used to be," Mom said. "Only he's much shyer than you were. Especially around girls."

"I'm setting him up on a date with a goddamn movie star. This girl's a dreamboat," I said.

"I don't have to do what you say," Tom told me. "And I don't have to talk to you if I don't want to."

"Who the hell do you talk to?" I asked.

"He's got lots of friends at school," Mom insisted. "They refer to him as a real chatterbox."

I said, "Chatterbox? This whole town's gone nuts and killed Sigmund Freud."

"You think you're so funny," Tom said.

"Sometimes I do, chatterbox," I said meanly. "Sometimes I don't."

"Pat, you're upsetting Tom," Mom said.

"I'm trying to talk to you, Tom. Brother to brother. So we could get to know each other just a little bit. I was in college and then out teaching when you and Tim were growing up. You're an adult now. We could get to like each other."

"You're not the Mr. Popular you think you are," Tom said. "Carol Ann doesn't like you worth a damn either. Everybody in my school thinks you're nothing but a nigger lover."

I made a hostile move toward Tom, but Mom was quicker and inserted herself between her two angry sons.

"I *am* a nigger lover," I told Tom. "And I'm proud to be one and proud to have put this worthless, racist South far behind me. And congrats, Tom, you're the first Conroy child I've ever heard use that soul-killing word."

"I know my rights and I can use any word I want to use," Tom said.

"Then get ready to have a fistfight with me," I said, sputtering. "And, Mom, this is what you get for sending Tom to a segregated academy. Have a talk with Tom. Something's going on," I said, preparing to leave the house.

"Tom is by far the most normal and nicest of my children," Mom said. "You've always been my favorite, haven't you, Tom?"

She hugged Tom, and he pulled away because no one in the family is comfortable with even the most modest rituals of affection. Generally, affection is as difficult as the mating of sea urchins to us, and only my brother Tim seems to have emerged from our childhood with much talent for the tender harmonies provided by human touch. The rest of us recoil from any emotional displays as if someone had thrown a fer-de-lance into our laps. Touch was electrified and painful to us. My father disfigured touch with his powerful fists—my mother brought a mountain coldness to even the simplest gestures of human affection. My rebellion lay in the fact that I'd hug anything that moved, but I knew the origins of that fakery of emotion. Today, I'll hug a fire hydrant because no one hugged me as a child.

In the summer of 1982, when Tom was in his early twenties, I brought my whole family to Fripp knowing it was the last summer I would likely see Mom alive. We rented a duplex on a tidal creek and I set a crab pot every day, which provided my mother with a constant supply of she-crab soup, crab cakes, and crab salad. My second wife, Lenore, and my mom got along well, and Mom had fallen in love with her Italian-born granddaughter, Susannah. My small daughter was at her most fetching that summer, spending long hours walking the beach and collecting seashells with my mother. Since my brothers and sisters came around on weekends, the summer often took on the feel of some corrupted homecoming. Dad even came down to visit several times; Mom and John were cordial and gentle with him, much to the relief of the Conroy children.

In the hottest days of August, Mom and I would rise early for a swim in the Atlantic and repeat the process in the late afternoon. Often I would watch Mom jog a mile down the beach, then jog back to the place I was swimming. She looked coltish and buoyant, and she would return to the ocean, panting. "I'm going to beat this thing. I can listen to my body telling me the secret things, and I can beat this thing at its own game."

"Attagirl," I would encourage her.

On one weekend, all the kids came down except Carol Ann, and we had one of our last great times as a family. Mom adored playing grande dame with her children and grandchildren, and she was getting stronger and more animated as each day passed. We were cooking burgers on a grill. The boys were sitting around in the blistering August heat when I heard my brother Jim say, "Where's Tom? I haven't seen him the last three times I've been down here."

"Come to think of it," Tim said, "neither have I."

"I don't see the downside," Mike said. "It's when you see Tom that the trouble begins."

"Pat, you've been here all summer," Jim said. "You laid eyes on him?"

I said, "At the beginning of the summer, a lot. But I've not seen him once in August."

When we brought the cheeseburgers into the house to eat, brother Mike asked my mother a direct question. "Where's Tom? None of us has seen him around much."

"Oh, he met this very nice retired couple who've taken a real shine to him. Some of you don't know this, but Tom can be a real charmer when he puts his mind to it," she replied.

"I've never seen him be charming," Jim said.

"Tommy's a sweetie pie," Mike's wife, Jean, said.

"Tom hates Conroy males," Terrye, Tim's wife, said, adding another layer of tension to the night. "Just like everyone else."

"You ever taken a look at your family, Terrye?" Jim lashed back. "Talk about fucked-up."

"Mom doesn't need this," I warned them. "We're here for her."

"Oh, pious one," the brothers sang out to me. Then Jim said, "Where's Carol when we need her?"

During the last week before my return to Atlanta, I went over for a late-afternoon drink with Mom and John. Mom was looking healthier than she had since her ordeal had begun. Her complexion was coming back, and her whole body was turning pretty as ripe fruit. When we heard the front door open, we turned in our seats and saw Tom walking, nearly staggering, toward his room. We smelled him before we saw him, and it would not have surprised me if a flock of buzzards were circling above our house.

My mother put her hands on her face when she saw Tom's pitiful condition. He smelled like roadkill left too long in the sun. Again I watched him stagger and I ran to him, put his arm around my shoulder, and helped him get to his bedroom. When I saw his face and arms, I was horrified. Several deer ticks were on his face, arms, and neck. Mosquitoes had ravaged the rest of his body, and it seemed my brother had lost at least fifteen pounds.

I pushed him into a hot shower and scrubbed his head with brushes and soap and washed his hair three times before I satisfied myself that he was clean enough to pass a Citadel inspection.

Then I took some tweezers to pull the ticks out of his skin, after which I dabbed a cotton ball of alcohol on each small wound. Some of the ticks I pulled out of Tom's flesh must have been in residence for a time long enough to grow to disproportionate size.

"Ouch. Ouch. Ouch," Tom would say every time a tick came out. "I'm gonna tell Mom on you."

"Just bear with me, kid. One of these places gets infected and there's no telling what might happen."

Turning him over, I went for the ticks on his stomach, and he seemed to relax into the procedure until I reached his genitals.

"The dick's off-limits," he said, covering himself demurely.

"Who says so? Your dick's probably got ticks around it," I said.

"It's sacred territory. I'll do it when you leave."

"Is that a promise?"

"There's something kind of homosexual about this," he said, eyeing me suspiciously.

"Yeah, I'm a gay man who gets my rocks off taking ticks off other guy's dicks, you idiot."

"The genitalia is my personal bailiwick!" he shouted, then began raving in one of those unknown tongues of the schizophrenic, untranslatable and violent. He was also foaming at the mouth.

Tossing him the tweezers, I walked out of the room and said, "I'm going to send Mom in for the final inspection."

"Does it bother you that I hate your guts more than anyone in the world?" Tom said as I left to confront my mother.

Walking back into the distressed living room, I understood that Mom and John had heard every shouted word.

"Got anything interesting to fill me in on, Mom?" I asked, resuming my seat and noticing that Dr. Egan was checking out of the latest Conroy melodrama and retiring to his quarters upstairs.

My mother said, "I told you about that retired couple who've taken a liking to Tom. He's been staying with them at their beach home most of the summer. They've really been good to Tom."

"Yes, I can see that. What is the name of this wonderful couple, and where do they live on the beach?"

"I don't know their names, Pat. I haven't had the pleasure of meeting them. But I've talked to her on the phone, and she told me that Tom and his friends play a rowdy game of volleyball on the beach. She says it gets rough sometimes."

"I see. That explains everything. Tom is playing in a rowdy game of volleyball. He goes up for one kill shot after another. Guys are knocking the ball into one another's faces. They dive to save the ball from hitting the sand, they jump, they leap—and Tom manages to pick up a few ticks in the process. This family is gonna drive me insane. I'll go nuts. You can't enable Tom on this, Mom. It's much too serious and it's gone way too far. Tom's in trouble, Mom—in mental trouble. That was a half-dead kid I just cleaned up. We've got to figure out what's wrong and get the best possible help for him."

"Pat, I can't deal with this now. Not in my condition. Not at this time of my life. And please remember, Tom's my baby . . . he's always been the sweetest—my most normal child. That means everything. Everything to me as a mother."

I hugged her as she went silent, then said, "I'll take care of it, Mom. Don't think about it again. I'll figure out what's best to do. I'll take action—and responsibility. But Tom's not going to like it."

"Don't let anybody hurt or embarrass him," Mom said. "He's much prouder than my other children."

For the next two days I called up every friend I had in South Carolina and Georgia to ask for their advice on how to handle Tom's deteriorating situation. Everyone advised me against public mental hospitals, including my brothers Jim and Mike, who both worked at the state mental hospital in Columbia, known as Bull Street. Mike assured me that we could always use Bull Street as a homecoming of last resort, but he admitted that the mental hospital was more of a warehousing center than a place with state-of-the-art facilities and first-rate therapists.

Finally, I spoke with a psychiatrist at Peachford Hospital in Atlanta. He dealt with me in a deft, professional manner, telling me they could give me a solid evaluation of Tom within three months. The only problem was that the hospital charged a flat fee of seven thousand dollars a month. I considered my options and found I might have to do this. I told the doctor I would bring Tom to Peachford Hospital at least by Saturday night at seven. Demurring, the doctor said that Monday morning was a more convenient time for registry, when I exploded that I was talking about an emergency situation and that I could not even ensure that I could keep my brother alive until Monday.

I called Dad that same night to debrief him on what was going on in the dark heart of his former nuclear family. Dad could not take in any more news of insanity or psychosis and tried to make light comedy of it all. Mental illness was for my father what a whoopee cushion was for an unruly eight-year-old boy. It was an excuse for hilarity and a wanton denial of reality. If I brought up the subject of insanity in any discussion of Carol Ann or Tom, Dad countered with my lifelong habit of exaggeration—that he assured me was well known and discussed in the family.

"Dad," I said, "I don't have the time to argue with you. Tom is far sicker than Carol Ann ever thought she was. He's had a total psychotic breakdown. He's not making sense when he talks. We've got to get him to start eating again. He was alone in the woods for a week, maybe two. He was catatonic. He dropped out of the cuckoo's nest, Dad. You've got to help me on this. Mom can't. She just can't."

"Why can't your mother help?" Dad asked. "Tom lives with her."

"Because Mom's dying. She's not going to be here this time next year."

"My boy's not one to look at the world with rose-colored glasses," Dad teased, and I hung up in anger.

The following morning, Lenore went to Atlanta with the rest of the family while I stayed on Fripp and looked into making arrangements for getting Tom into Peachford. My mother kissed her grandchildren and Lenore farewell, but there was a bittersweet leavetaking for all. My daughter Megan, who was a dead ringer for Peggy, to my mother's delight, had a hard time parting. The departure had the certain feel of last things to it.

In the late afternoon, I received a telephone call from Dr. Egan, who said, "Your mother received a phone call from her doctor, Dr. Steve Madden, Pat. You know the drill. She needs you now. Right now."

I drove over to her house in an instant and raced to the couch she always chose to do her serious grieving on. She had been crying and kept it up as I held on as though riding the backdrafts of a storm, and I held her shoulders as they trembled. I didn't know what had happened, but I was appalled at the timing of it.

"Steve called," she told me. "I've gone out of remission again. It's the last time. He may save me one last time, but then it'll come again quickly and it'll kill me. It'll kill me for sure, son. There's nothing that anyone in the world can do about it."

"Then turn to God, Mama. You've always put your faith in him. Embrace him. When do you have to go back to the hospital?" I asked.

"Steve Madden wants to start the chemo as soon as possible. Next Tuesday at the latest," she answered.

"Fine. I'll get Tom settled, then get to you by Tuesday," I said. "We'll fight it again, Mama. We'll do it together."

"This time it's going to be really rough," she said. "This won't be the time for sissies, son."

"You'll have a fucking warrior beside your bed, Mom, and that's a promise," I said, the bravado matching the sheer terror raging inside me.

The journey to Atlanta the next day marked one of the most sur-real and anxiety-ridden of my life. Whatever psychotic state Tom found himself in still had a hammerlock on his mind. He spoke nonsense for the most part, then launched into rounds of pure lucidity, when I would try to comfort him and put him at ease.

I had asked my nine-year-old stepdaughter, Emily, to ride up with me and Tom. Lenore's daughter Emily had a poisonous relationship with her whole family as well as the planet Earth. She had survived the accusations of sexual assault she made against her father, as well as what came across to me as her mother's unadulterated hatred of her. During the past, I'd noticed that she and Tom not only got along really well, they also enjoyed spending time with each other. On the trip, Emily made clever use of Tom's moments of lucidity, and it actually relaxed him to hear of Emily's own animated and frequent bouts of insanity.

"You don't seem crazy to me, Tom. I say crazy things all the time. I just can't help it. Listen to what I said to Pat the other day: 'I'd rather kill frogs than love you.'"

Tom laughed out loud when he heard that, so Emily said, "I'd rather bite the heads off snakes than love Pat."

"I'd let it go at that, Emily," I suggested.

"Yeah, Pat thinks I'm hilarious, but thinks I go too far," Emily said.

"Look who's talking," Tom said, which got a laugh out of me.

Forty miles outside of Atlanta, Tom seemed to enter some home-land of composure, or maybe just recognition. He started to tell me about anxiety attacks that he couldn't control or turn back, that they seemed to eat his flesh and suck his blood at the same time. He talked about stealing booze from Dr. Egan's liquor cabinet, but even the alcohol could not control or slow the immense power and threat he felt with almost every drop of air he breathed. He thought his stomach was devouring itself, imploding inside his body softly, like some corrupted nectar.

One night he woke up calm for the first time in weeks, and voices were directing him, giving him soft orders, so he dressed in the dark and the voices directed him to the Fripp Island bridge. He thought they would order him to kill himself in the outgoing tides on a very stormy night, but their plans were different. They wanted him to live, but in an Arcadian place, a modern Eden, a place far away from the strife and anger that he had grown up around in the Conroy family. They took him into the deepest woods of Hunting Island and told him to lie down beside a log. He felt at home, protected. Rattlesnakes came up to lick his shoes. Deer would lick the salt from his sweaty stillborn face, though he didn't know how long he lay there in silence and motionless, maybe more than a week. He had often heard of catatonia, but never about the peacefulness of catatonia. He could never remember being so happy.

In Conyers, Georgia, he returned to the morbid nonsense of his incipient madness, and I braced myself for the task of getting my brother Tom into either Peachford Hospital or Bull Street. When I arrived at my house on Peachtree Circle, I realized that I had made a serious strategic error in my hour of arrival. The street was lined with distinguished automobiles and elegant couples of tuxedoed men and immaculately dressed women, making their slow passage down the driveway I shared with our inimitable neighbors, Knox and Carolyn Dobbins. Carolyn was a partner at King and Spaulding, the most prestigious law firm in Atlanta, and they had been planning their elegant soiree for many months. I was distracted as I moved my station wagon and joined the slow procession that led to the Dobbinses' festooned backyard, with its open bars and its catered dinner with piles of smoked salmon, mounds of Beluga caviar, and a butcher carrying a rare roast beef for the lawyers and their spouses.

At the entranceway to the back garden a receiving line led by Carolyn and Knox formed that steered the forward motion and forced me to bring the car to a complete stop, with powerful lawyers and their attractive wives still flowing past my car and some of them rapping on the window, calling out my name in recognition.

Looking to my right, I saw that my brother Tom appeared ready to bolt. Emily opened the back door and parted her way through a sea of party dresses, entering the front door of our house. Her abandonment troubled Tom, who said that he wanted to do the same thing, that the crowd was making him crazy. Reaching over, I tried to massage the muscles of his shoulders, but both were as tight as coiled steel. Human touch could not soften them; nor could my voice calm the maelstrom raging inside him.

Finally, Knox Dobbins realized the dilemma and ran down the driveway to free me from the crowd so I could slide into my own small parking space.

"Thanks, Knox," I said through the window. "You saved the day."

"Sorry for the holdup, neighbor," he said, running back to rejoin Carolyn in the reception line.

On my right, I heard a disturbing humming noise, half human and half bird of prey. It was the sound of a breakdown happening two feet away from me.

"Peachford will be nice for you, Tom," I told him. "They'll get you medicine to calm you down. You'll sleep for a long time. It'll be quiet there."

Since I had not noticed he had removed his seat belt, he caught me by surprise when he leaped from the car running. So startled was I by the move that I struggled with my own seat belt before I came out of the car in a sprint. By the time I spotted Tom, he was pushing his way with uncommon rudeness and desperation through the beautifully dressed invitees to Knox and Carolyn's Ansley Park party. I knew I would have to become like an out-of-shape linebacker and hustle my way through that crowd with the same indefensible brusqueness Tom had used. I couldn't see myself tackling Tom and rolling on the ground in a death grip, scuffing the tops of dress shoes and the delicate high heels of Atlanta women with such pretty feet. I stood paralyzed with inaction as Tom's head disappeared from sight and seemed to turn north toward Peachtree Street. As I tried to make my way through the friendly crowd, lawyers I knew and admired accosted me, and they introduced me to friends of theirs at King and Spaulding I had never met. By the time I reached Peachtree Circle, I realized I had lost my brother Tom to all the fates and dangers of the city of Atlanta, with night coming in fast.

Before I called my father in full knowledge that I would face incoming rounds of his snarky Irish humor, I fixed myself a stiff drink and told Lenore the leading highlights of the day. Then I rang my father's number and he answered on the first ring.

"Where's Tom?" Dad asked.

"I don't know. I lost him."

"You *lost* him?" I could hear the fury in Dad's voice, the sudden kind that rose up like a sandstorm. "He was your responsibility."

I explained what happened and the confusion caused by Knox and Carolyn's cocktail party and my surprise at the suddenness of Tom's flight and his swiftness afoot as he weaved his way through the crowd.

Dad said, "I'm not interested about your report on a track meet. Just tell me where he is now."

"The last time I saw him, Dad, he was heading in your direction. I'm hoping he just walks to your place and checks in for the night," I said. "But I wouldn't count on it."

"He's always preferred my pad to those fancy damn living quarters that you love to live in," Dad said.

"This is going to be hard for you," I said. "But Tom is a real danger to himself, and I think other people aren't safe around him either. He's so paranoid he could kill anyone who got in his way."

"You've never been one to carry a happy tune," Dad taunted.

"Tom's life is in danger," I said. "That's all I can tell you."

"I'll bet you're dead wrong, pal," Dad said. "Again your powers of exaggeration have gotten the best of you."

"I'll call you in the morning," I said.

All that night, Dad rode up and down Peachtree and Piedmont roads searching for his lost son. Later, he told me how surprised he was by the number of men he discovered who just walked out their lives in a city asleep upon itself. He was about to give up when he spotted Tom near Lenox Center, following the path laid out by the subway tracks leading into the city. He pulled up beside Tom and said, "I hear Pat pissed you off. Jump in, Tom. I'll take you over to my place."

Without making a sound, Tom got into Dad's car at five in the morning. Neither said a word as Dad took him back to his top-floor suite in the Darlington apartments.

Though I woke up late, I called my father to see whether there had been any developments.

"Developments? I'd say yes, there's been a slight development. I found Tom at oh five hundred hours, picked him up, and he's in great spirits. Mary's over here cooking him pancakes and he's eating them like he's a horse—never seen a boy with a better appetite. We've been laughing about you and your pitiful attempt to put him in a mental hospital. Tom's more together than you've been on your best day. We've been laughing about what an asshole you can be when you try to make the whole family see the world as you see it. Tom thinks you're just a bully who never got over the prestige of being the firstborn."

"Oh, to be the firstborn Conroy child," I mocked. "There was a high honor I could never live down. Listen to me now, Dad. I'm not calling you again until six tonight. When I call you then, you'll know everything, big shot. You'll know all you need to know. Welcome to a crash course in madness."

At that moment, I could've hammered Dad to the floor with a tire iron. Yet my anger was now playing busboy to my anxiety about what was happening. I was highly prone to breakdowns, as I had proven to everyone's satisfaction many times in my life, and could feel the disintegration and unraveling taking place all around me. But if I failed my family at this critical avenue of fates colliding under the signs of chaos, I could not figure who could rise up and take my place. At this moment, I could not afford the luxury of one of the crackups I was famous for.

At six, I called my father's apartment and Mary answered, one of my father's great women friends he'd met at the Darlington over the years. I could hear two men screaming in the background. Dad grabbed the phone and he was sobbing hysterically. He could not utter a communicable word to me, but just blubbered in his misery.

"Dad, I'm truly sorry. I waited too long and it was unbearably mean of me. But I'm coming over now and I'll take care of it," I told him.

When I exited the elevator on the fifteenth floor, the purest pandemonium had broken loose, and I walked in on a scene I found troubling to the core. My brother Tom was screaming, talking a meaningless blather and cursing as he crawled toward me and the elevators. He kept reaching back to punch Dad's face as Dad held on to his legs and tried to slow his progress. Ten terrified women were peeking out their doors. I heard one of them say, "Should I call the police, Colonel?" Dad screamed, "No!" Another said, "I have a gun, Colonel. Do you want to use it on your son?"

"No!" Dad wailed in despair.

Then the oldest brother moved into position. I stopped Tom's forward progress by putting my Docksider against his face, pinning his head to the floor.

"Hey, baby Tom. The games are over. Your oldest brother has arrived. And you know what we big brothers do best? We love to kick the asses of our baby brothers because they're weak and pathetic and can't defend themselves."

"You're hurting me. Get your foot off my face," Tom cried.

"Dad, you let go of Tom and get back to your room. You ladies can return to your own lives, because this show is over," I said.

"Don't hurt my boy," Dad pleaded with me.

"Shut up, Dad," I said. "Get back to your room."

"Now, Tom," I continued, "since you seem to like crawling better than walking, I want you to turn around and crawl back to Dad's. If you try to get up, I'm going to think you'll want to fight me. If you fight me, I'll kill you. If I kill you, I'll be sad for a day or two, but that's all it'll be. So let's get this show on the road."

Tom began crawling on all fours toward Dad's in a passage that must have been humiliating to him. When he entered Dad's apartment again, I pointed out a chair for him to sit in. Earlier that day a doctor friend had given me a bunch of Valium and sedatives to calm Tom.

"Open your mouth," I said. "I got some pills for you."

"I don't have to do one fucking thing you say. Fuck you. I'm not opening my mouth!" Tom shouted.

"Then I'm going to break your jaw," I said, measuring it with my right fist.

His mouth popped open and I threw three tablets down his throat and made sure he swallowed them when I poured a glass of water down him.

Tom was furious and still rowdy when he looked at me with withering contempt and said to Dad, "You know, there's something about that guy I never liked."

This phrase would later become one of the catchphrases of Conroy family life. Even then, it got Tom the first laugh of the evening from Mary, Dad, and me. For the next five years, anytime my personality irritated one of my siblings, I would hear them say, often in unison, "You know, there's something about that guy I never liked."

Going home later that evening, after the pills had calmed Tom down, I felt the partial wreckage of myself as I made my way down a dark Peachtree Street. The confrontation with Tom had sickened me and filled me with a fully earned self-loathing. I called my brother Mike to see whether we could still get Tom into Bull Street the next day, since Dad had decided Peachford was too expensive.

"I was an asshole to Tom tonight, Mike," I confessed. "He terrified me more than I can tell you. So what did I do? I turned into Dad."

"Pat, I've worked with crazy people my whole life. Sometimes they're nice, and sometimes they're scary as hell."

Using an abbreviated version, I recounted most of the violent, fragmented incidents of that nightmarish scene on the fifteenth floor of the Darlington apartments.

"You stepped on his face?" Mike asked.

"Yes, I stepped on his face. He was dragging Dad along the floor, trying to get to the elevator. He was hitting Dad with his fists, trying to knock him off him."

"Why do I like this scene?" Mike said, chuckling.

"Because no one deserved it more than Dad," I said.

"Here's what's great about Bull Street, Pat. It's free. And I can check on Tom two or three times a day. Everybody up here knows about the Conroy family. We'll take real good care of him, and the whole place will take an interest in protecting Tom and getting him better."

"That's what I needed to hear," I said. "I'll see you as soon as I can tomorrow. Anything else I need to know?"

Mike said, "One more thing."

"What's that?" I asked.

"There's something about that guy I never liked." Mike was laughing when he hung up the phone. And so was I.

. . .

We left Atlanta at nine the next morning, and Tom's craziness had taken a catatonic turn during the night. We found him sluggish as I belted him up in the backseat of my car. Whenever he talked, it came out as gibberish, and untranslatable, even though Dad tried to engage him in conversation for the entire high-strung, jittery trip. In those four hours, I learned how psychotic my brother really was. The thought first hit me that he was most likely a paranoid schizophrenic, and would be for his entire lifetime. Despair filled me to the brim, as it would every day for the rest of Tom's life.

My three brothers were waiting when we drove up on the grounds of the South Carolina State Hospital. Mike took immediate charge, leading Tom into the building, where papers awaiting his signature were waiting. Dad and I would not see Tom again that day or for many to follow. We ate lunch at Yesterdays, where all my brothers had worked during college, including Tom. They had a bar stool with a Great Santini plaque where Dad always sat when he came in for a drink. The owners, who cherished my father and brothers, treated us as royalty. When Dad and I walked back to the car for the journey home, he got in and began weeping over the fate of his youngest son. I too burst into tears and cried as hard as I ever had, the first time I'd ever done so with my father. It would not be our last, nor the last time we would do it for Tom. Dad recovered faster than I did and started to compose himself as my head leaned against the steering wheel.

Finally, I lifted my head up, dried my eyes, and turned the ignition on. As I eased the car into the traffic of Five Points, my father said to me, "What a fucking pussy you turned out to be." He said it with affection this time, not malice.

I was thirty-nine years old then, a tired veteran of the weird-ass ruffled strangeness of the Conroy family dilemma. For years I had studied it, judged it, renounced and ridiculed it, scoffed at it and held it up to the light. I was sorry I'd been born to such strange, volcanic people. I would never forgive the Conroy family for making me a stranger and an illegal alien in my own life. Love came in wounded and frantic ways to my dismaying family, but love it was.

When we stopped for gas, we both headed for the men's room to wash our tearstained faces, the Great Santini and me. It was another good day for us as father and son. But the residue of that bipolar day would haunt me for the rest of my life. Now I knew for sure that when I was pressed hard and with my back against the wall, something would always snap inside me, and I would face a perilous world in the full-voiced, savage fury of the man I was born to be. During crisis or breakdown, I would put on my father's flight jacket, grab the throttle of his warplane, and turn the gaze of the Great Santini toward every squadron maneuvering the night skies in pursuit of me. Despite all my protestations and refusals, I was, at last, revealed to be Santini's, and by a boy who had no defenses to stop my utter renunciation of him.

My brother Tom never spoke to me again.

CHAPTER 14

The End to It All

I t was a bleak, windswept day when I entered Eisenhower Army Medical Center for the last time. Dr. Egan had called all of Peg's children, and most sat around the waiting room looking like death-row criminals. My brothers and I hugged one another more solidly than we normally did. With this embrace, we were acknowledging the end of it all, the final extinction of that pilot light of love our mother protected during the gale-force slipstreams of our lives.

"It's over," Jim said.

"She'll leave here in a casket," Tim agreed.

"Hey, she's beaten this before," I said.

"You haven't seen her today," Mike said.

"Can I visit her now?" I asked. "Is anyone with her?"

"Your worst nightmare is in there with her," Jim said. "Carol flew into town."

"Jesus of Nazareth," I muttered, and started down the hall.

Halfway to my mother's room, I heard what seemed to me the most horrible noise to pass through a human throat. I could hear my mother's strangled, desperate breath hurtling out of her body in thunderclaps. Steadying myself on the far wall, I regained feeling in my legs as I tried to accustom myself to this wet, devouring sound. My mother would have killed herself if she knew what her final aria of death would be. The noise was undignified, unladylike, and un-Peggy-ish. I later learned my mother had lost her cough reflex and the air kept forcing itself through streams of mucus it couldn't expel.

Turning the corner, I slammed into the wall of Mom's horrible breathing. I watched the rise and fall of her breasts as her lungs struggled valiantly to remain alive. A numbness seized my entire body, and tears streamed down my face as I absorbed the stunning news that my mother would never leave this room alive. Though the warnings had shaken me, I still came to that hospital with an optimism that my mother's reservoirs of pure strength would pull her through again. I banished that hope forever as I tried to acclimate myself to the gruesome sound track of her dying.

Then I spotted a pair of eyes watching me with utter malice. Carol Ann was lying beside Mom with her left arm propped under Mom's neck and her right arm wrapped around her shoulder. Carol Ann looked like a novice wrestler on amateur night. From my point of view, it appeared that Carol Ann was trying to strangle Peg.

"Why're you in bed with Mom?" I asked.

"I made a vow that she would die in my arms," she said.

"She seems to be having a bit of trouble breathing. You've got her in a headlock."

"My love for Mom is deep and mysterious and eternal. As a poet, I see things that are denied to ordinary people. It's beyond language or comprehension. Though she ruined my childhood with her bitterness that I was not the Southern belle of her dreams, I have come to the deep and literary comprehension of our relationship. We were goddesses of war locked in mortal combat."

I was considering the happy option of beating up my sister to test how a goddess of war did in a fistfight, when Dr. Steve Madden and John Egan walked through the door. Dr. Madden had fallen in love with my mother when she became his patient, joining a long line of handsome men in her life. He immediately saw the problem in Carol Ann's awkward embrace of Mom and said, "Carol, we need to let your mother's head rest on the pillow, because you might obstruct the flow of air she's getting."

"I plan for her to die in my arms," Carol Ann said.

"There'll be plenty of time for all of that," Dr. Madden said. "Now we need to provide her with as much comfort as possible. There's a chance that people in comas can still hear what's going on around them. No arguments, no noise, no drama."

"Ah, Doctor, I see you've become wise in the ways of the Conroy family," I said.

"I've had experience with many families," Steve Madden replied.

For three harrowing days, Carol Ann, John Egan, and I lingered over Mom in a deathwatch as ancient as time. When I heard that Mom might be able to hear us speaking in the room, I ran down to my car and found a book of poetry that Jonathan Galassi had edited and sent to me the previous week. Because Jonathan, who had exquisite taste in poetry, had selected the poems, I knew the book would be a perfect accompaniment to my mother's dying hours. I began at the first poem and read slowly, at first in pain, and then in great pleasure as these poems began to work their strange magic on me, Carol Ann, and, I hoped, my mother. A languor hung in the room as some of the most beautiful words in the English language poured over us in both harsh and silken folds. Since my mother had read so much poetry to Carol Ann and me when we were children, it calmed the warring beasts that flared up between the two of us. Because Mom had made the language such a happy voyage for both of us, it seemed fitting to fill her last days with the honeycomb and vinegar cruets of poems that spoke of love, eternity, earthly beauty, and even nothingness. The world is poetry's most dauntless calling—its most urgent business. It pleased me that this woman born to the cruelest poverty could rise out of those murderous origins and lie dying with a poet and a novelist in loving attendance of her. When sister Carol Ann's book of poetry *The Beauty Wars* was published by Norton in 1991, it pained me that my mother was not alive to celebrate the happy occasion.

For three days I read to my mother, and on the third day I finished the book. When I went out on a hamburger run, I discovered, by accident, that Augusta had wonderful Chinese restaurants run by the offspring of the Chinese laborers who built the Augusta canal earlier in the century. A routine set in, which we operated with admirable efficiency. In the morning, John would go in with his wife for a couple of hours and I would run errands. I had suggested to Carol Ann that she let John have some time with Mom alone, but Carol Ann nixed that idea immediately, because she might miss that moment of final extinguishment.

I believe it was a Saturday when I noticed that the Augusta paper said it was November 17. I also remember watching a football game with John in the afternoon. In the waiting room, I chose a chair with a view of the long hallway leading to my mother's room. Some team scored a touchdown; then I checked the hall and I saw two nurses leading a stricken Carol Ann toward us. Carol Ann's face told of my mom's death with a purified articulateness. It had happened, and I would spend the rest of my life motherless. Grabbing John's wrist, I leaned over and whispered in his ear, "Brace yourself, John. Mom just died." John went slack-jawed and into immediate shock. I helped him rise to his feet as tears streamed down his face.

Now, I had planned this scenario for the moment of Mom's death—I saw myself as the stoical, heroic man of courageous forbearance who would comfort the elderly, the women, and the children. I was a Marine brat and a Citadel man who knew about the confinement of emotions and feelings. I knew how a man should react in such a situation—I was thinking Humphrey Bogart, Cool Hand Luke, and Han Solo—guys like that.

Carol Ann was pure wreckage when I hugged her in the hall. Her face looked hammered and misshapen, as if some great internal scream was forming inside her.

"Mom died in my arms," she told me. "I was holding her, telling her how much I loved her and how I would honor her passing with poems of exquisite beauty and style."

"You tell her that your brothers and sisters are going to miss her, too?" I asked, sorry for the words as soon as they came out of my mouth.

"You did not earn the privilege of farewell," she retorted. "I never left her side. You guys didn't put in the time. She died in my arms."

Gathering John on my left arm and Carol Ann on my right, I led a sad procession down this hallway for the last time. In the days I had been there, I had grown accustomed to my mother's ghastly death rattle, but I had not prepared for a sound that was the most chilling of all. I had not prepared myself for silence. Despite my John Wayne fantasies, when I made the turn into her room and found it noiseless, I fell apart. I heard someone screaming, "No, no, no!" and was surprised to trace the source back to myself. My eyes flooded with tears, and I covered my mother's face with kisses and tried to pull her to me. I had nurses sprinting from their stations to see the source of the mayhem. That despairing sound came out of me. I was screaming and shouting and making a complete horse's ass of myself when I heard Carol Ann's voice behind me.

She said, in a detached, observatory tone, "You're lucky you can cry. It'll be years before I can shed a single tear for her. She destroyed my whole life and was my worst enemy. Even so, I forgave her long ago. I forgave her for all the crimes she committed against her daughter, which were too many to count. I told her I forgave her everything as she died in my arms. Also, I've found it in my heart to forgive Dad, who was a monster when I was growing up. But he was stupid, macho, and unevolved. So I've let him off the hook, too. I've forgiven both our parents even though they were unspeakable to me. Now I only have one mortal enemy left in my life, one that I can never forgive his crimes against me, one whom I hate more than Mom and Dad. But I've got my eyes on him and I'll never take my gaze away from him. Pat, that enemy is you."

She emphasized the "you" so that its fury echoed around the room. But I was on the move now and swift in my shock, so I flew out of that room like a fox hearing the approach of hounds behind him. I bolted out of that hospital and into the Augusta night. Something had broken in me that had once been good, and I had the rest of my life to figure out what it was.

. . .

My mother's funeral was a rather uneventful, sober one by Conroy family standards. The family seemed so grief-stricken by her death that we were in no shape to help John Egan prepare for the funeral. I should have written Mom a rip-roaring eulogy, and Carol Ann should have sent her out with a poem, but all we did was cry. One time, I looked over at my brothers and at my brother-in-law, and all six of us had our heads down, crying openly and without shame. I thought that tableau would have touched Mom to the core. I heard crying all over the church. At some point, she had become a beloved figure in Beaufort.

PART THREE

. . . .

CHAPTER 15

Tom's Leap, Carol Ann's Ball of Tears

My brother Tom was the prettiest child our parents produced. His features lent all the handsomeness that symmetry and structure could add to a face. His hair was a brown that seemed stolen from the pelts of otters; his eyes were blue lapis lazuli and as haunted as those of a wounded songbird. Tom was born to hurt. All the family craziness was thrown into the awful country behind his eyes. The rest of us could teach one another what there was to know about sadness, but Tom would teach us all we needed to know about tragedy. He tore our hearts out and left an indissoluble emptiness in his place. From Tom, we accepted the black scar that would carry us through the rest of our lives. In the middle of one of the hottest days in August of 1994, something set off one of Tom's convulsive rages. Tom walked to a fourteen-story building in Columbia, took the elevator to the roof, and hurled himself into the summertime air until his body exploded against the pavement below. Among his brothers and sisters, we still barely mention Tom's name, even though he killed himself almost two decades ago. He was only thirty-four years old.

There is a business side to a sudden death that none of us could imagine. At five in the morning at my home on Fripp Island where I now lived, I received a phone call from my brother Mike. Mike was weeping as he told me the devastating news. He had been Tom's caretaker in Columbia who watched over him with heroic forbearance, often bailing Tom out of jail or taking him to the mental hospital when Tom refused to take his medicine. Mike made sure Tom had all the food he needed, stocking the apartment Dad had bought for Tom. He shepherded Tom and looked out for his needs. Tom's suicide devastated my brother Mike; his crying was earned, and deeply so.

"Tom's dead," Mike said the early morning when he called me; then he wept for several minutes. "He leaped off a building in Columbia. Dead when he hit the ground. You know that Jean's cousin runs a funeral home in Lexington? Because it's so hot and the body was so mangled, he declared it 'a disaster body.'"

"What does that mean?" I asked. "We've got to make sure all the kids get here. Have you called Carol?"

"Yeah. That was fun. Let me warn you, Pat: After she went out of her mind, she kept repeating that she was the only one who truly loved Tom."

"I know the drill," I said. Then Mike and I cried together, both of us breaking down at the thought of Tom's last minute on earth . . . for his helplessness, his agony that we could never touch or share with him—our carelessness in how we loved him, because we discovered ourselves raised in a family where no one showed us how to love. For us, love was a circle and a labyrinth; all its passages and cul-de-sacs found themselves guarded by monsters of our own creation. Within us, love grew as slowly as stalactites in a cave, formed by calcite drips of water, one drop at a time. We had lost Tom, and I believe every one of us felt that his loss came from a failure of our family's capacity to rally anyone into a safe harbor where one could rest a disabled self. I believe that Mike and I wept because we could not love Tom enough. Mike was wrong about that, however. He did everything for my youngest brother. I had not done a thing for the kid my whole life except to step on his face.

When I composed myself enough to speak, I asked Mike, "What about Dad? My God, he's gonna take this hard. He had a real soft spot for Tom."

"It was awful telling Dad," Mike said. "He's driving down from

Atlanta. Wait a minute, Pat. He's pulling into my yard right now. It'll take him a while to get inside. He's slowing down bad."

Dad needed both hips replaced, but carried a mortal fear of the surgeon's knife and the loss of control under anesthesia. He would die limping, as all his sons will do in their time. When he finally reached Mike's phone, Dad was crying. I let Dad's tears come until he composed himself enough to speak.

"I'm so sorry about Tom," I said, and then I broke again.

Dad waited for me to finish, then said, "Tom was my baby. My baby boy, Pat. He never had a chance, not a fighting chance at doing anything. Tom always got the short end of the stick."

"What are we going to do about the funeral?" I asked. "It sounds like we have to work fast."

"I've got a call in to my brother Jim," Dad said. "I want him to conduct the funeral service. He'll be assisted by the local parish priest. We're burying him in Beaufort so that he'll be near his mother."

"Dad, the Catholic Church used to teach that suicides went to hell," I said. "I don't want to hear any of that shit, or we're going to be burying some priests alongside Tom."

"The church changed on that," Dad told me. "They understand mental illness now."

"I'm happy to hear it," I said.

"I'm coming down to Beaufort as soon as I leave Mike's," he said. "I'll stay with Kathy and Bobby Joe. Can you put up the other kids and their families at Fripp?"

"Send all of them out here," I said. "I've got plenty of room. If you think of anything else I can do, please let me know."

"Can you cook for everybody?" Dad asked, then added, "I'd like to order shrimp and grits, Frogmore stew, and maybe some of your crab cakes."

"Consider it done," I said. "Do you need me to pick anyone up at the airport?"

"I'll let you know. This all happened so fast, I've had trouble getting my old bearings. It's a decision-making time, and I find myself unable to make any kind of decision."

"Rely on your kids," I said.

"I'm going to rely on Kathy when I get to Beaufort," Dad said. "You've always been a hothead, and no one can depend on you in these kinds of situations."

"Try not to do that until after the funeral," I suggested.

"Do what?" he demanded.

"Divide your children. Set up wedges between us. There's going to be enough pressure on everyone, Dad. Try to forget you're an asshole for the next forty-eight hours, okay?"

Again, Dad burst into tears, and I wished I hadn't said those nasty words to him. But I said them and regretted them as soon as they came out of my mouth. But the family was on its way now, bursting with grief and powerlessness as we gathered to bury the most delicate among us.

Except for Mike and Tim, we had done little for Tom alive, but his death was a stake through all of our hearts. Instead of making us forget our past, it made us remember it in clear detail. We punished ourselves for not knowing Tom better. Whatever wars he fought within himself, he provided us with no access, no way of easing his torment in a world that was hostile to people like him. We beat ourselves up for not providing a safer hermitage for Tom, but all of us were uncomfortable trying to find answers for one another.

The wick of the fire burned fast and hot as we tried to coordinate the arrival of family and friends into Beaufort. Kathy and Dad bought a coffin and a grave site at Copeland Funeral Home. It was a natural part of small-town life that we went to the funeral director whose wife Judy had been in Gene Norris's English class with me. Mr. Norris, who had been my favorite teacher at Beaufort High School, came over often during the short but incandescent hours it took to get Tom's body into the ground. Some of the Chicago relatives came, but the only one I remember was Father Jim, who would serve as chief celebrant of the mass for the dead and deliver the eulogy in praise of Tom's life. Dad's kids almost revolted when we heard that news. Father Jim was not just a mediocre speaker; he could put a colony of hummingbirds to sleep. Not only had Father Jim beaten me up when I was a ten-year-old kid, he had also slapped around some of the other brothers. He was not a popular choice.

But Jim was Dad's brother, and Dad got to make all the calls when it came to the burial of Tom. None of us had ever witnessed our dad so undone and pathetic as he whimpered his way through the long hours before Tom's funeral. The rest of the family had slipped into our own collective state of shock, with Mike and Tim too disturbed to do anything but suffer with open-faced grief.

Tim and his wife, Terrye, came down the semicircular drive beneath the palmetto forest I adored at the Fripp house. After we had hugged one another and cried into one another's arms, Tim said one word: "Liquor."

Pointing the way, I said, "There's plenty more where that came from."

"I can't think of any other way to get through this," said Tim through tears.

"Drugs," said Terrye, and we all laughed.

Then the ladies of Fripp Island began to show up with hams and fried chicken, shrimp gumbo, pies, cakes, and congealed salads. They brought enough food to feed the entire family for a week, and I came close to weeping each time one of these splendid women brought something to feed my hurt family. Because I'd been so prone to breakdown for so long, I had kept a low profile on Fripp and didn't know whether people even knew I lived there. They did. They turned out in droves to bring food as we tried to deal with the terrible death of our brother whose body had exploded on a Columbia street. Among those ladies who brought food, I watched Kathy leading my grief-stricken sister Carol Ann across Remora Drive. "Something horrible this way comes," I said.

Behind me Tim said, "More liquor. Less food."

I had not seen Carol Ann for ten years, not since she issued me my walking papers out of her life after Mom's death. Periodically, she would write me a letter extorting money out of me. My friend Bernie Schein remembers one that I handed him while I was on the phone calling Carol Ann at her apartment on New York's Lower East Side. It stunned Bernie that Carol Ann threatened to cut her own throat if I didn't send her five thousand dollars. On the phone, I told Carol Ann that I'd send the check through FedEx when I got off the phone. Bernie was screaming at me, "You can't put up with that kind of blackmail! That's awful for Carol and awful for you!"

"But I know she won't slit her throat for a while," I said.

"How many letters do you get like that?" Bernie asked.

"It's down to two or three a year," I said. "Usually she hits up Dad."

"Does he give in to her demands, too?" Bernie asked.

"The power of suicide is enormous and Carol knows it," I replied. "She understands how to manipulate all the airways of guilt. She uses her childhood as a weapon against us."

"Would Peg have fallen for her bullshit?" Bernie asked.

"From Mom, Carol wouldn't have gotten one nickel with an Indian butt-fucking a buffalo on it. Peg would've laughed her ass off and told Carol never to call her again with that line of bullshit."

"Be like Peg," Bernie suggested. "You're setting a terrible precedent for Carol. You and your dad are both turning her into an asshole."

"She's crazy, Bernie, and she's mean," I explained. "She's learned to be an asshole all by herself."

There lives a ferocious narcissist in the heart of the psychotic that unravels the family circle. By taking on the role of madness after Tom proved that his own had the capacity to create the empty space that would torment us all for the rest of our lives, Carol Ann assumed Tom's mantle of suffering for herself. With unbecoming zeal, Carol Ann took her rightful place as the one most hurt in the family sweepstakes. From that day on, she could manipulate all of us, because we lived in the immortal shadow of the Cornell Arms Apartments, where Tom had leaped into the black Carolina night. Carol Ann could wield her madness like a sword that could find our arterial blood in thin air. Tom became an undone prince in the tarot deck she invented out of her own troubled soul and used to keen effect against us. Because Carol Ann had no use for redemption, she brought her glittering powers of malice to Tom's funeral. Not only did we have to deal with the aftershocks of Tom's death, we had to listen to Carol Ann's skewed reasons why it happened. It would turn out to be worse than we could imagine.

When I opened the door to greet Carol Ann, I saw that she had assumed the role of chief mourner, the only one in the shallow Conroy family who could understand the vastness of Tom's despair. She would show us every pathway and lane that crisscrossed the country of the psychotic. She wore her trouble like a series of merit badges that she displayed on a sleeve of heraldry. Carol Ann had come south to drive us all nuts, and she did a commendable job of it.

In the decade of the nineties, I was having breakdowns at regular intervals and was suicidal much of the time. My divorce from Lenore had nearly broken me, and I was just beginning to realize that I would most probably never see my beloved daughter Susannah again. With the direction and help of Dr. Marion O'Neill, I was managing to keep myself alive. When Carol Ann learned about my war against depression, she pooh-poohed it as some amateur version of the real thing. She and Tom held monopoly on the psychic pain produced by the far-flung craziness of our family.

Even as I write these words criticizing Carol Ann, I find myself filling up with apprehension and dread. Her talismanic powers over me extended into the deepest realms of self. The Family Crazy has complete control of any family's hard-earned serenity. Carol Ann had threatened suicide so many times it became as rote to me as a weather report in South Carolina calling for high temperatures in the summer. But I write this with pure certainty that Carol Ann will turn these words into the bituminous fire of her anger. When she reads this, will I get a call that Carol Ann has leaped from a building in New York, set herself on fire, hanged herself in a closet, or cut her wrists until her body is bloodless and accusatory and something I have to live with the rest of my life?

Since I remain the primary eyewitness to the hallucinatory epic of her childhood, I know that my parents left her on the shores as part of the wreckages of their own past. Both of them hated Carol Ann's originality, her otherness, the poet who threw fistfuls of words like a bright bird of paradise. Her mind was a traveling circus of marvels and magic-making, and my parents never saw it. Carol Ann had arrived at a house full of grief, but hers was the only one that counted.

I opened the door to Carol Ann, and her face was like a mirror that could only receive images of Tom. His death now lived in her face and her swollen eyes. Tom belonged to her now. She would become the self-appointed keeper of the flame. But her expression was a mass of inconsolable anguish. We hugged on the porch, bonding for a lot of different reasons. I walked her from the door in tears. For a while we just cried together over Tom and for all of us.

When Carol Ann got control of herself, she looked at me and said, "God, Tom hated your guts. He always called you his kidnapper, his abductor. He never forgave you for forcing him to go to Bull Street."

"It wasn't my finest hour," I said.

She shook her head. "Tom said you were worse than Dad, and that's the worst thing someone can say about another person."

"Tom scared me," I said. "I thought he might do something terrible to himself—like jump off a building."

"Tom had nothing to do with jumping off that building," she said. "Everyone in the family conspired to throw him to his death. It was a long time in coming, but all of us are responsible for his being there."

"Speak for yourself."

"Tom and I were very close. We talked to each other by phone all the time. He hated you the worst, then Dad, and he was starting to really hate Mike's guts."

"Mike took care of Tom on a daily basis, Carol. Don't say a word to Mike," I pleaded. "He may never get over this."

"I'll suffer for this more than anyone in the Conroy family, but I'll keep Tom's memory alive with my art, with my poems to honor him."

"If you can, Carol, try to be easy on us. The next couple of days are going to be tough on everybody," I said.

"I'll go easy on one condition," she said. "Nobody can imply that Tom was crazy. He was the sanest of all Conroys. He was the only sane person this family has produced. I'll claw the eyes out of anyone who even suggests that our brother was insane. He was heroic and carried the weight of this whole nutty clan on his shoulders. But he was the only normal child Peg and Don produced. The rest of us are either nuts, or assholes like you and my other brothers."

"There is the small fact that Tom killed himself," I said. "That he jumped from the roof of a building. Some people might draw a conclusion from that."

"He was the only sane one. It's the world that's crazy. I've written a poem for Tom. I'll read it at his funeral if you don't do a eulogy. I won't stand for you to write a eulogy for a man who hated your guts," she announced.

"I'll leave it to you," I said.

"And I don't want to talk to anyone," she said. "My grief is so much greater than everyone else's I'll want to be left alone."

"I think that'll be easy to arrange."

"Is that one of your swaggering, chauvinist jokes?" she demanded to know.

"Yeah, I think I was trying to lighten things up," I admitted.

"You ought to hear what my feminist friends in New York say about you. I can't begin to describe the hatred," she said.

"They don't know me, Carol. They've never met me."

"Men like you repulse them."

"I think they'd find I'm a much nicer person than you," I responded.

"Do you have to try to win every single argument? Do you know you've always used your wit and sarcasm to silence me? You're my greatest censor. You want to tape my mouth shut. You run from the truth. The sisterhood has set me free, and nothing you ever say can hurt me again."

"When are you getting back to the sisterhood?" I asked. My patience had worn thin and I was thinking that ten years without Carol Ann just wasn't long enough.

My sister Kathy came to relieve me of guard duty with Carol Ann. Seeing her was a relief, because after Mom died, Kathy, a registered nurse, had come into her own as a woman. She performed gallant service as a peacemaker and courier, delivering messages from both sides during the border skirmishes that broke out around her. Because there was no one else who fit the job description, Kathy could bring the warring sides to the peace table to get us through our most perilous times. As she was the middle child of our family, both the older and the younger kids listened to her counsel. Dad was putty in her hands, and even Carol Ann could be swayed by Kathy's soft-spoken reasonableness. Kathy brought a simplicity and kindness to my own overrun house, but she looked drained by the runaway emotions of the last twelve hours. I was dizzy with the fast-moving events that didn't seem to leave any time for reflection, or even prayer. People were coming into

Beaufort from everywhere. As I dressed for Tom's funeral, my fury at Carol Ann drenched me with sweat, and I had to take a second shower. I discovered that you could cry as hard as you wished in a shower and no one would know.

When I drove to the funeral home, I heard from the front door the beginning of the recitation of the rosary. I knew that some of the Conroy relatives from Chicago had shown up for Dad. It was the ancient Irish way, and it seemed appropriate to me.

Because of Dad and his gathering of the Chicago clan, the ceremony turned into a commemoration of Tom's life. There was not a thing Southern about it, but there were touches of Roscommon here and hints of Galway there. Father Jim passed out holy cards with Tom's name and the date of his death on them. My brothers Mike and Jim noticed a mistake on the card that was both morbid and droll. In near hysteria, Mike and Jim pulled me into a side room while the rosary continued its monotonous cycle as the grievers dedicated their prayers toward Tom's casket. Jim showed me the offending card, but I failed to see what errors Father Jim had made in his first act as the celebrant of Tom's funeral mass. Then it came to me with a shining clarity. The mass for the dead was in honor of Timothy Patrick Conroy, not Thomas Patrick Conroy. Breaking away from the rosary sayers, Tim found us as he was studying the offending card.

"Can you guys believe this shit?" Tim said in disbelief. "Even for this pain-in-the-ass family, this is too nutso. Don't you guys agree?"

"Sorry you're dead, Tim," Jim said. "But it had to happen someday."

Mike said, "It's kind of a relief. We thought it was Tom who jumped to his death. Thank God it was you."

"Yeah," I agreed. "Tom's death was rough going, but losing Tim is much easier on everybody."

"Basically, no one gives a shit if it was Tim," said Jim. "It'd be a happy ending to this whole affair."

"I've got the worst brothers in the worst family that ever lived in South Carolina," Tim said, then addressed me. "Carol's on the warpath again, Pat. She hates you in a way the rest of us never thought about."

"Have you watched her eyes when Pat comes into a room?" Mike said. "It must be hard to be hated that much."

"No, I hate all you guys that much," Tim said.

"Shut up, Tim. You're dead," said Jim.

Mike said, "I need to go out and collect those cards."

As Mike turned back to the drone of the rosary, Tim warned me, "Be careful about Carol, Pat. She's sitting off in one corner, all by herself. She's crying harder than anyone. She cries and blows her nose, then does the strangest thing—she doesn't throw any of the tissues away. She rolls them up into a ball, like she needs some proof that her grief is more real than all the rest of ours."

"That's because Tom was the sanest of all of us," Jim said. "In fact, he was the only sane one among us. Tom wasn't mentally ill, but all the rest of us are bat-shit crazy."

"Carol may have a point," I said.

"Hell, she sounds like a prophet to me," Tim said, as he headed back for the final Hail Marys on the rosary. Jim and I lingered behind, sorrowing over our lost brother.

Returning to the main room, I stood with Dad and Kathy and the brothers as we thanked the Beaufortonians for coming to be with the Conroy family on this alarming night. Beaufort was always good to the family in our suffering. A contingent of Tom's friends had driven down from Columbia, and we welcomed them for their appreciation of a brother who did not seem to want it from us. His best friends from high school came around, and so did Tom's teachers at the Beaufort Academy, where Tom had graduated. Gene Norris did not let me out of his sight, but I saw him laying hands of comfort on my brothers and sisters. In all the strange twists of life, my father and Gene Norris had managed to become fast friends, and there existed an affection between them that only deepened as they grew older. Gene understood that Dad's job description was to kill our nation's enemies, and nothing in his job hinted at any obligation to be a good father or husband. Over the years, Gene had taught hundreds of the children of Marines. Often Gene became the translator of our roughneck fathers and tried to explain the great pressures that drove them to cruelty, impassiveness, and drink. Gene taught me my first baby steps in how to go about not hating my father, and I've been grateful to him since. Though it took years to accomplish, Gene had performed quiet miracles while teaching the children of violent men. Beside him was my high school principal, Bill Dufford, who was also trying to bring comfort to my dad and brothers. It amazed me how lucky the Conroy family was to have Beaufort and the teachers who would love us the rest of our lives.

In her own corner of solitude, Carol Ann's multidimensional grief seemed volatile, and somewhat self-aggrandizing to me. She stared at me with a baleful grimace, and she meant me no good. But I thought I could stand anything for a single day, and that included Carol Ann's observation that I was more responsible for Tom's death than anyone. When the service began, Carol Ann had managed to stockpile her moistened tissues into a glob the size of a tennis ball. By the time we walked out into the torrid night, it had grown to the size of a base-ball, and Carol Ann was treating it as some kind of totem or omen of despoiled ruin. At last, Tom had brought the Conroy family to its collective knees. The whole architecture our house was built on was in danger of collapse. As the rest of us composed ourselves, Carol Ann's sadness grew uncontrollable and threatened to spill over into violence.

"Whatever she does is okay," Mike said to the rest of us. "This thing's killing all of us, so let's just let her act it out. It's not like crazy is new to us."

After the wake, over a nightcap, my brothers and I talked about all the things that could go wrong with the funeral.

"Everything," the four of us said in unison, and we laughed as soon as we said it.

"Pat," Mike said, "you sit by Dad and take care of him. I've never seen him broken up like this. This killed something in him."

"What happened on Tom's last night, Mike?" Jim asked. "Were there signs that he was so nuts?"

Mike left the room and went to bed and wanted no part of the discussion of the events of the night before. He wanted no talk about Tom's suicide, and as far as I know, has never had one since the night Tom leaped off the top story of the Cornell Arms. Because Mike had been responsible for Tom's care on a daily basis, he could never for-give himself for this nightmare that took place on his watch. On one occasion, a mentally ill drug addict beat Tom half to death when Tom brought the dangerous loser back to his house to spend the night. In every crisis, and there were lots of them, Mike was there to clean up the blood and tears and throw out the homeless and the drug addicts who would steal everything Tom owned. His other brothers and sister Kathy were grateful to him without measure. Rarely do we even broach the subject with Mike, thinking that he has suffered enough.

Going over to replenish Tim's drink, I said, "Tell us what you know, Tim. You were closest to Tom. He loved you the best."

"That's because Tom and I agreed that this family fucked us up more than any of the other kids. Mom quit raising us. Dad didn't show any interest in us until after we were raised."

"You can't blame poor Dad for that," Jim said. "With you, there was nothing to work with."

"Control yourself, Jimbo," I suggested.

Then Tim moved us into the morning hours of the same day we lost a brother forever. It was a night of complete dissolution and break-down, one we'd all grow accustomed to over the years. If Tom took his meds, his schizophrenia was controllable and he was able to live his Columbia life as a drifter and an alcoholic who had a home to return to that provided safety when he got off the streets. But there were times when he rebelled from the tyranny of the antipsychotic drugs that emptied him out and loosened the control he felt he required to live a normal, self-actualized life. Tom longed for wholeness, for a complete immersion into the natural world, where he would not be branded by his strangeness.

Tim was telling the story well, relaxing into a flow of well-chosen words that riveted Jim and me to our seats in a sleeping house. When he looked straight at me, Tim asked whether I remembered that night of pure lunacy when Tom went nuts on the top floor of the Darlington apartments in Atlanta.

"Remember it?" I said. "It changed my whole life. I don't think I was ever so afraid of anything. I was hoping to get out of the hallway without Tom killing me and Dad both. We committed him to Bull Street the very next day."

"You bastard," Jim said. "No wonder Tom killed himself."

Tim explained that Jim had never seen Tom's psychotic seizures, which were uncontrollable. When Tom went crazy, you thought everyone he encountered was in mortal danger. He carried such an aura of menace that he turned everyone around him into nervous, creeping things who had lost their humanity for Tom and acquired a meaningfulness only in the obstacles they provided for him. Tom had a capacity for hatred that was breathtaking in its heat-seeking destructiveness. That was the way it was in his first phone call early that morning, Tim told Jim and me.

"Why didn't Mike just run over there and throw a Valium down his throat?" I asked.

"Oh, there's a pharmacist in the building?" Tim said. "It doesn't work that way, bro."

"Somebody could've done something," Jim said.

"It doesn't matter anymore, bro. Mike and I both fucked up with Tom. And I wish I'd done things differently, but I didn't," Tim said.

Tim told us that it started out to be a dismal night, but it got out of control fast. Tom would find himself so removed from reality he would create a freakish world that only he could decipher. In the few times he called me in his most psychotic state, I could barely register the fact that he was speaking English. Another time, Tom had spent over a month in jail when he spelled his name in such gibberish that Dad didn't recognize it when he traveled from jail to jail searching for his son.

Always, these states seemed beyond anything we'd seen Carol Ann endure. Her illness seemed manageable, crystalline in her acceptance of the augers of our family's destructiveness. While Carol Ann could pinpoint the source of her great troubles, Tom's mind deteriorated into a volcanic upheaval where limits did not exist.

On the night Tom died, he called Mike and woke him up, demanding that Mike bring him over some money right that minute. Mike told him he would bring money the next morning, and suggested that Tom try to get some sleep.

Instead, Tom went wild on the phone. No one would listen to him, he claimed; no one would help him in his time of greatest need, but it was his money and a part of the inheritance of his family he had earned by being the ultimate victim of the fucked-up Conroy family. Mike would hang up and Tom would call screaming again. After the next hang up, Mike turned off his phone. Tim guessed that this had all taken place at three in the morning. Then Tom began to call Tim.

"Jim, you never heard Tom when he got like this. He was so irrational that nothing he said made any sense. He was so violent that you thought he might kill you or himself at any moment. Jean used to ask Mike if she could go over to help Tom. Mike never let her go because he knew Tom might break every bone in her body before Mike could reach them. This family owes Mike a great debt. He took care of Tom for the last fifteen years, and Tom made Mike's life a nightmare."

"What did Tom say to you when he called you?" Jim asked Tim.

"Cuckoo's-nest time. Remember how I loved Ken Kesey's novel and the Jack Nicholson movie? After I saw that movie, I was always hoping I would find me an Indian. One who could free me from all pain. Tom called me begging for help. But I'd seen him this way before, saying that Dad butt-fucked him. Pat did the same thing. All the brothers butt-fucked him for his entire life." Then Tim added, "I promised Tom I'd come up to Columbia when I woke up. Then I got Mike's hysterical phone call. Jean told me that she heard Mike screaming when the cops came to tell him about Tom. He just screamed over and over again and began hyperventilating to the point that she thought her husband might die of the shock."

"Great family to be born in," Jim said.

"The only family we got," Tim replied.

I said, "Boys, we need to sleep as much as we can. Tomorrow looks like it's going to be a long, long day."

And a long day it became.

When Dad rolled in at seven in the morning, I made coffee and breakfast, or hope I did. Over the years, the siblings have tried to cobble together the skin and tangles of that disjointed day. Although we knew we were not up to the task, we were being gentle with one another and let each know that any way we handled Tom's funeral was all right with the rest of us. Because of Carol Ann, we knew there was going to be a cold immersion into melodrama in a way we could not anticipate.

Carol Ann entered the house, her eyes still misting with a grief too brutal to endure. The rings beneath her swollen eyes were purple with a rage that had nowhere to go. Still, she was weeping violently and without hope or comfort. Her moistened ball of tear-soaked tissue had passed the size of a big-league baseball and was fast heading toward the diameter of a softball. I brought her a trash basket to relieve her of the sodden mess she carried in her hands, but she was quick to snap at me, "My tears are the only thing I've got left of Tom. The only way he'll know of the real love I felt for him. I've written a poem for his funeral and I don't want to hear any of your prose shit."

"None of my prose shit," I said. "That's a promise."

"I'll write poems about him that will make sure he lives forever, but I forbid you ever to write about him," she said.

"I've told you before, Carol," I said. "I don't ask *your* permission to write anything—or anyone else's, for that matter."

"Are you writing about him in your new book?" she asked.

"Yes, I am," I said. "And I was going to have his character, John Hardin McCall, kill himself. But no longer. The book is too sad by half. It couldn't endure the weight of my brother's breakdown and suicide."

"If you ever say Tom had a breakdown again, I'll sock you in the face," she said.

"You sock me in the face and I'll beat the living shit out of you and toss your body in the casket with Tom," I said, enraged, but sorry the words had flown out of me and regretting them immediately.

"I hang around writers in New York who are respected around the world. They think you write trash for the mob," she said.

"Tell it to someone who gives a shit, Carol."

Turning from her, I went over to join Kathy and the brothers in a semicircle around Dad, who sat enclosed in a sorrow as tightly built as an A-6 cockpit. Dad worried about the details of the funeral, obsessing that things be done right and proper for Tom.

"Kath?" he said. "Do you think anyone will come to the funeral?"

"We don't know, Dad," she said. "The obituary came out this morning, so a lot of people won't even know about it."

"Maybe we should put it off for a day," he said, fretting.

"Have to get Tom into the ground, Dad," Mike explained again.

At ten o'clock, the men from Copeland's arrived wearing their funeral-home faces and serious suits. Gathering in the yard, we took our assigned seats in the three limousines that were transferring us to St. Peter's Catholic Church. Mike assigned me a seat next to Dad and told me to take care of him during the entire ordeal. Carol Ann rode in the same limo, eyeing me as if I were a poison toadstool in the forest, yet afraid she would miss something profound Dad had to say about the death of his youngest son. The rest of us granted Dad any leeway he needed on the day of Tom's interment. Something had broken in Dad that seemed unfixable, and how he chose to react was his own business. The rest of us were having trouble enough.

Always full of surprises, Carol Ann opened the right-hand door and leaped out of a still-moving limousine in front of the church. She sprinted up to Curt Copeland, who was waiting beside Tom's casket, and began screaming at our unprepared funeral director. What the screaming was about we didn't find out until later. But I saw my brother-in-law, Bobby Joe Harvey, walk over to Carol Ann and Curt, and watched when Carol Ann turned her wrath on Bobby Joe. Crestfallen, Bobby Joe returned to the family as we lined up to enter the church.

Later, we discovered that Carol Ann had jumped out of the moving vehicle to confront Curt Copeland off guard. She screamed at him that he had been part of fucking her out of being one of her mother's pallbearers, and that she, as a part of the feminist nation, would never allow such an injustice to occur again. Furthermore, she demanded that she would proudly bear the weight of her brother's body all the way to the grave. No one knew this piece of stagecraft had gone on before our eyes until we had taken our place with the family in the front right pews.

When we entered the church, we had all broken down when we saw the church filled up with mourners who had come to stand beside us as we grieved the loss of Tom. Again, the town of Beaufort had come through for the Conroy family with a display of generosity that took all of us by surprise. Beside me, I heard my father's sudden intake of breath as he gauged the size of the crowd. I thought he might fall to his knees in a gesture of pure gratitude. In droves, they'd turned out for my mother, and twice that number had answered the bell for Tom in the newly built Catholic church that was three times as large as the old St. Peter's.

Father James P. Conroy of the Davenport, Iowa, diocese came out to lead the congregation, and he seemed confused by the change of scenery. Some of us weren't sure Father Jim had ever met our local priest.

My brother Jim moaned in displeasure behind me: "Dad, why did you pick the worst goddamn speaker in the history of the Catholic Church to do Tom's funeral?"

"Settle down, Jim," said Bobby Joe.

Tim asked in surprise, "Why're you here, Bobby Joe? You're supposed to be with the pallbearers."

Bobby Joe explained, "Carol kicked me off. Told me to go sit with her sicko family."

"Go knock the shit out of her, Bobby Joe," Jim said.

"Jim, you've got to quit talking like that," Bobby Joe said. "Show the proper respect."

I leaned back from trying to comfort my father and said to Bobby Joe, "Brother Jim goes crazy at all funerals and marriages. No one knows why. Just let him say what he needs to. It doesn't mean anything."

Father Jim approached the podium to deliver his eulogy for his nephew. I held out hope that my uncle would come up with the most inspired words of his lackluster career as a public speaker. As soon as he began to speak, I knew it would be far worse than I'd imagined. My brothers were harrumphing and grumbling from the beginning of his talk to its merciful ending. For Dad, we needed something that would refresh the soul and comfort the faithful.

Father Jim looked down at his speech, and I could see a nearsighted squint and the flooded altar lights causing him to shift his head and crane his neck, seeking an angle of vision where he could read his own words to a breathless, nervous audience.

Finally, he began to speak. "Today, we come together to celebrate the life of Timothy Patrick Conroy."

I turned around and said to Tim, "How does it feel to attend your own funeral? Sorry you're still dead, Tim."

"Tim attended the University of Southern Colorado," said Father Jim, and I thought there could be an open rebellion by my South Carolina Gamecock–loving brothers.

"What the hell?" Mike gasped. "Tom's never even been to Colorado."

"He can't see the page," I said, my father's weeping growing more pronounced the deeper we went into the ceremony. He had started to sob, and no sound on earth could have been more devastating to his kids.

"The worst part is over," I told him.

I could not have been more wrong, as my brothers would remind me for the rest of my life. Because I was trying to lay soft hands on Dad, I forgot all about Carol Ann waiting cobralike in the center of the pallbearers, who had never seen nor heard about her.

In innocence, they listened to the monotonous voice of my uncle, who was starting to wing it when he reached the major high points of his thoughts about his nephew.

"I'm the pastor at St. Anthony's Parish in downtown Davenport; we have a huge number of homeless in our community, but our outreach program makes sure they are taken care of. As you probably know, a lot of the homeless are simply mentally ill with nowhere to go."

When the words "mentally ill" were spoken aloud, a round, greasy object was tossed in the air among the astonished group of pallbearers. It rose about five feet; then it was snatched angrily by a small, womanly hand.

"Did you see that?" Mike asked.

"Who in the hell is playing catch at our brother's funeral?" Tim added.

"This whole town's gonna think we're bananas—completely off our rockers—and they're going to be right. Who brought a softball to this joyful occasion?" Jim said.

Kathy whispered, "Calm down. It's Carol and her ball of tears. She warned us that she'd make a scene if anyone said Tom was mentally ill."

"Just hang on," I said. "We've got to get through this."

Father Jim continued, and unfortunately he got stuck in the same vein. "The homeless come by and we feed them twice a day. At lunch, we fix them all a sandwich and give them all a buck. I can't tell you how good it makes the mentally ill feel when they've got some money in their pocket."

Again the tear-laden softball found itself flung into midair, this time glistening with too many tears to mention. But Father Jim had not completed his thought on the subject and offered, "Also, Don and I have got a brother who's what you might call seriously mentally ill."

Again, the object of Carol Ann's sorrow took flight, even higher this time.

When Uncle Jim made his next error of judgment, I was ready for the moment. As I listened to Father Jim, I heard him continue to talk about his outreach program: "Now, our brother Jack has been seriously wacked-out for a long time, yet he's doing better. He lines up each day with the mentally ill and I give him a sandwich and a dollar. Even though he's my brother, he gets no special treatment from me just because he's mentally ill."

By then, I had positioned myself where I was looking toward the back of the church. When Carol Ann let loose on her final toss of protest and futility, I saw three-fourths of the congregation with their heads tilting as they followed the fetid mound of tissue on its last flight. On its way down, Carol Ann had to move to her right to snatch her ball off the playing field.

Then I heard a collective moan come up from my family as Carol Ann made her way up to the podium to read a poem she had written in commemoration of Tom's life. She called it "The Deer Man," and it had appeared in Carol Ann's marvelous book *The Beauty Wars*. It is a book about unbearable hurt, but it is written with a fly-by-night eloquence that moves me. "The Deer Man" tells the story in all its misdirected power and energy of that week that our catatonic brother had gone to heal himself on Hunting Island by lying down in a pine hummock as still as a veil of lichen. It made a portion of beauty out of a disturbing moment when my mother and I watched a tick-covered, irrational young man who had made his stillness such a success that the island deer used the sweat from his body as a salt lick. The poem was a lovely tribute to our lost brother, which Carol Ann read as though it were a devotional she stole from a secret litany in her garden of language. The poem moved me and helped me make it through that dark ceremony.

But I was part of a family lost in sorrow, who would insist on grieving in their own way. Jim tapped me on the shoulder and said, "Now

I know why Tom killed himself—he always hated shitty poetry. That was the shittiest poem I ever heard."

Sotto voce, I said, "Easy, dark one. We're almost finished here. We'll bury Tom, then go home."

The funeral had collapsed my father from the middle, and his constant sobbing made his grief almost unbearable. Since none of his kids had ever witnessed such profound sorrow from our Dad before, it caused a field of profound disturbance in each of us.

When we returned home after the burial, the women of Fripp ministered to us by their soft laying of hands and their preparing food for all who needed to be fed. My great friend Mary Wilson Smith fed a multitude that day and organized the Fripp women, who arrived in waves from afternoon till night. As Conroys, strangers in every town we ever entered, we both acknowledged and appreciated their labor for us. The food was plentiful and delicious and seemed to arrive as an endless bounty.

Sometime over the long course of that afternoon, I managed to talk to all my siblings alone, except for the unapproachable Carol Ann. We talked about Dad and his remarkable devastation over Tom's suicide. Before this event, none of us had been quite sure that Dad loved us. His breakdown over Tom was proof enough of Dad's ability to demonstrate love for his kids and served as a window on his soul. He loved us, in his own way, with all his heart, but he had trouble demonstrating that love, which made him just like the rest of his children. From that day forward, my long war against Dad came to an end. The Conroy children wiped that slate clean. I was coming up to my fiftieth birthday. It embarrassed me what a mess I'd made of my life, and casting stones at my own parents lacked the allure for me it once had in my fire-eating youth. Forgiven at last, my father sat in a chair in the living room, not even trying to control his crying. His kids surrounded him, because his love of Tom provided us an understanding of his own love of all of us. It was a day of surreal, uncommon beauty.

Carol Ann chose to have nothing to do with any of her family or friends of Tom's, and headed for the edge of the lagoon behind my house, where she paced for hours smoking cigarettes and talking to the air, gesturing wildly at the osprey-haunted sky and the mullet-clefted lagoon. Our guests were able to watch Carol Ann's antics as she performed before a full house. She could not have drawn more attention to herself if she had hired a marching band to follow her.

"Conroy," Mary Wilson Smith said as she walked to my side and we joined a sizable contingent of guests watching Carol Ann's performance, "has anyone ever told you that your family's crazy?"

"Yeah, Mary," I said, as I watched Carol Ann speaking to something the rest of us couldn't see.

"I feel the need to call nine-one-one and get some boys to throw a net over Carol and haul her away," Mary said.

"She'll be gone by tomorrow," I said. "Back to New York. That's how poets act, Mary."

"You're bad enough as it is, Pat, writing novels," she said. "I'd better not catch you writing any poetry."

"No poetry for me," I promised her.

When Carol Ann left for Kathy's house, she rode with Dad and Bobby Joe and failed to say good-bye to any of the rest of us. After they left, tempers began to flare as the pressures of the day caught up with us. Jim walked into the den, where Tim and his friends from high school had spent the entire day reminiscing, and he announced, "Tim, is there anything else we can do for you or your loser friends? Is there any other drink we can fix or plate we can wash?" Tim answered with a string of epithets that were forgivable under the circumstances. Mike and I made a move to get Jim out of the line of fire, but he was in a hotheaded mood.

Mike said, "Tim's getting through this in his way, Jim. He's laughing and drinking with his friends. It may not be our way, but it's Tim's. Let him be."

Jim calmed down, then said, "Did Tim give you his poem after the funeral?"

"He gave me a piece of paper," Mike said. "I haven't had the time to read it. Busy day, you know."

"I think you boys'll find it worth your time," Jim said.

In the nearly empty house, I reached into my jacket pocket and pulled out a piece of paper that had Tim's handwriting on it. When Carol Ann's book *The Beauty Wars* came out, all of us fixated on page fifteen, which was not exactly a poem but carried a title that caught all of our attention: "The Great Santini's wild, sleek children." Though we did not rate a complete poem, she named each of us with the moniker of one of the aircraft Dad flew in his career. I believe she took some time and pleasure in putting all of the Conroy children into our father's phantom squadron. I was Skyhawk, and Carol Ann named herself Dauntless. Mike became Corsair; Kathy, Avenger; Jim was dubbed Hellcat; Tim was baptized Panther; and Tom carried the poetic name of Pilot Dawn to his death.

Since Tim and I took the most delight in the quality of Carol Ann's poetry and the value of her book, we took the naming of the winged children of Santini with great seriousness. Tim's poem that he passed around after Tom's funeral was pure homage to Carol Ann and her work. But it also offered a bended knee toward our family's attraction to absurdity and a misshapen sense of humor that could induce either laughter or dismay.

Tim had taken Carol Ann's homage to her family and put his own twist on the subject matter. Instead of fighter planes, Tim named all his siblings after fast-food restaurants. The idea struck me as both ludicrous and hilarious. I read my own name first, "Pat—What a burger"; Carol Ann's was "Wendy's," and Mike carried the moniker of "Bessinger's Barbeque"; Kathy was honored with "Bojangles"; Jim was "Long John Silver." Tim called himself "Yesterdays"—the restaurant the brothers had worked in during college. Tom was "Applebee's."

Hearing the laughter of his brothers drew Tim into our circle, where he delighted in our taking pleasure in his attempt at poetry. He gave us the names of all the different fast-food joints he considered, then explained why he made the choices he made.

"You only got one of them wrong. Completely wrong," Jim said.

"Tell me. I can still change it," Tim said.

"Tom. You got him wrong," Jim said.

I said, "It sounds pretty good to me. Applebee's sounds about right."

"I like it," Mike agreed.

"It's all wrong," Jim insisted. "If you think about it, Tom should've been called 'IHOP.'"

"Why?" Tim asked.

Jim said in the shadowy darkness where he stood, "Didn't Tom just 'hop' off a fourteen-story building?"

"My God, the dark one speaks," I said.

"The evil one," Mike said. "MLD. Most Like Dad. A monster. Jim, you're far worse than any of us could imagine." Then the Conroy group started laughing, though we hated ourselves for it. It was a terrible ending for an unspeakable day that was indefensible and Conroyesque.

Five years later, I was shopping in Publix when a stranger approached to ask me who was hurling the softball toward the rafters during my brother Tom's funeral. Though I could not answer the man's question, my laughter carried me through the arugula and the Belgian endive. In the way of my world, there are some things that don't lend themselves to explanation.

CHAPTER 16

Losing Carol Ann

My sister Carol Ann lived a valiant, unpraised childhood, but one of almost unbearable solitude. She was a prize for any family to engender, but she passed much of her time unnoticed. By any measure, she was a pretty girl who didn't measure up to her mother's lofty standards. Despite herself, Peg Conroy had a careless gift for making her two daughters feel unattractive.

But my mother carried a dream of poets and novelists inside of her that her fixation on physical beauty could not touch. Mom drenched our childhood with poems and children's books, then let fly with *Gone with the Wind* when Carol Ann and I were both closer to infancy than to adolescence. Slowly Mom began to read us the books she wanted to read, and this habit lasted until I got to high school, when Carol Ann and I could fill out our own flight plans at the library desk.

But there was one story of our reading life that our mother made perfect—and no novelist or poet could add a word to improve it. The year we moved to the pretty coastal town of New Bern, North Carolina, my second-grade year, was when my mother read *The Diary of Anne Frank* to her children.

As a young boy, I was caught up in the immediacy and brightness of Anne Frank's unmistakable voice. I studied photographs of Anne Frank and noted how pretty she was, and how she looked exactly as I expected her to look: fresh and knowing and—this was important to me—smarter than the adults around her. I fell in love with Anne Frank and have never fallen out of love with her.

But my mother did not prepare her children for the abruptness of the diary's ending. Anne's voice went silent after the Nazis invaded her family's attic hideaway, a place I visit every time I find myself in the watery, cross-stitched city of Amsterdam.

"What happened to Anne, Mama?" I asked.

"Why'd she stop writing?" Carol Ann asked.

And my Georgia-born mother began telling us about the coming of the Nazi beast, the cattle cars, the gas chambers, and the murder of six million Jews, including babies and children and the lovely Anne Frank. I will always honor my mother when I think of the words she spoke next. "Carol Ann and Pat, listen to me. I want to raise a family that will hide Jews."

And I will always adore the spirit of my sister Carol Ann, who asked me to walk next door to Mrs. Orringer's house. Mrs. Orringer came to the door, dressed in grand flamboyance.

"Yes, children? What is it?"

My sister Carol Ann looked up into Mrs. Orringer's eyes and said with a child's simplicity and ardor, "Mrs. Orringer, don't worry about anything."

"What are you talking about, child?"

"We will hide you," Carol Ann said.

"What?" Mrs. Orringer asked.

"We will hide you," Carol Ann repeated.

. . .

Another memory comes to mind, when Carol Ann was five years old, and the last of the Nolen family came to pay their respects to Stanny for the loss of her husband. The visit took on a nightmarish aspect when one of Stanny's second or third cousins started telling stories, mostly about himself. When displeased, Stanny's eyes could assume a hooded, cobra look, while my mother's eyes could turn a biting blue.

The cousin was a vintage Southern boy of that era, strong and willowy, sporting a blond crew cut so sharp that it looked like it could cut your finger. He fascinated me because I'd never seen a man so young take over the conversation from his elders. Then he told a story that is fabled in our family mythology, yet firmly and resolutely denied. He told about going to a Klan meeting outside of Jacksonville, Alabama, when the group he was riding with spotted a five-year-old "nigger boy" playing alongside the road. As a joke, they picked the boy up to give him a joyride, but the little boy screamed in terror. Some of the men wanted to drop him off. Instead, the driver accelerated his car to a hundred miles an hour and threw the boy off a high bluff located somewhere between the two towns.

"We felt like we'd done a pretty good night's work for the Klan," he said, his smugness filling the room.

Then we heard it, the keening, the primitive call of inconsolable women, and turned to see it coming from Carol Ann. It began low-pitched, then rose in fury and register until finally she approached the unstrung cousin with her finger pointing straight at him: "Evil. You are evil—get out of this house. Get out right now."

I didn't know what the word "evil" meant until I heard it raw and nasty coming from my sister's lips.

The cousin said, "Ain't anybody gonna whup her? She deserves to be whupped. I'll be glad to do it."

"You touch my daughter and I'll cut your heart out," my mother said coldly. "Now, you leave and go back to what brought you."

"Never come calling at my door again," Stanny said. "I don't know a damn one of you, and I sure as hell ain't gonna correct that. Git. Go on down the driveway."

"Make them leave our house," Carol Ann moaned, the ancestral moan still putting her fury in parentheses.

"We heard you were strange, Margaret," a girl cousin said.

"Not strange enough for that part of the South," Stanny answered, and that accursed branch of the cousinry slouched down the driveway.

I thought my sister Carol Ann was the bravest, most admirable person on earth. But how did she know all of this when she was so young? The story of Carol Ann facing down a family Klansman burned like a brand into my brain. Even then, I marked the moment when she packed a wallop of social courage I always lacked. Wordless, I'd watched the exchange with knee-knocking terror.

Afterward, I was so shaken up that Mom and Stanny explained to us that the boy was just a bigmouthed braggart and that was how some white boys in the rural South got their kicks—boasting about the killing of colored people. Even Stanny wouldn't explain how she was related to the crew-cut guy, and we never heard him mentioned again.

"Call the cops," Carol Ann demanded.

Stanny took time to explain: "Even if that boy did what he said, no white jury would convict him for killing a colored person."

"We're raising you in an evil land," my mother said. "But we're not raising you to be like him." And she never again took us to Piedmont, Alabama, during our childhood.

Later, however, Carol Ann would enter dangerous waters with my mother every time she opened her mouth. Now I know what Mom was expecting in a Southern daughter: a darling girl with an adorable laugh and a love for jewelry and girlie clothes. She wanted a conventional, presentable girl who would one day attend cotillions and debutante balls with a retinue of young men begging for a place on her dance card.

My sister was nothing like the daughter my mother dreamed of when she appeared on March 10, 1947. Mom raised Carol Ann and me to be writers, failing to take in the strangeness of poets and the long gestation period required of novelists. Every time my sister spoke her mind, she generated a savage reaction in my mother. At an early age, I got the distinct impression that there was something about Carol Ann that both my parents hated. With odd skills of articulation, she spoke truths her parents were not interested in hearing.

But the enmity between my mother and sister was growing malignant as I entered eighth grade at Blessed Sacrament School in Alexandria, Virginia. After we returned home from school, Mom would begin picking away at Carol Ann on everything from her appearance to her posture. Instead of just letting those criticisms go, my sister would fire back wounding volleys of her own, and a no-holds-barred mother-daughter catfight would break out. Prisoners were never taken and wounds were never cauterized. The words flashed like razors and the fight would move upstairs, where Carol Ann and I had pine-paneled bedrooms of our own. Retreating to my bedroom, I would close the door, but the waterworks of their personal fury battered against my walls like waves. They brought the ferocity of leopards to their howling encounters.

"Young lady," Mom said, "what does it feel like to know everything in the world?"

"Better than being you—knowing nothing," Carol Ann said. "You didn't even go to college."

Wham! I heard a broom whistle through the air, a new weapon my mother brought to the art of warfare against her voluble daughter.

"I hope that made you feel good, Mother. Hitting a ten-year-old in the face with a broom."

"Just shut up. You always have to have the last word. I promise you this, young lady: You won't have the last word today."

"If that makes you feel better, Mother," Carol Ann said, raising the ante.

The broom whistled again and hit my sister. Carol Ann was not one to suffer in silence. She screamed as though she'd had a breast removed by a cutlass, a signal that I should enter the fray. All three of us had memorized all the steps of the macabre dance many years ago.

"Oh, the golden boy has arrived. Hello, Mr. Sunshine. I was so hoping you would make your heroic entrance before Mom beat me to death with her broom," Carol Ann mocked.

Bam! Mom swung the broom again and caught Carol Ann hard on the chin, eliciting the same animal cry of hurt as before. I grabbed the broom and twisted it out of Mom's hands.

"No broom, Mom," I pleaded. "Please just ignore her."

"I won't let her get the last word in!" Mom screamed. "So help me God, I'll beat her to death with my fists if I have to."

"I think that's a very fair thing to ask, Mother," Carol Ann said.

Mom lunged for Carol Ann with her fists flying, but I grabbed her from behind. "Carol, just shut the hell up and I'll take Mom downstairs."

"Gosh, Mother, it must be so nice for you to have the normal son, the adored one. It's a shame he's as stupid as you are. Hell, you're reading Edna Ferber and acting like she's Jane Austen."

Again, Mom charged and caught a hunk of Carol Ann's brown hair. She would've pulled it out if I'd not been there to loosen her grip.

"Now, I want you to shut up and let Mom get downstairs before you can say a word," I cried.

"Have you ever noticed that you're not king of the world?" my sister declared.

My mother returned armed with the broom and almost brought Carol Ann to the floor with a well-aimed sock to the back of the head. Again, I fought the broom away from Mom, this time throwing it down the stairway. When I returned to the field of battle, Mom had Carol Ann in a stranglehold and had fought her to the floor.

"You seem to love being cruel, Mother," my sister said, "just like the beast you married."

"Shut up! Shut up! You'll not have the last word today, even if I have to knock every single tooth out of your head!"

I picked my sister off the floor, then covered her mouth with my hand. Limber and strong, she fought me and spit on my hand as I yelled for Mom to make her escape.

"Ha! I got the last word," Mom said in triumph as she ran downstairs. Carol Ann would've tried to take my fingers off if I had not released her fast and pushed her toward the window. Quickly, she spun and challenged me, spitting in my face and trying to claw my eyes out of their sockets. Finally, exhausted, we both sank to the linoleum, breathing hard.

Finally I said, "Who the hell is Jane Austen?"

"Poor idiot golden boy. You've got nothing written all over you. You try to make these idiots like you, but they never will. I'll hate you forever for holding my mouth shut. Can you spell 'forever,' golden one? Altar boy asshole."

Though the change was a slow one, it had an inevitability about it. My parents were drawing me slowly into their enemy camp, where I became Carol Ann's chief interpreter and the vilest traitor she would ever invite beside her council fires.

So I grew up with this unripened mind, a sister who sounded like a teenager trapped in a child's body. In a chrysalis of words, a poet was growing up beside me; because of her infinite curiosity I walked through the ruby mine of her consciousness as she made jewelry from the language she and I shared.

I had once thought Carol Ann and I were as close as any siblings could get. Her mind delighted me in all its trailblazing discoveries. When Dad served his first tour in Vietnam, I was a sophomore at The Citadel and came home that Easter to a continuing civil war between Carol Ann and my mother. Again, the broom was the weapon of choice.

Early in the evening hours, I awoke to a screaming physical fight that I had come to expect at The Citadel when two men clashed over a girl.

I rushed into the TV room, where I saw the broom bash against the side of Carol Ann's head.

"You might beat me to death, Mother," Carol Ann said, "but it'll only make me much more famous among female writers who know about the martyrs in their midst."

"I'd like to make you a goddamn martyr tonight, you little bitch!" Mom screamed.

"What's the problem?" I asked.

"Oh, go back upstairs and clean a sword or something," Carol Ann sneered. "You do know they sent you to the worst college on earth. It doesn't have a literary reputation because it doesn't have a reputation at all. You'll go to Vietnam and die in the paddies with boys with the lowest IQs."

"Let me beat her to death, Pat. You're just wasting time."

"What's this fight about?" I asked.

"I'm watching a British play to the end. I've become an actor this year," Carol Ann said.

"She's got a nothing part in Thornton Wilder's *Our Town*—nothing to write home about," Mom said.

"Then you need your sleep, Carol Ann," I said, walking over to turn off the TV.

"You ever turn that TV off again while I'm watching it, I'll turn you into fish food for the next day," Carol Ann said.

I intercepted Mom's next baseball-bat swing of her broom.

"Carol Ann, I don't want to have to kill you," I said, "But it would actually feel good, the way you're acting."

"Oh, son of Don, progeny of Zeus, chattel maker of women, since I'm a girl, I'm just roach dung in the field for the golden issue of Apollo. Though he acts like a sun god, Pat is a war god and Carol Ann is his immortal enemy. I'll bring you down with my poetry. My art will put you into your grave. You'll write for Hallmark cards."

I always cherished these moments when my sister made her long-winded mythological and psychological attacks on my character. I found them erudite, hilarious, and perfectly close to the mark. Though I knew I dealt with a chickenhearted assimilation in my dealings with adults, I never saw the wisdom in alienating them to the core, as Carol Ann was so apt to do. I liked it when Mom kissed me rather than putting me to the floor with a broom. It was Carol Ann's belief that an artist had to be a rebel in constant war with the world around her. She would bring the world to its knees with her poetry, and I would make them kneel at the communion rail with the shit I wrote. When we were kids and all the way through college, Carol Ann Conroy and I were locked together in a two-step dance to survive the windchill factor of our parents' marriage. For twenty-five years, we kept up a running commentary on the hopelessness of our situation in fashioning some kind of normal life from the ruins of the Conroys' undermined hermitage.

Early and often we remarked about the real damage our parents had inflicted on us and wondered drearily about the fates of our younger brothers and sisters. To us, Peg and Don did not appear to grow more facile with the art of parenting as they aged. When we left home for college, it seemed like an escape from the pages of a blighted hymnal. Though I hated the plebe year at The Citadel, I also believe that Carol Ann caught some sickness of her lonely spirit in her first six months of Winthrop, but neither of us gave serious thought to returning to that scene of breakage that had produced us. Not that our folks would welcome us home. When a Conroy kid went off to college, there was no bed to come home to, no chest of drawers or a closet, or bathroom privileges, or even a place at the dinner table. You had to squeeze your way in, find how the house worked without your participation, and hope for a mattress on a basement floor to sleep on. College became not only our new home, but also our destiny. There was no such thing as looking back.

Of all the people I've ever talked to about literature and books, Carol Ann was the most insightful. She possessed a natural gift for summation and a broad-minded affection for other writers' work. We grew up believing both of us would be writers. At the time, I didn't think we had any reasonable chance to succeed at this ambition, since our education was sketchy and run-of-the-mill. There were long odds against us, but neither of us cared, and both were innocent in the extreme.

The break between us was gradual, but I now believe inevitable. When Carol Ann was in college, she made a bold move by announcing to the family that she was a lesbian. It was the summer of 1969, when Dad was in Vietnam, and Carol Ann came to Beaufort with her roommate from Winthrop, Chris Cinque. I'd never spent any time with her friend Chris, but Carol Ann had written great letters about her steadfastness, charm, and reserve. She had stated that Chris Cinque was the perfect roommate for her.

At the request of my mother, Carol Ann had come down for the weekend so the happy Conroy family could pose for a group photograph for my father's camp desk in Vietnam. After dinner Carol Ann made her disruptive but colorful move. She charged into the kitchen with her blue eyes flashing her desire to take center stage, with Chris trailing like a fledging bird behind her. Carol Ann cried out, "I have an announcement to make." All eyes in the room turned to her as she stood there, her booted feet set solidly on kitchen tiles and her face filled with righteousness.

"I am a lesbian!" she shouted. "I am a bull dyke."

My mother hurled herself around, undone like I'd never seen her before. Then she began chanting, "I knew it. I knew it all along. I knew from the morning she was born. Something was off. I couldn't put my finger on it. I couldn't name it. But she's always been off. Now I'll never have grandchildren. I wanted so much to have grandchildren."

As I helped my mother to her feet, I said to her, "Just look around, Mom—you've got three grandchildren looking at you."

"I'm proud to be a lesbian, Mother!" Carol Ann said, still in shouting mode. "I'm proud to be a bull dyke. I'll shout it from the rooftops, from the highest trees."

"Subtly done, Carol Ann," I said as I helped Mom into a kitchen chair.

"I'm declaring who I am. It's important to me that all of you accept me as a beloved sister and as a lesbian."

In complete innocence, my mother looked at pretty Chris Cinque and asked, "Is Chris a lesbian, too?"

This brought Chris and Carol Ann to the point of collapse, and they held each other as their laughter reached hysteric proportions.

I felt a tug at my fingertips and I looked down to see little Jessica and her puzzled face beneath me.

"Daddy," Jessica asked, "what is a dyke?"

"Jesus God," I moaned, and then said, "Let me think about this for a sec. A dyke. Yes. It's coming to me. Got it. You know that story I read to you girls? The one about that brave little Dutch boy who put his finger in the dike? Well, Carol does that. She runs around and finds holes in dikes and dams and holds her finger in them." Then I turned to Barbara to ask, "Don't you think it's time to put the girls to bed?"

"Oh, no," Barbara said, "I wouldn't miss this show for anything."

Stanny jumped in and said, "You aren't a lesbian, Carol Ann. I've sailed around the world five times and I can guarantee you're not a lesbian. I'm worldly, you know."

"Are you calling me a liar, Stanny?" Carol Ann said. "I thought you, as a gallant woman, would accept this with the love and courage it requires. In the South, I'll have very few people supporting me in the racist, lesbian-hating world that surrounds me. But you? The great traveler in our family, who has been everywhere and done everything? You've been the great experiencer of the family, the voyager, the Odysseus traveling for years to get back home. If you fail me, where will I turn?"

"Don't know, but you aren't close to being a lesbian," Stanny said with maddening certainty.

My mother said, "Can't we change the subject? It's getting rather boring."

Again Carol Ann lit up like a Roman candle and exploded. "My sexuality is boring? Do you realize you're putting a stake in my heart by saying something that stupid and insensitive? Look at me. I'm your daughter. The hated, tormented first daughter. See me, Mother. For the first time in your life, please try to see me."

"I see you, I see you," Mom said. "So now will you shut up?"

"No, I won't, Mother. No one shall muzzle me or silence me again. I've come out of the closet and into the streets. For the first time I've come into the light, and I love the light and I'll never be hurled into darkness again."

"She's the farthest thing from a lesbian I've ever seen," Stanny continued. "She's not even close."

Carol Ann started haranguing Stanny about the rights of women and the history of women's liberation, ending with a thrilling, "Stanny, when you were born, women weren't even permitted to vote."

"Listening to you run your mouth tonight, I kinda see the point," my mother said unhelpfully.

The mother and daughter exercise flared up again, and I jumped between the antagonists and kept them away from each other. Both women were ready to claw each other's eyeballs clear out of their heads, and they were trading epithets that were growing more profane by the second. I saw Barbara moving the kids out of the battle zone and I heard my grandmother say something that seemed irrelevant to the intellectual social discussion that was under present review:

"Carol Ann's never even been to Beirut."

When I got Carol Ann to retreat to the doorway, near where she and Chris held hands and Mom was sitting again facing Stanny, I assumed my natural role of peacemaker between the two women. It had been my role since I was a child.

"Let's discuss this calmly," I said.

Carol Ann rolled her eyes and said to Chris, "This is the part of my brother I hate the most. The kindly one. The Goody Two-shoes. The perfect one. U Thant. The ambassador to the peaceful kingdom."

"Shut up, Carol Ann," I said, "or I'll beat the living shit out of you and leave you for dead."

"That's what he really wants—to silence womanhood," she declared. "To threaten us with bodily harm. But I'm telling you this right now, buster: Womanhood won't be tamed or condescended to or have our mouths taped shut again. We are billions and we are on the move."

"Before I tape your mouth shut, Carol, I'd like to say something to you," I said.

"Say it," she said.

"You're my oldest sister. You and I grew up together. Learned to read together. You know I adored you and admired you from the time I was a little boy to this very night. We're as close as any brother and sister I've ever met. I think you are a great poet and great person."

"Cut the bullshit," Carol Ann said. "Get on with it."

"You've had a difficult life in a difficult family. But you and I survived. By staying together, you and I got through the worst of things. We did it by loving and trusting each other. Trust me now. Mom will get over it. Stanny judges no one. Your brothers and sisters all love you like I do, like Mom does. But I don't think you stage-managed this announcement very well. I believe it could be done in private. But if you're a lesbian, I'll accept it. If you love Chris Cinque, I'll love Chris. So will your family. Except for Dad. You're on your own with Dad. He could kill you for all I know. I don't even know what lesbians do to each other and I don't care. But if that's who you are, I'm fine with it. I support it and I hope you're happy the rest of your life."

Carol Ann threw herself into my arms and both of us trembled with emotion. Then I led Carol Ann to Mom and they embraced each other and cried. I hugged Chris and the whole room restored itself into a quiet equilibrium.

Later that evening, still in the kitchen, we were at the table talking about that day's events. I was curious about something and I asked Carol Ann, "Why this lightning strike, Carol Ann, why this blitzkrieg into Beaufort, bringing us these tidings of good joy?"

Carol Ann and Chris were at the sink washing dishes, and she said, "I had to work fast. I needed to tell you tonight because I'm insisting that Chris be included in the family photograph we send to Dad."

My mother exploded beside me. "Over my dead body! She's not a member of our family and she never will be."

"She's a member of my family, and I say she'll be in this photograph," Carol Ann retorted. "Or I'll refuse to be in it."

"That's fine with me, young lady," my mother snarled.

"I've never heard of such a thing," Stanny said. "A lesbian in a Southern family photo."

"Quiet, Stanny," I said. "Don't get yourself involved in this. Carol Ann, are there any more surprises? Any more hand grenades you want to lob into this kitchen?

"No. That's the last one," she said. "But I resent you calling my lover a hand grenade."

"Mom," I said as I pulled up a chair beside her, "this is just a photograph. Dad won't even notice there's someone else in the picture. Tell him Carol Ann's roommate was down for the weekend and we wanted to see if he even noticed a stranger in the family lineup. It doesn't have to be a big deal."

"It's a big deal to me," Mom said.

"Ladies, ladies, ladies," I began, then stopped, tongue-tied, and couldn't think of one thing to say, but out of perverse frustration I said, "Mom, Chris is going to be in our goddamn family portrait or I'm not going to be; nor will any of the other kids."

"You can't make an ultimatum like that," my mother said.

"I just did, and I meant every word of it."

Carol Ann turned to Chris and said, "Golden boy comes through again."

"It's just not right," my mother said, but with an echo of surrender in her voice.

Later, in the living room, we gathered for a glass of wine before we went to bed. It had been a hard day in the Conroy household, but we were long accustomed to high drama and angry voices. We were battle-scared veterans of many fractious skirmishes of both the body and spirit. The wounds of the night would heal and the tempers would be smoothed by sleep and darkness.

But Carol Ann asked my mother whether there was anything about lesbianism that troubled her, or whether she and Chris could answer any questions that would set her mind at ease.

My mother thought about it, then said, "Yes, I've always been curious about lesbianism." I had never heard her mention the word in my entire life. "There is something I'd like to know. When you and Chris make love, if that's what you call it—"

"That's what we call it, Peggy," said Chris.

"Well, whatever, but when you do to each other what you do, who takes the 'male' role? You or Chris?"

"We don't play roles like that," Carol Ann explained.

"Oh, come on. You asked if I was interested or not, and I'd just like to know which one of you plays the male aggressor, who makes the aggressive animal-like moves toward the more feminine of the two."

Finally, Carol Ann had come to the end of her patience, and she stood up and put her jackbooted foot up on the arm of Mom's chair. She rolled up the cuff of her overalls to the knee, tightened the muscles in her arms, and growled with apelike ferocity, "Mother, it's *me*."

My mother fled out into the night.

The next day we arrived at Ned Brown's studio for our family portrait. It remains, by far, my favorite family portrait. One can study the clothing styles and the haircuts of that unlovely era. Take your time doing it. In that pyramid of faces, I see much of my life passing by in review. The long hair on the boys I attribute to my mother's not handing out money to pay for haircuts more than I do to the sixties. The cheap eyeglasses on the boys are one of my mother's trademarks. My brother Tim's shirt belongs in a museum somewhere. Mom is radiant after the tumultuous dinner at my house the evening before. Always, when I see my lost brother, Tom, there is a heartache that'll never heal. My children and my wife are lovely and I look happy.

Yet the centerpiece of the entire photograph will be Chris Cinque, with her slight Mona Lisa smile as she sits separated by a resilient sea of Conroys from her lover, Carol Ann. Though they broke up more than thirty years ago, I still love the moment when a distant cousin or an old friend tries to match the fresh faces in the photograph with the older faces we now carry around with us. Most of them can identify every one of them with a little bit of help, but they're flummoxed by the mysterious stranger who anchors the left flank of the photo.

Though I've told this story hundreds of times over the years, I never cracked the case about what Stanny meant by saying that Carol Ann had "never even been to Beirut." Years later, when I took Stanny to lunch at Morrison's Cafeteria in Atlanta, she and I were talking about the family when she brought up the subject of Carol Ann and her love life.

"She don't still insist on calling her own self a lesbian, does she now?" Stanny asked.

"She sure does," I said. "And it's still a sensitive subject with her."

"Does she now? Well, she's making a fool of herself if you happen to ask me." Stanny ate her food as slowly as a manatee. Then she said again, "Carol's never been to Beirut."

"What do you mean by that, Stanny?" I said. "Who cares if you've been to Beirut or not?"

"Pat, it only makes sense if you look at it literally. Only people who're from Lebanon can be real lesbians."

I hollered with laughter and drew some unwanted attention to our table. "I get it, Stanny. I finally get it. Growing up in Piedmont, they taught you that people from Lebanon were called lesbians."

"That's what they're called everywhere," Stanny said, not giving an inch. "It's not just Piedmont. Carol's people are Scotch-Irish on my side of the family and pure Irish on your daddy's side. She needs to learn these things, needs to study a little geography."

. . .

Following Chris northward, Carol Ann audited courses at the Iowa Writers' Workshop, where Chris majored in the theater arts. Moving to Minneapolis afterward, both established themselves in the arts community of that good-hearted city. Carol Ann's drift out of our family circle became almost complete, even though I took my young daughters to vacation with my sister and Chris at the north shore of Lake Superior for three summers in a row. During our last summer there, Carol Ann informed me that she would no longer call herself Carol Ann, that no one in the cutthroat world of poetry would take a double-named Southern woman seriously.

Eventually, Carol Ann and Chris drifted apart, and all the Conroys mourned the loss of Chris. Carol Ann moved to start a new life in the New York poetry world, and has befriended poets as distinguished as Sharon Olds and Galway Kinnell. Her family sees her now at funerals and weddings, but she mostly spends her time in the East Village, where the smells of curry and tandoori chicken spice the air leading to the East River. Though Carol Ann was born with a greater verbal gift than I possess, her poems form as slowly as Ming vases in her cunning hands. Her light-infused poems are webs of silk and gossamer. She condenses the Conroy freight down to a cell of light and a pearl of black sorrow.

Basically, Carol Ann has not talked to me since the death of our mother in 1984, and our brother ten years later. Though I don't like the silence that has sprung up between us, I know it's all part of living a high-strung and troubled life. It's also a part of being the brother of a poet.

CHAPTER 17

Escape from San Francisco

When I grew up, I found the word "father" to be an obscenity. Dad's cruelty was a mass of the catechumens for me, a religious protocol that became confused in my mind with the unimaginable suffering of the Catholic martyrs. I confused God the father with the terrible reign of suffering that the Great Santini brought to the art of fathering. He bewildered his children by failing to know a single one of us. Then, after Tom's suicide, he seemed to understand in a sudden rush of prescience and light how desperately he needed us.

My mother's divorcing him had torn my father apart. None of us quite knew how crazy in love he was with Peg. The completeness and integrity of that devotion came to us only in the shock of her leave-taking. His face was dark with her abandonment for the rest of his life. Though he expressed great puzzlement over her dereliction of duty, I tried to make her reasons clear to him when he arrived for his daily coffee at my apartment on Maddox Drive in Atlanta from 1976 to 1980, when we lived near each other.

"Why'd you beat her up?" I'd ask him in the privacy of my living room.

"I never touched your mother in her life," he said. "That's bullshit you made up to sell your books."

"I remember lots of times you slapped her around," I said. "So does she."

"When people invent lies about you," Dad said, "what're you supposed to do? How do you go about protecting yourself?"

"Admit you did it," I said. "Come clean, Dad. Confession is good for the soul. That's what our silly-ass church preaches."

"Kathy doesn't think I ever touched your mother," he said. "She thinks you made it all up."

"Why did she testify under oath that you beat Mom up, then?" I asked. "She was the only one of your kids to testify against you in the divorce case. I'm still ashamed of myself for not telling the court what a prick you'd been."

"I could've sued you for character assassination for that shitty book you wrote about me," he said.

"I get the night sweats when you make threats like that, Dad."

He laughed and said, "The only reason I hold off on litigation, jocko, is my love for the magnificent seven, my great bunch of kids. Remember, high culture came out of my joint. Two writers out of seven kids—it ain't bad. And remember, too, I fathered a poet. I'm betting that Carol kicks your ass when all is said and done. She thinks you write for the poor idiot who reads just to pass the time away. She and her friends have much higher aspirations. To tell you the truth, I think your sister's really onto something. I like her poetry a hundred times better than your prose, which I personally think is horseshit."

"Dad, I'm impressed you're so enamored with her poetry. May I ask you to name your favorite poem she's written?"

"I've got to think," Dad said. "I love all her shit."

"Just name one, proud father of poets," I said.

Dad began to laugh. He had a wonderful laugh when he was caught in the open, after carrying a conversation to a height he couldn't come down from. He delighted in speaking about his passion for literature, but loved even more when he found himself exposed as a preening, empty vessel.

For the rest of his life, I would listen to Dad give his saturnine view of books he'd never read and poetry he never knew existed. By then,

Dad thought of himself as a literary figure, a surprise ranking that no one enjoyed more than he did.

In those years, I said terrible things to my father. When I think about the things I said to Don Conroy, I understand that I shamed myself with my own immense capacity for a murderous litany of the crimes he committed against his family. To his credit, Dad absorbed these daily attacks with patience and alacrity. Some days I was pouring it on with such violence that I found myself standing over him, screaming. Though I was trying to unleash the dark secrets he carried inside him, I was letting myself display a bloodletting portrait of the scar tissue covering my own soul. By holding my father accountable, I was offering irrefutable proof that I was his most violent son. By confronting Dad, I exposed myself and my flawed, incorrect view of myself as a softer, more sensitive version of my father.

My rage would engulf me and I'd lose my temper so many times, I failed to bring any relief to the existential suffering that overwhelmed me. So many times, I exhausted myself. I found hatred leaching me of both energy and hope. When I finished and collapsed back again in my chair, my anger was spent for the day. Dad waited for my seizures of spirit to run their course; then he would break his own code of silence and say, "Is the morning lecture over, sports fans? Surely you can drum up one more a-trocity that your poor old dad used to torture his poor family with. Surely there's something you've left out. Maybe I popped you on the fanny after you practiced for First Communion. There must be something you left out."

"I'll think of it tomorrow," I said.

"You make me out to be some o-gree. The other kids think you're full of crap. Though it goes against my better nature, I've got to believe my other kids are onto something. Carol says you've got a bad case of writer's angst," Dad said.

"What do you mean by 'angst'?" I asked him.

"Ha, thought you had me on that one," Dad said, roostering with pleasure. "Angst is what a writer feels when he can't write worth a shit."

Always Dad could bring an end to these morning matinees by making me laugh. He had an instinct for deflating a pretentious quality I brought to my complaints. Though I thought I was calling on my father to defend and explain himself, Dad outlasted me by the stubbornness he brought to denial. Never once did he admit to abusing us. Nor do I think I ever lit a fire on his shallow trench of emotions. He would listen to my grievances with a disinterested look in his cornflower-blue eyes—those extraordinary eyes that brought nightmares to the daydreams of North Korean infantry trying to establish bridgeheads on rivers whose names meant nothing to Americans. There was something staunch and heroic about his reaction to my version of the story of our life. I thought during these overcaffeinated sessions that I'd uncover every flaw in his line of defense. Instead, faced with his steadfastness, I exposed every single thing I hated about myself. On leaving, Dad would say, "Same time tomorrow. Try to work up some new material, jocko."

It was during those years that I discovered parts of our life I could tell Dad that would delight him. To my absolute dismay, I seemed to be one of the only members of my family who recalled anything of our history together. What the Conroys brought to memory was all erasure and blank slates. But I remembered some happy or funny times that pleased Dad.

"Do you remember the time you were in the bathroom and our box turtle moved out to crawl on your shoe? You screamed like a python had wrapped around your leg."

"Give a guy a break. Your mother and you were village weirdos about bringing beasts into the old domicile," Dad said. "I was a city boy, and I thought your mother was nuts about snakes and shit like that."

My mother had a fixation on snakes that I remember from a very young age. Because I was close to Grandpa Peek, I knew a lot about my mother's upbringing in the primitive Baptist Church. She never mentioned the Baptist Church when she raised her seven children, and it remained an area of obscurity in our spiritual makeup.

By marrying a Catholic, my mother had chosen a surefire way to alienate every member of her Piedmont clan and many of the Southern civilians who worked at the bases where Dad flew his fighter planes. After an apprenticeship in the octopus grip of Catholic nuns, we knew for certain our mother didn't know a single thing about the church she had joined as a very young woman. It was not until I was at The Citadel that the thought occurred to me that my mother had grown up in a sect of snake handlers.

We were living in Manassas, Virginia, when I was three and Carol Ann was one. Mom and Dad were walking on the rocks of a pristine river with a hardwood forest growing to the border of the mountain-fed stream. Carol Ann was riding piggyback on my father. With my father I watched as Mom knelt down and lifted a snake from the river. She held it up and displayed it to my father. "Don, be careful. Don't move. This is a cottonmouth moccasin. It can kill all of us with one bite. Watch out. We must've stumbled on a nest of them. Look, they're all around us."

Snake heads appeared close to every rock. I heard my father scream once, then take off over the rocks toward the shore, as nimble as a ballerina. My mother laughed so hard that I thought we'd both fall into the swift-moving stream. As he made his way back to the car, Dad was still screaming, and I watched Carol Ann bobbing up and down, gamely holding on to my father's ears. It was the same week that a filly turned around and bit my leg in a moment that made me forever afraid of horses. As a teenager, when I asked Mom about the story of the river, we both laughed at the memory. Mom admitted she'd lied about the cottonmouth moccasins. Instead, the snakes were nonvenomous water snakes, but to her constant joy, all snakes to Don were deadly killers whose bites could take even the strongest Marine to the ground.

Over the years, and especially in the inviolate forest behind our apartment in Cherry Point, I could find my mother an unlimited number of snakes. In a boyhood of overturned logs and hidden nests, I brought my mother a series of snakes she used to terrorize my father with when he returned home from his squadron. Once I scored with a copperhead, another time with a very angry rattlesnake, and finally, in the pièce de résistance of my serpent-hunting career, I brought home a deadly coral snake from the pinelands of Florida when we were visiting Uncle Russ's house in Pierson.

In my mom's favorite story about Dad's flying career, he crash-landed a Corsair on an abandoned airfield near New Bern, North Carolina. His cockpit was on fire, so Dad leaped out on his left wing to escape the burning plane. He saw two rattlesnakes lying close to where he was about to land. In his fear of snakes, he ran back through the burning cockpit and saved himself by leaping off the right wing and racing through the overgrown runway to the woods. Snakes became Mom's amulet against my father's explosiveness. He could slap her and she would run to my closet to pull out my snake-for-the-day that I had to release the next day where I found it. But twice, I remember observing scenes of Mom chasing Dad out of the house as she held a harmless grass snake as though it were a razor-sharp cutlass.

Later, I began to wonder whether the handling of snakes in the mountain country of Alabama was part of some elemental climax of her Sunday services. It might very well be true. When I was doing family research for this book, I stumbled across a great-grandfather who was pastor of a church on Sand Mountain, Alabama, which is the heart of the legendary mountaineers whose faith is so strong they lift rattlesnakes into the shaking air of faith and know that their passion for the Lord would protect them from the venom of all the diamond-headed snakes brought in to test the borderlines of their belief. I believe now that my mother was raised in such a church, but she left all that behind her when she became a Roman Catholic.

. . .

As the years went by, I thought the Santini wars were over for good when they roused themselves for one more showdown. In the early 1990s, I was living in San Francisco when my father fired off the latest retort from the fields of rancor. Barbra Streisand's movie version of *The Prince of Tides* was about to hit the multiplexes around the nation. It was a very difficult time in my life. I could feel that phantom ship of madness pull into port to harm me again. My beloved stepdaughter Emily had entered into her own period of breakdown and had tried to kill herself on several occasions. My marriage to Lenore was falling apart, and I didn't believe my good friend Tim Belk would live for another year. I was in the middle of writing *Beach Music*, the book that would bring my depression to bright fruition and send my life reeling off balance once again. In September of 1991, my father called me. His tone of buoyancy and gloating told me he had scored what he believed was a major victory in the cultural wars between us.

"You seen the new *Atlanta* magazine, pal? You might as well start waving a flag of surrender. I won the race. I won the sweepstakes. Vince Coppola exposes you for the lying asshole you really are. People've been calling from everywhere. My fellow Marines are over the top that you've finally been given your due, and everyone in Atlanta knows about the sack of shit you've become. But I've got a big heart, and I'll humbly accept your apology if you're on your knees when you give it."

"Gosh, Daddikins," I said from my home office in San Francisco, "you sound like you're reborn. Now calm down and explain your hysteria to me."

"No one's gonna believe a word you write after they read this shit."

Dad had bought so many copies of the magazine to send to friends and relatives, it took him nearly a week to find one to send to me.

Vince Coppola, a journalist I had met several times in the *Newsweek* office when I went to lunch with the bureau chief, Vern Smith, had hit upon a lodestone of an idea. I could acknowledge that in the very first reading. Vince Coppola entitled his article "The Great Santini Talks Back." In the new movie, the father portrayed as an abusive, uneducated shrimper brought back recurrent echoes of the harsh father in *The Great Santini*. Vince thought it would make a fascinating article that would offer insight into my family's predicament. As a writer of the family saga, I had become a figure of both enlightenment and betrayal. The brilliance of the article is that Vince gave voice only to Dad, my siblings, and Barbara, my first wife. He had no need for my rebuttal. I'd already had my say and told my story.

The article begins with the most extraordinary portrait of my father, a stunning photograph by Caroline Joe. If anyone ever doubts my father's dashing handsomeness, they need to study this photograph, which tells exactly about the bravado of the fighter pilot and his in-your-face aggressiveness as a man. Dad was one good-looking son of a bitch, and he'd dressed up in his tuxedo with his rows of military decorations over his heart. In his left hand he holds a cigar, and in his right, he makes a fist that he theoretically beat my mother with. His smile is a joker's smile, as though he were laughing at the preposterousness of his son's work.

The piece began with the explosive publication of *The Great Santini* in 1976, and my father's nuclear response to this event. But soon, my dad was being interviewed on talk shows and panels, "debating his son, arguing the finer points of parenting, and driving a car with a Santini license plate on the front bumper."

My sister Kathy said, "He—my father—decided he was going to love being a celebrity. It dawned on him: he could be more famous than Pat." Then Vince related the story of my writing an introduction to the book by Mary Edward Wertsch called *Military Brats*, in which I accused Don Conroy by his own name for the first time. "I grew up thinking my father would one day kill me."

My father's retort to this calumny was classic and pure Santini. He was discussing my trouble with writing anything that might resemble the truth of what happened, and said to Vince, "He had an ideal childhood . . . an ideal childhood. Not even close to being unhappy. He didn't turn out that bad . . . one of the best writers in the country . . . . Pat's an opportunist. Look at the bottom line. He found out by writing the way he does, he has a captive audience . . . all the women of America, all the do-gooders, all the bleeding hearts . . . all the psychiatrists. They love that kind of crap."

When I first read the article in San Francisco, I knew Vince Coppola had given me a priceless gift. Though I had confronted my dad with every single trauma he'd inflicted on his family, I could not get him to admit a thing or to articulate his coward's mythology of his own history with his family. Gloating and preening for the camera, he strutted his stuff and told his own version of events for the first time. Dad's mocking disapproval of my book held no surprise for me. Since the publication of *The Great Santini*, Dad had made a cottage industry out of mocking the book and the unreliable memory of the wanton, father-loathing son who wrote it. In his bottomless naïveté, Dad thought this would be the final word about the whole Santini affair, and that his exoneration from my charges against him would finally happen.

I got something of real value from the article. I noticed that Vince had not evoked a single response from my brothers, who refused his request for interviews. From the time the book hit town, my brothers had risen up as one to ratify my memories of events that took place in Dad's fearsome home. Kathy remembered nothing, as I long suspected, and I couldn't even get a conversation going with Carol Ann, so I knew Vince's chances were minuscule with her. She didn't return Vince's phone call, and I understood that the chief witness to my humiliation would never be called to testify on my behalf. Dad subsidized Carol Ann's entire writing life, and she had been on his dole since my mother's death.

But there was something in the article that shocked me profoundly. My first wife, Barbara, who had always been as articulate as she was pretty, talked about me as a father to our three girls. A frozen piece of tundra calved off and fell into arctic waters as I realized I was going to see my own fathering exposed to the world for the first time. Here are Barbara's words as they're recorded for this story:

"'Don was a wonderful grandfather to my three girls,' says Barbara Conroy. 'He never had an angry word for them. He'd come by after school and drive them to dental appointments. He'd take them to Six Flags. He was the only adult I knew who had a season ticket.'"

"What is suggested but left unsaid in the course of the long interview is that Don has proved himself a loving, more involved grandfather than the haunted, overwrought Pat has been a father."

"'Pat never laid a hand on them, never yelled,' Barbara makes clear. 'He tried to maintain a relationship, but Pat's very intimidating. He can make you feel like two cents, and if you mess up, he'll mention it every time for the next 10 years.'"

Barbara's assessment of me as a husband and a father held up very well to any scrutiny or excuse I could conjure up in defense of my flawed parenting. That I was intimidating is a hard fact and I'd rather not know that about myself. But it stands up strong as the truth of the matter. As the son of Santini and a knife-wielding mountain girl from Alabama, I was born with a fighter's blood inside me. For my entire life, I tried to control a temper that threatened all the dikes and levees I had set up for the rainy seasons. But my wives and children feared me and trembled at my approach. For me, that was proof that my life had been a failure in all the ways that were important to me. There was a stinging authority in Barbara's voice, a truthfulness that required no argument or commentary from me. I had wanted to be what I could not become—a good father and husband.

The article arrived a month before *The Prince of Tides* had its San Francisco debut. My stepdaughter tried to kill herself twice in that week bedazzled with parties and breakdowns. Once again, I found myself on the outer edge of a crackup of my own; I could feel the engines warming up inside me, and I knew that this one was going to be the worst of all. The task I set for myself was to get through the black voyage of spirit without killing myself. As Emily grew worse and her despair seemed bottomless and untouchable, I tried to ingest her sorrow into myself, thinking I could go to war with the demons that were threatening her life. Instead, my own temporal agony grew worse, and I could feel myself falling into the grave I'd dug for myself. When the festivities were finally over, I fled to Fripp Island and spent the rest of that decade in an act of recovery of spirit that I thought was beyond retrieval.

That breakdown hunted me down and found paradise in my damaged life as a man.

I wrote a letter to the editor about Vince Coppola's article. My father called me as soon as he read my off-the-nose rebuttal of his own story of his family's life.

He said, "I can't figure if you're more a piece of shit than you are a monkey-assed son of a bitch."

"Dad, that hurts my feelings," I said.

"You don't play fair," he whined. "If you don't play fair, how does a guy get his two cents in? I mean, this is such high-class bullshit that it leaves me no room to maneuver. I look like an asshole no matter what I say."

"You put yourself in a tough position, Dad," I argued.

"You're a sack of shit," Dad said. "Even my brothers are laughing their asses off at me."

"You gave me the opening," I said. "And aren't you kind of proud about the way I conducted the fight?"

"You're lower than whale dung that sits at the bottom of the sea."

My letter to *Atlanta* magazine:

I read Vince Coppola's fascinating piece about my father and was delighted to know I'd been raised, not by the Great Santini, but by St. Francis of Assisi. I thought I was the fiction writer in my family, but even I was breathless when my father described my childhood as though I were the eldest Von Trapp singer in The Sound of Music.

It hurt when Dad called me "an opportunist" and that I've found out by writing the way I do that I have a "captive audience: all the women in America, all the do-gooders, all the bleeding hearts, all the liberals, all the psychiatrists."

My self-composure melted like snow when I was confronted by the irrefutable truth of my father's testimony.

Don Conroy was nothing like the man I described in The Great Santini. *He was much more like Mother Teresa, and I remember him going around the neighborhood repairing the broken wings of songbirds, cooking nutritious meals for shut-ins, coaching wheelchair–bound children for the Special Olympics and cleansing the wounds of lepers with his flight jacket. In his spare time, he also taught Gregorian chant to Down's syndrome children, ran a softball league for retired Sisters of Mercy, and gathered healthy soul-food recipes for a nursing home full of blind, diabetic black women. He translated these recipes into braille.*

When he first developed the stigmata (the five wounds of Christ appearing on his hands, feet, and side), he could no longer control a flight stick and had to retire from the Marine Corps.

But I lied about that, too. Dad was never in the Marine Corps. He made his living as a beautician and a manicurist and in his spare time he did Judy Garland impersonations in select clubs around the area. My mother divorced him when he began singing off-key.

If you believe Dad's version of my childhood, I thought you might believe anything. But that's another story.

Pat Conroy, San Francisco

Meanwhile, I tried to rush a novel into print. I took inventory of my life and came to the conclusion that I'd been clinically depressed for most if not all of my adult years. I had always wanted to live in San Francisco, but I wanted to love it more after I moved there. My wife, Lenore, got caught up in the whirlpool of high society, a place I had no desire to be a part of, yet I went along with it because Lenore was in the middle of trying to cure something untouchable from the rude childhood she had loathed in Brooklyn. The death of so many friends from AIDS exacted a visible toll on me, and the death of two Southern friends brought me to my knees. On one night, I attended a birthday party for Herb Caen, a journalist I had long revered, at a baronial dance at the Fairmont hotel. And the next day I sat and held the hands of young men who would be dead in a matter of weeks. I went to dozens of fancy-Dan parties in my two years spent on Presidio Avenue. Though I came to that magnificent city for many reasons, I didn't come there to grow shallow.

Toward the end of my time in that timeless city where the sound of foghorns was as lonely as the cry of gulls, I was struck by a car in the intersection of a four-way stop sign near our house. When I saw that I was going to get hit, I turned my body so my back and buttocks could absorb the blow. I somersaulted over the hood of the car, turned upside down, was cut by the windshield wiper on the cheek, then landed on my feet in some miraculous finish. A woman was driving and her husband started beating her with his fists while screaming that she was a worthless bitch.

My cue had sounded and I rushed into the breach, banging on the windows and telling the man to stop hitting that woman.

"I can hit my wife anytime I want to, you nosy bastard," he yelled back.

"Get out of here before I start beating you!" I screamed.

They disappeared and drove toward whatever destiny they were fulfilling. I didn't get their address or phone number or the make of their car. When I entered the house, I had nothing of proof to memorialize the encounter. But the next two months I spent as an invalid crucified to my bed. The pain immobilized me. When I went to the bathroom, I was in danger of falling every time. Unfortunately for my wife, I learned something deal-breaking about Lenore. Whenever we woke up in the morning, she would ask me whether I felt better. Usually I'd answer, "Worse, I feel much worse." Without hesitance, Lenore would answer with two words: "Shit," followed by a quick, explosive, "Fuck." One of the kids would bring me breakfast, a maid would bring me lunch, and one of the kids would bring me dinner as the sun entered on the soft-gliding slipstream of the fierce Western horizon. For sixty days, I studied the rooftops of San Francisco, which I found as comforting and intricate as latticework. During this drifting, worried time of my life, I continued my vast project of self-improvement and read Robert Musil's *The Man Without Qualities* and James Joyce's unreadable, pretentious novel *Finnegans Wake*. Both novels stank up the landfill, and I spent the rest of purgatory in the hands of John Fowles and the many pleasures of *Daniel Martin*, which became one of my favorite books after the forced march in full gear through the impenetrable mangrove swamps of Musil and Joyce.

During this time, I felt like a shut-in locked in the turret of a medieval castle. I spent much of my life alone praying for a novel to present itself in a form that would light an interior fire in me and attract readers at the same time. But all my days, I found myself with a need for conversation and friendship after I had wrestled with the aching loneliness of the English language. In San Francisco, except for Tim Belk, I found myself cut off from the stimulating conversation of friends. As I thought about this painful isolation and incurable solitude, I finally figured out that Lenore had isolated me from all the friends I had brought to our marriage. Because she was merciless and conniving, I found myself in my late forties facing a loneliness that cut like a horse's bite. Into this vacuum I heard a woman's voice, and it was calling out my name.

Before my back went out, the loveliest woman imaginable came up to talk to me at a party. She approached me, and we began talking easily. She was a great reader and was selling screenplays in Hollywood, near where she had grown up on a farm in the Los Angeles area. Her name was Sylvia Peto, and her marriage to the glass artist Dale Chihuly was winding down at a rapid pace. Before she left the party, Sylvia said, "Pat, you are aware that your wife hates you, aren't you? If not, everyone else in this room knows it."

She began calling me every day, and we'd always speak for more than an hour. She too found herself locked into a loveless marriage, and our histories floated out to meet each other in the middle of San Francisco Bay. I was crazy in love with her and had forgotten what that rare concoction of the spirit was like. I told her every story of my life and tried to leave nothing out. I'm still shocked I did not marry this woman, but she and I both underestimated my capacity for breakdown. I began my longest season as a likely suicide. It cost me the love of this fabulous woman, and making love to her was like a form of communion to me. One day, I hope to get to write a novel praising her for her intervention into my collapsed and hopeless life. She deserved much better than me, and I pray she found it.

Though the doctors could find nothing odd in the X-rays they took of my spine, they decided to operate to see whether they could find something by opening me up. After the operation, the surgeon told me that he had found a fragment of spine, shaped like an arrowhead, that had floated into my sciatic nerve. When I got on the elevator to go home, Lenore told friends I burst into tears, I was so happy to be returning to my home. I wept and couldn't help it, but I was weeping not because of any joy in the homecoming, but because I inhabited a loveless home, and one where I couldn't depend on my wife to take care of me.

"I will not die with this woman at my side," I promised myself in secret.

Lenore told me when we got back to the house, "I've always hated sickrooms and invalids. I just can't stand it, and it's nothing I can help."

"You make it very clear, Lenore," I said.

That night I called my father, who was staying at Kathy's house in Beaufort.

"I'm coming home, Dad," I said. "I'm a very unhappy man."

"You're married to a jerk," he said. "C'mon home and we'll take care of you. You need a good shot of family. We'll snap you right out of it."

A week later, I took a flight to Savannah, and my father was there to meet me. I almost fell apart with gratitude when I saw him. I'd been running away from him for my entire life—now I was home to stay. I needed a dad to take care of me.

CHAPTER 18

Don and the Chicago Irish

Whenever I go to Chicago, that city of winds and fog-horns and calloused hands, I'm always a stranger on arrival and a stranger when I leave. It should not be so. My father was as marked by the stockyards and railroad freight yards as Studs Lonigan was. When I read Saul Bellow's psalm to the city, the immortal *The Adventures of Augie March*, I felt cheated out of a natural birthright. The streets of the city should flow through my veins in rivers of green dye, but Chicago will always remain a part of my life I never got to live. My father bragged about Chicago almost every day, making it sound like the prince of rough-hewn cities, where the Irish had escaped the potato famine to embrace a new, all-enfolding destiny. Growing up, I knew nothing about Chicago, and Ireland was nothing but a sundered worrisome canker on each Irish soul. Though my father reigned as the most grotesque of Irish Catholic males, I never knew the origins of his blue-collar crudeness. In my high school years, my dad grew enraged as I went through the works of Shakespeare, Dickens, Thackeray, Hardy, and Austen.

"They write in the enemy's language. Plus, the Irish write a lot better than the English," Dad said with that air of authority backed up by nothing but wishful thinking.

"What Irishmen should Pat and I read to catch up on the genius of the Irish?" Mom asked him.

My father could not name a single Irish author of note, much to my mother's delight. Chicago was the great mystery of my childhood— Ireland the black hole, a secret frigate moving angry men and contraband through my bloodstream.

Whenever I came to Chicago to sign books, I never told my father's family that I was arriving, because some of them had humiliated me when my first book came out. One distant cousin really liked *The Water Is Wide*, calling it my "book about the niggers." At the time, I could get that same response in the South, and my patience for it on the shores of Lake Michigan wore out fast.

Even so, my lines at signings in Chicago have been long, enthusiastic ones, and my name has attracted a lot of attention for a long time. When I signed at Marshall Field's in 1980, it was big news among the Chicago Conroys and represented some healing of their broken spirits in the new world. I'd never heard of Marshall Field's and couldn't make out what all the fuss was about.

But over and over again, I would sign books for Irish Catholics who bought my books only because I was an Irish Catholic, which took me by surprise.

"When are you going to write a book about being an Irish Catholic raised in Chicago?" a hundred Irishmen and -women have asked me.

"I don't know a single thing about growing up Irish Catholic here," I responded.

"Why not?" I'd be asked. "Your name is Pat Conroy, and it doesn't get any more Irish than that. Where'd your father live?"

"On Bishop Street," I'd reply.

More than a few times, I'd be answered, "It's all niggers now."

This is how I learned that Chicago was as racist as Birmingham in its most primitive years. It surprised me, because I believed that an oppressed people like the Irish would have a great national compassion for a group that suffered as much as the blacks have. Yet, as I visited Chicago more often, I came to believe it was as racist and ethnically polarized in a mean, rather careless kind of way as any city on earth. It was a municipal sport for every ethnic group to hate every other ethnic group. Chicago seemed to have a meat-eating gift for it.

In 1986, *The Prince of Tides* was published, making the largest splash of any book I'll ever write. When I got off in Chicago on my book tour, the climate of the city itself had changed for me. After being driven to the hotel, I was delivered to a restaurant where I was to have lunch with Mayor Richard Daley and his charming wife, Maggie. To be honest, I think Mrs. Daley was the only member of her family who had read the novel, but she was curious about its origins and asked smart questions. Maggie talked about books with grace and ease, then brought up the inevitable Chicago story—"When are you going to write a book about the South Side Irish?" Again, I had to disclose my ignorance of the subject, but Maggie and the mayor promised me limitless access to men and women who could tell me everything I would need to know.

"But that's research," I said. "That's not living a life."

"Just pretend," pretty Maggie said. "Just make it up and no one will know the difference."

Though more reserved and watchful than his wife, Mayor Daley started talking about his own Irish childhood, which seemed to have left him with a serious sense of responsibility, but not much time to be a child. Like all of the Chicago Irish, he was a huge White Sox fan, and it was some mark of baptism that never wore off. He told me that his children were more fanatical than he and Maggie. They both had wanted to move to a beautiful house in the northern section of the city, but his children rebelled because it would put the Daley family into the heart of the city where Chicago Cubs fans were most numerous and loudmouthed. While he explained that bit of ephemera, I observed the obeisance of the waitstaff at the front of the house, and I felt like I was eating with some exiled Irish king. He wore his power well, but I would not have wanted to cross the man. If he'd taken a strong dislike to me, I could envision being picked up for speeding ten or fifteen times on my way to the airport.

Among my father's relatives, my luncheon with the Daleys took on mythic proportions, the kind that transform a family's destiny on a hard new continent. My uncle Willie, aunt Marge, and uncle Jim took special pleasure in my relating every word spoken to the most untouchable family of Irish renown in the history of Chicago.

My relationship with Aunt Marge had its bumps and sharp corners from the beginning. Marge is a six-foot Catholic nun who could hit a softball as far as her brothers and had the charming habit of swatting her nieces and nephews across the room with a squidlike arm. "It's my love pat to the kids," she would say, as another Conroy nephew went flying across the room.

Marge could punch with the best of them and drink with the worst of them. In Chicago's Irish community, there was enough priest worship and nun euphoria to stop a lesser religion in its tracks. In fact, the fanaticism of Catholicism among Irish Catholics seems one of their least attractive qualities. All critical thinking seems to stop at the holy water font near the front door.

As a Catholic boy growing up in the South, I bought the whole program without caveat or discouraging word. In my final years at The Citadel, I thought my faith endangered, so I persuaded Reverend James Hopwood to open up the new chapel every day. I went there to fight off my transfiguring doubt about my religion with an avalanche of the Eucharist. Father Hopwood met me on a daily basis in the year that I felt my faith slipping away. The priest's generosity could not stem the tides of my incoming apostasy, however. I'd been set on fire by Vatican II and saw a church I could fall in love with. With the death of John XXIII, I began to lose the faith of my forefathers.

Several times, over many years, I've asked my brother Mike what he remembers from his Chicago visits.

"Nothing," he says. "Not a single thing."

"Oh, c'mon, Mike," I nudge. "You were in a younger generation. Surely you saw things that Carol and I missed."

"You didn't miss anything, because nothing happened. Look, Kathy, Jim, and I got to Chicago three times at the most. We learned the Irish were awful to their kids. Big surprise. We knew that from Dad. They'd hole us up in our bedroom while they took over the basement, where they played pinochle and the aunts danced to Uncle Willie's shitty music."

"Did they take you to any museums?" I asked.

"What museums?" Mike said. "I didn't know there was one in town. After Kathy graduated from Beaufort High School, we drove to Chicago to attend a graduation party for our cousin Chrissie Huth.

They made a real big deal out of it, but no one knew our sister Kathy's name. Hell, they didn't know any of us, and our grandparents didn't seem to know or care whether we were alive."

Brother Jim said, "Because of Mom, we weren't considered to be Irish, or even Catholic. We were like hitchhikers through their lives."

Despite myself, I kept running into the open propellers of my Chicago family's sensibility, often without knowing what I was doing. When I was on business in the city in the mid-eighties, my father asked me to drop by and see his family, because his mother had been under the weather lately. I arrived for dinner with a beloved Houghton Mifflin sales rep, Dana Baylor, who brought me to Uncle Willie's house in the Polish neighborhood where he spent the last half of his life. Neither my father nor my relatives informed me that Grandma Conroy was in the last stages of an active and violent form of Alzheimer's. The family, of course, pretended she had a bad case of the flu.

At the front door, Dana was making plans to meet me for breakfast when Grandma Conroy roared out of her bedroom like a harridan. Making a race for the door with her strange, unkempt coiffure sticking up a foot in the air, she went straight on the attack with me and poor Dana.

Now, there is nothing funny about Alzheimer's disease and I fear it more than any disease on earth. It has swept through my family like a plague, and it's difficult to deal with and to bear. My grandmother had become pathetic. But my long dislike of her had stopped up the valves of pity, so I watched her approach toward me and Dana with a wary eye.

Grandma screamed out, "Are you two fucking? That's what it looks like to me. I can smell it all over you."

I watched the heels of Dana's shoes as they sprinted down the walkway to her car and she yelled that I would see her for breakfast the next morning. Turning toward the group, I could feel the collective relief from the family that the secret of Grandma's illness now was part of the Southern narrative. Shaken by the encounter, I sat down to a meal of Uncle Willie's famous Italian meatball pasta, which was an abomination to the spirit of Italian cuisine. My grandmother took her place at the head of the table and stared me down with a cobralike hatred I could not mollify.

As the bowl passed into the hands of my grandma, she picked up a meatball and bounced it off my face, leaving a red stain of pasta sauce on my cheekbone. In silence, I wiped my face, then heard Sister Marge and her raucous laughter hee-hawing.

"Now Pat's been baptized by Maw. She still has a strong arm," Aunt Marge said.

Uncle Ed added, "And throws with accuracy."

Uncle Willie could barely contain his mirth and reloaded the pasta bowl. Within a minute she had inked my face with three well-placed meatballs that splattered each time they hit. When she ran out of meatballs, she began hurling handfuls of undercooked pasta that draped from my shoulders like some freakish Medusa's hair. The uncles and aunts screamed with laughter as each assault was delivered, but no one was much surprised when I ran from the table, cleaned up in the bathroom, and asked Uncle Willie to take me to the Roosevelt Hotel.

"Oh, he's too good to stay here. He's got to put his shoes under a bed at the Roosevelt," Uncle Willie mocked.

"I signed a contract with the publishing company," I said. "I sleep where they tell me to sleep."

"Part of the job," said my uncle Ed, the youngest and most successful member of the family.

"I think he's just got the big head," Aunt Mary said.

"I'm going out," I said. "It's been such a pleasure to get to know Dad's family better."

It was the last time I ever saw my grandmother, who died when I was living in Italy. I went to the Vatican to light a candle and have a mass said for the repose of her soul. It brought me into a larger family, denied to me, and I felt like a good little Irish Catholic for the first time in my life. My father and his family believe in the Church as unquestioning believers all set on autopilot. The rosary was the special province of Father Jim, who could utter it without a trace of adoration to cut through its repetitive lines. When Uncle Jim said the mass, there was not an ounce of awe or mystery when he lifted the host into the air and turned bread into the living, bleeding entity of Christ. Without ecstasy, the mass is a puppet show with human hands. But that's the promise the Catholic Church always contains, heirlooms of priceless beauty formed from texts of the New Testament. That the church has let itself slide into the bloat and agues of its worst self is utterly repugnant. Among the choices of the world, there are many forms the Catholic Church may take, and for rigidity and suppression, there is none more disgraceful and gaudier than the liturgy debauched by the Irish Catholic Church. If there were no doctrine of hell, there would be no need for such a church at all. It's one of the heart murmurs that has degraded Ireland for me.

There is a submerged Atlantis that overwhelms the immigrant and brings almost everyone who claims to be Irish to his or her collective, nostalgic knees. Ireland is a scattered nation, and my family is part of a great, damaged tribe obsessed with exile. My father once gave yearly donations to the Irish Republican Army. He and I almost had a fistfight when I found out about it.

"You raised me to avoid killing the innocent," I said.

"Then I raised you wrong," he said. "In Ireland, anything goes."

"Raise an army, uniform them, arm them, and meet the enemy on a common field of battle," was my argument.

"Study geography. That doesn't work in Ireland," he said.

"Study philosophy; the terrorists are the lowest scum on earth," I said, our voices growing louder.

"Not when they're Irish," Dad said. "Then they're heroes beyond compare."

"Did everybody stupid leave Ireland during the potato famine?" I asked.

Dad answered, "No, we left a few idiots behind. Guys like you."

One of the reasons I had moved to San Francisco in 1989 was to be near my friend Tim Belk who was dying of AIDS. It was a time of the uneasy rule of death in San Francisco, where boys died impoverished and alone in squalid hotels in the Tenderloin. Tim and I made it our mission to hunt out Southern boys abandoned by their families, disgusted by their homosexuality, and left to die alone. We had our work cut out for us.

During early work among these suffering boys, I gave an interview to *San Francisco Focus* magazine. Surprising me, the editor, Amy Rennert, interviewed me about a subject I had rarely considered: my Irishness. Her questions sank like depth charges, but it has been part of my nature and my belief system that I'd answer any question I was asked by a legitimate reporter. So I let loose on the Irish for the first time, and it wasn't pretty.

I admitted that I knew not a single thing about my Irish heritage—from Dingle to a dingle berry. What I knew about St. Patrick's Day is that Dad would come home drunk and beat me up, so the day took on some of the characteristics of Kristallnacht to me. Without my knowledge, the mooncalf bedlam of Ireland had filled me with an incurable anxiety, an uncontrollable temper, a tendency to abuse alcohol, a stubbornness I found both repellent and incurable, and a tendency to always think I'm right. What a screwed-up legacy this hard-hearted island left to me.

What I didn't know when I conducted the interview was that San Francisco was a thoroughly Irish city. I thought it was a city of gay guys in the Castro District, vegetarians in the Haight, Italians in North Beach, and Maoists from the universities—but the swarm of Irishmen who attacked me (with perfect justification) did so with an insider knowledge that I lacked. I had guys hopping off bar stools all over the city ready to fistfight me for the honor of the old country. After that article, I could never go into Harringtons Bar and Grill again. The bartender at the Washington Square Bar and Grill, Michael McCourt, told me why the interview was so incendiary: "You said about the Irish what we think of ourselves. But we hate the Irish mick who spills the news to the Brits and everyone else."

"What can I do to change the perception?" I asked Michael.

"Nothing. You're dead meat in this town among the Irish," he replied.

Michael was always telling me that his brother Frank was writing a book about growing up in a poor Irish family in the homeland. "Watch for it. It's called *Angela's Ashes*. One thing you forgot to say about the Irish: We can write our asses off."

This interview followed me wherever I went, even up in the larger

Irish community out of New York. There began a long, intense struggle to bring me back into the fold. But my marriage was falling apart, and yet again, I was beginning the long process of coming undone in the hundred vestibules of my own soul. Breakdowns were common to me by then, and I attributed them to that sour Irish gene, but could cast plenty of blame on my washed-in-the-blood-of-the-lamb Southern roots also. Taken together it looked like a wicked combination of destinies—Irish and Southern, forming a comfortable birthplace for lunatics, nutcases, borderlines, and psychos. I could not blame everything on a bar fight in Galway when I also had the smoldering fires of white-lightning smoking in a copper coil off Sand Mountain, Alabama.

In 1996, I left San Francisco forever, then flew to Dublin when *Beach Music* came out. I went on the Gay Byrne show that night, the only television show I'd ever been on that seemed to be watched by an entire country. On my first appearance, Gay Byrne, a witty and urbane man whom I liked immediately, asked whether I still had any relatives in Ireland. Before my trip began, I asked my father that exact question and he answered, "Nope. Not a single one. They up and left for Chicago."

"Dad," I said, "that's impossible."

He answered, "There's not a single Conroy left in Ireland. When our family decides to do something, we do it right. We're stubborn in that kind of way."

By the time I left the Gay Byrne show that night, I had a list of more than two hundred phone numbers and addresses of people who claimed to be direct relatives of my father and me and had genealogy charts to prove it. A whole nation of Irish Conroys were ready to receive me. Their notes were more than welcoming.

The next day I signed books at a store not too far from the post office where the 1916 insurrection had begun, and three blocks from where my maternal great-grandfather, James P. Hunt, was born—both of which were unknown facts to my father. As I went in to sign books I could not help but notice that hundreds of Irishmen and -women had assembled at my table. They could not've been more cordial to me. They talked easily about the lost generation, the inhuman perfidy of the English, the devastation of their loss of a million young Irishmen to the American shores, and their infinite pride in Irishmen who kept the suppressed and mythic tongues of the Gaelic tradition alive in our own take on English prose. Though one Dubliner issued me a warning when he said I was lucky to have been part of the immigration and made my way out of mean-spirited Ireland. When I asked him what he was talking about, he said, "If you'd been born in Ireland, we'd have ripped you apart and mocked your talent, and laughed at your presumption to be something you're clearly not."

"You do that to your own people?" I asked. "Why would you do that?"

"The Irish are great debunkers of one another," he said. "No one sticks his head above the tulip fields or we knock him down to size. You're from off . . . so we give you a pass."

"Not in Chicago, they don't," I told him. But the man had left my table quickly and brought me back a book entitled *The Art of Irish Debunking*.

It was a good trip for me and helped me understand the artillery fire of put-downs I always received when I traveled unarmed through my father's relatives.

. . .

Yet Ireland stayed inside me, a disapproving moon throwing out a scant light. I began to read the histories and texts that would open Ireland up to me, seeking to find a guidance system that would allow me some compassion for this island I didn't understand. My own history of being Irish was so brutish that it seemed like a blight on my soul. I found myself soused with a hatred I did not need or want.

In my boyhood, everyone who hit me was Irish, from my father to his brothers and sisters, to the nuns and priests who taught me, so I perceived Ireland as a nation hateful to children and cruel to wives. But as I read, I learned the role of England in one of the most monstrous occupations possible. England turned a dark country into a black-hearted, despairing one. If the tides of history had flowed in a different pattern, I would have spoken and written in Gaelic. I learned about Pádraic Ó Conaire of Galway, who was a celebrated modern writer in the old language. The translation of his name is Pat Conroy. Deep in me, Ireland lived in some indiscoverable shell of sorcery. Though I could deny it a thousand times, I could feel the surge of Ireland on my tongue and in my bloodstream. I could not place it, nor put it in some tortoiseshell box. But I could not write an English sentence without the Irish Sea splashing it with seawater. For so long I'd looked upon myself as a Southern writer and nothing else that this new supplicant for my attention caught me by surprise. Because my name has such an aggressive Irish finality to it, it caught me unprepared when I discovered the American Irish community had become proud of me. It both pleased and troubled me.

In the year before he died, my father came into my house at Fripp Island and began sorting through my mail. During that last year, he disturbed me in my writing room only one time. He knocked on the door of my office with a cane.

"Get out of here!" I yelled.

"It's your beloved father, son," Dad said.

"The guy who beat me half to death when I was a kid?" I said.

"Oh, you're not back to that old chestnut, are you?"

I said, "I like that old chestnut."

"I like this letter," Dad said. "I'd like you to do this, son, and forget for a minute that you're the biggest pain in the ass in America."

The formal letter was an invitation from President Bill Clinton to join a group of American citizens, mostly Irishmen and -women, at a rally for a peace settlement that he was organizing and attending in both Northern Ireland and the Republic to the south. As an Irish American writer, I was invited to attend and participate, as was William Kennedy, a writer I revered from Albany, New York. I wrote back that I was pleased to be included and considered it a high honor.

My father drove me to the airport in Charleston and said to me, "The IRA is agreeing to a cease-fire. Try not to be a loudmouth."

I was not a loudmouth and took great pleasure in meeting some of the most prominent Irish Americans alive. Being in *Air Force Two* seemed more like a meeting in some great hallway of a cruise ship, where the talk was bracing and serious and unhindered. Most on board were veterans of trying to bring peace to the two intractable sides, religious and political leaders who had spent their whole lives working on the subject of the Irish peace movement. These were realists who knew how promising the stakes were and how elusive an actual settlement was going to be. I looked forward to a relaxing and intellectual trip. I couldn't have been more wrong.

That delegation to Ireland worked from early morning to late night. En masse, we attended meetings so boring that the droning voices could induce comalike states in hamsters. In one meeting near the Belfast harbor, we were listening to a beelike man drone on in a free-fire zone of statistics, when there was a vicious attack on America from an Orangeman who opposed all peace treaties with Irish Catholics. He was voluble and insulting, and I waited for the two politicians leading our stupefied group to answer this upstart with sharp words of their own. One was a former governor of South Carolina, Richard Riley, who was now secretary of education. The other was a black, charismatic man named Ron Williams, who would die in a plane crash in the fog of the Balkans shortly after this trip was done. The problem was that both men were sound asleep, as exhausted and bored as the rest of us. But two aides awoke them and they both came out of their slumber eloquent and adroit, and argued toe-to-toe with the Ulsterman for the next ten minutes.

Ah, I thought, the United States is well represented here—from sleep to fiery replies the men awoke to defend their country's interests with flair and passion. I thought our country lucky to have them working for us.

After endless meetings and parties and speeches, I began to get some sense of how important the work was here. I tried to talk to many politicians from Northern Ireland who represented the English side, and felt the same quicksilver power of their fierce love of the country above the borderline of Ireland. Their patriotism was very moving to me.

One day I found myself taking a piss by Gerry Adams, the president of Sinn Féin, who was one of the great movers behind the disarmament of the IRA. "Hey, Gerry?" I said. "Can you guys quit this bullshit? No guns and bombs. Can you help bring this about?"

He looked at me and said, "Yes, I think it's possible. That's why we've gathered here."

But most of the trip centered around President Clinton and a series of speeches that he gave outlining what America wanted to accomplish at these talks. He was elegant, precise, and elliptical when it came to the specifics to be worked out. Though I watched him address the parliaments of both the north and south of Ireland, it was when Bill Clinton took to the streets to address the people that I saw the real genius of the man. Not once did it occur to me that an entire foreign nation could fall in love with an American president. It was a certain incendiary love, driven by the passion and the attractive charms of the man that he could spread like pollen across the ground. If I complained about our workload, the president and Mrs. Clinton were on a schedule five times more arduous, and I never saw a harder-working man or woman in my life. The ecstasy of those Irish crowds invigorated the president, and he responded by setting them ablaze for all the possibilities of the future. I saw him wade into crowds, and for the first time realized that the world of politics was of a religious nature, and that there was the need for leaders to rise above their worst instincts and to teach people to rise up to their own finest. Bill Clinton made the Irish people long for a peace that was long overdue. You could feel the immensity of his belief in the country as he lifted his voice to address as equals the folks who wore orange and the people of the green. It was a great thing to be a part of. It made my heart ache for all I had lost by not being raised an Irishman.

When Dad picked me up from the airport, I was still emotional and exhausted from the trip. We did not speak until Dad turned on Highway 17 to Beaufort.

"Well?" Dad finally said.

I had brought back melancholy and an inspirited sense of hope from the journey, and I said, "Ireland, Dad, poor Ireland."

"Fuck you," Dad said.

I laughed out loud and said, "Dad, those two words might make you the greatest philosopher in the history of Ireland."

"The only thing I regret is that I never got to kill an Ulsterman," Dad said, his lips a tight line, like a disrupted border.

"I think there's a chance of peace," I said. "There're still a lot of assholes like you on both sides, but there's a chance."

"Fuck you. Could you keep up with the ball scores when you were gone?" he asked.

"Yeah, I did, Dad."

"That's all that counts," he said. "I think the Bears'll be loaded this year."

"Ireland," I said to Dad. "It's an amazing place. You should have let me know, Dad."

And thus it went between father and son during the last years of his life, when I finally made my own baffled and steadfast peace with Ireland.

CHAPTER 19

The Arcs

When my father retired from the Marine Corps, he took up a hobby that most of his children thought odd, but I found both eerie and uncomfortable. He started collecting photographs and newspaper clippings in large albums he called "the Archives," or, as it was later referred to in the family, "the Arcs." Before he died my father had assembled more than two hundred of these over-stuffed, chockablock volumes full of history and memorabilia. One thing that caused me deep embarrassment was that because of my own public life, "the Arcs" were heavily weighted toward the record keeping of my career. Though he included everything that he could muster up about my siblings, including class pictures and report cards, my presence in these spilling-out albums of record seemed oceanic and nearly pornographic to me.

"Dad, you've got to cut out this monkey business. Eventually it's going to hurt the kids' feelings," I said when he handed his labor-intensive handiwork to me.

"The kids love the Arcs as much as I do," Dad said. "We all like seeing Conroys kicking ass in the world around them."

"Eventually it's going to drive Carol nuts," I argued. "And she's borne me nothing but ill will since the day I started writing."

"It'll encourage her to write more poetry and get her name in the froufrou magazines. That stuff'll be great for the Arcs."

"It's unbalanced," I protested.

"It's history," Dad said.

One reason that Dad's fixation on the presentation of every interview or article written about me went against my grain was an incident in my senior year at Beaufort High School. Coming back from his squadron, Dad caught me red-handed as I was cutting out an article celebrating the game I'd played against the heavily favored Chicora High School out of Charleston. I'd scored thirty-six points, and an attendance record was set that majestic night. The article was so wonderful that I wanted it as a keepsake. I could look at it forever. Then my father made his surprise entry and caught me in an act of self-worship. He told me never to get the "big head" again or he'd slap it plumb out of me, so I never saved another article. It came as an utter shock that my father was doing it for me. In one of the earlier Arcs I discovered that article of my play against Chicora High, and realized that my father must have cut it out and saved it over many years. This act was not only a surprise; it forced me to look at my father in a far different way.

The Arcs were ambitious in their completion and wholeness of vision. If Mike and Jim came to visit Dad and attend a Braves game, the tickets were recorded with a sardonic commentary from the colonel. Whenever *The New York Times* presented me with bad reviews, my father would remark, "*The New York Times* sure doesn't like my boy." When Carol Ann asked for five thousand dollars for a dental emergency, Dad noted that she endured such emergencies each year, then wrote, "That girl has more teeth than a crocodile." Although my dad was the recording angel of the Arcs, they also emphasized a strange flaw in my father's character. As I have browsed through the Arcs in researching this book, I discovered that Dad had stolen much of what was in them from my mailbox. He pocketed the letters from big names—a handwritten note from Barbra Streisand, a letter from President Jimmy Carter and two from his wife, Rosalynn. He cadged a letter from Martin Scorsese asking whether I was interested in writing a film for him. At the time I'd have given up the last knuckle on my pinkie finger to work with Mr. Scorsese, but Dad got to the mailbox before I did, and I didn't see the letter until ten years later. There were letters from agents, editors, and publishers, and one from Alfred A. Knopf telling me that he and his wife considered *The Prince of Tides* to be a masterpiece. I mention that letter because it could have helped cure the insecurities and incapacitating doubt that every writer brings to the writing table. Many writers think we're nothing but poseurs and self-aggrandizing impostors, and those thoughts can drive us to destruction and madness. And any writer who claims otherwise is a liar and a bullshit artist whose work should be avoided at all costs.

When work was being done on my house at Fripp in the mid-nineties, I moved to Asheville, North Carolina, and took a place at Longchamps Apartment House with a superb view of the city below. The ghosts of Thomas Wolfe and F. Scott Fitzgerald still lingered in the mountain-circled town that was in the rapid process of becoming one of the most enchanting cities in the country. Even in the time I lived there, it was Birkenstock-happy and heading toward a gluten-free paradise. Dad was with me when I laid a rose on Thomas Wolfe's grave, as I tried to do every time I visited the town on my own.

"I love this man for making me want to be a writer," I said.

"You'll never be in his league, son," Dad said. "As far as I can tell, you're eating his jock."

"I don't care. He brought me to the dance, Dad," I said, happy that I had led him to this sacred ground to see the fountainhead of my career.

"I bet nobody builds a museum in a house you lived in," Dad said.

"You're right, Dad. I lived in twenty houses before I got to Beaufort."

In the spring of 1996, I received a phone call from my sister Kathy informing me that Dad was in the naval hospital in Beaufort in danger of dying from heart congestion. Though I was dating a wonderful woman in Asheville, Irene Jurzyk, whom I'd known as a writer in Atlanta, my life was moving me south and homeward. Several days before, I'd received a phone call from the son of the late, nonpareil poet James Dickey, who had once taught me in a poetry workshop at the University of South Carolina. I had read Mr. Dickey's obituary with obsessive interest. I realized that his death was going to establish a backlash against his life and work. His machismo was of an in-your-face variety mostly found in sumo wrestlers or inside linebackers. He made no adjustments for the rise of feminism or even the civil rights movement. There was something Southern as well as a tricky refusal to adjust his beliefs to fit the fashions of his day. He was a natural conservative who fought a lifelong rearguard battle against that most imposing foe—the future. He was more like my father than any man I've ever met, and, like Dad, I'd come to view him as part of my destiny in my love-hate relationship with the fraught, hardscrabble world of men.

"Pat, my dad's family and I would love you to do the eulogy for my father," Chris Dickey said when he called.

Though it caused me some pain, I said, "I've got to be honest with you, Chris. I didn't like your father very much. I avoided him like the plague after I left his classes."

"That doesn't necessarily rule you out, Pat," Chris said. I was not expecting such honesty in such a situation. "But from what I hear, you loved his writing," he added.

"I revered his writing. I always will," I said.

"Then we've got a deal," Chris said. "I've had my own problems with Dad."

So I found myself on the exquisite horseshoe-shaped arena that is the pride of the University of South Carolina, with a bright pool of writers in attendance and a decent crowd for the best Southern poet who ever lived—hell, let me be not shy; in my opinion James Dickey is the greatest American poet who ever lived, and that poetry sprang from a bloodstream made by God, and his language changed the way I thought about art itself. I tried to give him a rip-roaring farewell and honor the man with a missing plane formation of fighter planes, like I'd done for my father at the end of *The Great Santini*.

When I reached the podium above the manicured grass, the sun was shining so bright I could not read the eulogy I had prepared for my great teacher. I tried to adjust the yellow legal sheets and shift them out of the sunlight when I looked up and heard a building call out to me. I was looking at the shadow of the Cornell Arms for the first time in my life, the building my brother had plunged off on the night he died. One of my first acts after hearing about Tom was to read Dickey's poem "The Leap," which is written in perfect pitch and wonder at the suicide of a girl Dickey knew in elementary school who leaped to her death from a skyscraper after her life had proved impossible to live. Though

I've many flaws as a writer, some egregious, I've no trouble with the language of praise. I thanked the poet for all the things he told the hurt heart of a young man who came to his class for enlightenment. As I told Chris and Kevin and Bronwen Dickey, I considered delivering James Dickey's eulogy one of the highest honors of my lifetime. I got to fall in love with his children as an unasked-for bonus of the ceremony.

Two hours later, I was sitting in front of my bloated father, who lay on a hospital bed with his feet and legs swollen beyond all recognition. His heart was endangered by a rising tide inside him. In the workup for his treatment of the congestive heart failure, they had also performed a colonoscopy, though Dad had fought the doctors at the very idea of such an invasion of privacy.

"They took a Roto-Rooter up the sacred wazoo," Dad said. "I'd have fought them with my fists, but I didn't have the strength."

"What did they find?" I asked.

"Colon cancer," Dad stated. "Seems like I've had it for a long time. They're trying to set up some chemotherapy as soon as I'm strong enough to survive it."

"Survive it!" I yelled. "Has the goddamn military ever given you a colonoscopy before?"

"Negative. It's not required on the annual physical, and I sure didn't want to bring the subject up."

Putting my head in my hands, I said, "Dad, because military medicine is such a joke and a ripoff, you may die because your doctors were idiots."

"Your job is to pep me up, lift my spirit, sports fans. Hell, you're making me feel a little boo-hoo about my situation. I'm going to tell Kath on you."

"Tell Kathy anything you like," I said. "They can cure colon cancer, Dad, you goddamn idiot, if they get it in time. Yours sounds like it's spread all over the place."

"Hey, I need some happy time," Dad said. "You aren't making me happy. I'm going to tell Kath."

For the next several days, I stayed with Dad at the naval hospital and watched as his gargantuan feet and legs began to respond to the medication, and the swelling began to subside all through his body.

What gave me great hope was that the cancer was attacking one of the strongest men I've ever known, who brought an indomitable spirit to the gruff task of survival. In the next two years, the fires of life itself lit up his eyes, the eyes of a night fighter. It was an honor to watch such a man die and to know that I was that man's oldest son. Both of my parents died with exemplary courage and resolve, and in so doing, they proffered their children the finest of gifts—they taught us how to die.

When my father left the hospital, we took off on the first of many road trips we made during the last two years of his life. First, we went through Florida to see the Harper boys. We decided to keep off the interstates and take only the back roads down Highway 301 and through an almost deserted road along the eastern rim of the Okefenokee swamp and across the Florida state line. We never passed by an orange juice stand without picking up bags of oranges from the Indian River; nor did we ever pass an alligator farm where we didn't feed fish to the leaping gators. At Alexander Springs, we stopped for a long, delicious swim and dog-paddled over and above the gloomy caverns that served as a fountainhead for the creek that headed out into the forest toward the St. Johns River. The springs were too cold for the alligators, which Dad and I took as a sign from a loving God. As we drove into the pretty town of Ashton, Florida, we headed down an unpaved road toward Bobby Harper's house on the St. Johns River.

"What's unique about the St. Johns River?" Dad asked, as he used to when I was a boy and we'd get near the magical river.

"It flows north," I said.

"Good boy," Dad said. "I taught you kids about geography if nothing else."

Yes, he did, and I can still tell you all of the capital cities in the United States.

"What's the only other major river to flow north?" he asked.

"The Nile."

"Hey, talk about advantages. You bellyache all the time about what a horseshit life a military brat is forced to live. But show me a civilian kid who knows about the Nile. You ain't gonna find it. The military brat knows the world."

"It was worth it all because the Nile flows north," I said.

When we pulled up in front of cousin Bobby's house, the four Harper boys—Bobby, John, Mike, Russ—were waiting for us with their families, and they engulfed Dad with their country-boy love that always flowed north when it came to honoring my Chicago-born father. Though I never quite understood the grand relationship my father enjoyed with the Harper boys, it always moved me and caused me some slight agitation when I witnessed any gathering of the Harper tribe with my father at its dead center. They acted like some outlawed circus had arrived in town, with my Dad well rehearsed in his role as flashy, whip-happy ringmaster. For the next twenty-four hours, Dad would spin elaborate tales, and the Harper boys would answer him with applause and appreciation and a powerful surge of family solidarity that I found difficult to believe.

. . .

When I was a boy, I envied the Harper boys and the life they were leading more than anyone on earth. Since Uncle Russ was a dentist and a respected member of the community in Orlando and never planned to move, I wanted that kind of steadfastness in my own road-weary life. Aunt Helen was a beauty and soft-spoken, with a silky, accented Southern voice, who was incapable of any surprises or shocking eye-openers that would alter your view of her. The primitive Baptists of Sand Mountain, Alabama, had shaped her spiritual life out of the limestone and quarries of Piedmont. She was a pious and evangelical woman for her entire life. Whenever I spent the night with the Harper boys, Aunt Helen would send us to bed after a long reading from the King James Version of the Bible. The inflection of her voice was lovely, and the God of the Old Testament found one of his female soldiers passing His word on to her sons and nephews. The gorgeousness of language floated around her living room like tufts of cotton candy. I grew up believing that she was one of the great women of my life, and my sisters took me by surprise when they admitted to me later in life that they found Helen a priggish busybody who had tortured my mother about her divorce from Dad. Helen and Russ had swallowed my Father's Kool-Aid and took his side during those ruinous days when

Mom and Dad went their separate ways. I decided to forgive Helen and Russ for this lapse. I needed a perfect aunt and uncle to fill in for the crestfallen days of my youth, and they fit the bill admirably.

The Harper boys had prepared a large barbecue in honor of Dad's getting out of the hospital. Picnic tables overflowed with slow-cooked pork, and there were beautiful piles of blue crabs and shrimp taken from the St. Johns River. My father could not say a word without gales of appreciative laughter rising out of the semicircle of nephews surrounding him. The Harper boys had inoculated their own families with this bizarre form of Santini worship, and I saw my cousins of a new generation, Rusty, Benjamin, Robby, and Priscilla, all fall under Dad's spell. As I listened to him regale the Harper family with his bright compendium of stories, the Harper wives kept the table overflowing with coleslaw and potato salad and biscuits hot from the oven. I don't remember another soul speaking for the first two hours. It was a celebration of my father's victory over congestive heart failure. Then Cousin John asked, "Uncle Don, tell us about the chemotherapy and what's going to happen next."

"That's it, Johnny, break the spell. Make us get back to the subject of my untimely demise," Dad said.

"I didn't mean it that way," John said. "Honest, Uncle Don."

"You know how to make a fellow feel good," Dad said. "Why don't you get the undertaker on the phone and order me up a coffin while we're at it?"

"I just want to know how they're gonna cure you," John said.

I interrupted: "I'd love to hear it too, Johnny." Dad hadn't mentioned a word of his treatment to his kids.

Dad told them about his hospitalization. "They sent over a little guy whose name I can't remember or pronounce. [It was Dr. Majd Chahin.] He's this Iranian dude who seemed like he knew what he was doing. Course, how would I know what he was doing? It's all Greek to me, if you get my meaning. But he's the one they sent to repair the plumbing and all the other stuff."

"What's the other stuff, Uncle Don?" Cousin Russ asked.

"The stuff. The bad stuff. The stuff that's causing all the problems," Dad said.

"The cancer, Uncle Don?" John said.

"Yeah, that stuff. That's the bad stuff. Dr. Sinbad explained it to me."

"Who's Sinbad?" my cousin Mike Harper asked.

"My doctor. The Iranian whose name I can't pronounce. Since I can't pronounce his name, I've nicknamed him Sinbad. He seems to like it," Dad explained.

"Better make sure, Uncle Don," Russ warned.

"Well, he explained the process to me. I go in and he hooks me up with those jumper cables to the veins in my arms. Then he takes bags of stuff, hangs them up, then goes away for a couple of hours while I watch a ball game. The bag's got the good stuff. It gets inside of me and sends out a search party for the bad stuff. When the good stuff meets the bad stuff, they duke it out, and the good stuff beats the living stew out of the bad stuff. If it does its job right, the good stuff cuts down the nets and the bad stuff goes home to sulk. But that don't mean I'm out of the woods just yet. The bad stuff's going to make a comeback. I'll go out of commission . . ."

"Remission, Dad," I corrected.

"Whatever the wordsmith says, but when the bad stuff makes its comeback, Sinbad will be there waiting with a couple more sacks of the good stuff. Again, the good stuff goes looking for the bad and they duke it out again. We hope the good stuff kicks ass again—pardon the French, ladies. I'll do whatever Sinbad says. Hell, I'll fly a magic carpet for that guy. He seems to know his stuff and he talks a good game. But the bottom line is, the good stuff dukes it out with the bad stuff and that's the end of the tale. Over and out. Could we bring up a happier story?"

Over the last years of my father's life, I heard many versions of the same story, and it all devolved into a sacred crusade of good and evil played on a game board of mortality. Dad could get you rooting for the good stuff and giving a unanimous thumbs-down to the bad. I believe it had formed because of my father's inability to contemplate his own death, but his was as clear an explanation of chemotherapy that I've heard anywhere.

At five the next morning, Dad woke me up and said, "Reveille has sounded, soldier. I've got something to show you that you ain't going to believe, jocko."

"I'll believe it at ten in the morning, thanks," I said, turning my head in the darkness. "I haven't seen five in the morning since I left The Citadel."

"You're going to see this," Dad said, as he turned on the flashlight and we walked down the dock. Bobby's wife Lonnie handed us mugs of hot coffee as we went out to meet Bobby, who was waiting for us on the dock.

"Uncle Don wanted you to see this, Pat," Bobby said as he turned a huge flashlight into the deep-currented St. Johns River. When man-made light swept across a river or a swamp in the marsh-haunted waters of the Deep South, I knew that an alligator's eyes would glow like the light from Japanese lanterns. Over the years Dad and I had often seen the fiery witness of alligators to our passages on fishing trips with Uncle Russ. But in this moonless darkness we were stunned to see hundreds of gators regarding us with the carmine eyes of cold-blooded predators.

"Want to go for a morning swim, Dad?" I asked.

"That's a good idea, Uncle Don." Bobby grinned. "I'll come in after you give the okay signal."

"I wouldn't go into that water after a squadron had strafed that water clean of reptiles. I wouldn't put a single piggy of my left foot in that mess. Hell, I wouldn't live within five hundred miles of the St. Johns," Dad told him.

"Stay and hunt with us today," Cousin Rusty said. "We'll fry you guys up some gator tail. I guarantee that you and Pat'll love it."

"I made a pact with all the wild shit in the world," Dad said. "If it don't eat me, I won't eat it. I used to see packs of sharks following in the wake of aircraft carriers, and they really helped me concentrate on my landings. I'm proud of the fact that I never got my feet wet when I fought in the Pacific."

When we left the Harpers, we drove down back roads toward the Atlantic, where we made stops at Daytona Beach and Sanlando Springs and Rock Springs, places that the Conroy children had come to revere whenever Dad was waging war overseas. In Florida you are always near a bright-eyed source of water that flows with a quartzlike purity from a plunging hole in the dark Florida earth. We were especially fond of Rock Springs, which was undiscovered and often deserted and seemed to boil out of the rock like the birth of a powerful river. All of us felt disappointment when we returned as adults and Rock Springs seemed like a waterway that was barely larger than a creek. We had grown up and the springs had not.

Cousins Mike and John met us over at the assisted-living facility where Aunt Helen had been a resident for two years, suffering from dementia. Though I knew my father was disconcerted by the milieu of hospitals, he had spent a lifetime teasing and poking fun at Helen, who carried no weapon to resist his insistence on mocking every word out of her mouth. It was an Irish street urchin going after a backward Southern girl who was defenseless to ward off his aggression. But they had somehow managed to discover a way to love each other, and Dad was the only person I knew who could make Aunt Helen laugh.

Using two canes that he now needed to walk because of his bad hips, my dad passed a hundred beds of people in various stages of dementia and Alzheimer's disease. There were vases full of roses and jasmine and every other blossom that gave off a delicious scent, fitting the state of Florida—the place of flowers in our national dream. The sweetness of the arrangements cut through the odors of antiseptics and bedpans as thunderstricken relatives sat around their loved ones in agony about what to do or say to comfort such lifeless vessels of silence, where souls had passed on to the next dimension, but their hearts still beat in time and one could only guess whether they could still dream.

Unnerved and shaken to the core, my father observed the gallery of the city without memory or affect and said to me, "I'm giving you a direct order, sports fans."

"What is it, Dad?" I asked.

"If I ever get like this, you shoot me in the back of the head when they come to put me in such a place," he said. "Now promise me."

"Bang, bang," I said as quietly as I could. But Mike and John had heard the words Dad had spoken, and it had alarmed and upset them both.

Mike Harper said, "Uncle Don—you couldn't be more wrong about Mama. She understands everything that's going on around her."

John added, "She's sharp as a tack, Uncle Don. Nothing gets by her. She knows what's going on—at all times."

"That's great, Johnny," I said. "I heard it was much worse."

"Who's spreading that rumor?" John demanded.

"It's my horrible, untrustworthy sister Carol," I said.

"Carol Ann hasn't seen our parents in a coon's age." Mike snorted.

I explained, "Carol loathes everyone in our family until they start dying. Then she loves and cherishes them more than anyone else in our sick tribe."

As we approached the bed of Aunt Helen, we came to the washed-out face as blank as a tablet. Still, Aunt Helen was one of those beautiful Peek girls who had come out of the hill country of Georgia to make their marks and find their husbands in Atlanta. She was as polite and self-effacing as she'd been in her lifetime. But you could wave a lantern in front of her eyes and she would not even be aware of the light.

Dad said, very upset, "She doesn't know me from your Buick LeSabre, Pat."

Mike and John jumped to their mother's defense like guard dogs. "No, Uncle Don," Mike protested. "She knows everything that's going on. She doesn't miss a thing. Mama, you recognize Uncle Don, don't you? And that's his oldest son, Pat. You know, the oldest cousin. They're the Roman Catholics in the family. Look, Uncle Don, she sees both of you. She recognizes you both and understands everything that's going on. Man, she was always sharp as a tack."

"Mike should know, Uncle Don," John added. "He comes and sits by Mom every day. Sometimes he stays all day long. He really looks after her and makes sure she's treated right. It's a beautiful thing to watch."

My father was deeply shaken after our visit. As I drove through Orlando, I showed Dad the St. James Cathedral School at one corner, where I used to lead Orlando kids to safety as a member of the school patrol, then the outdoor basket where I scored my first two points as a basketball player, and the route I walked Carol Ann home on each day to the rat-infested house on Livingston Street. I pointed out the bridge on Lake Eola where Mom had bought her first landscape painting and stopped her young family, most of whom were still in their infancy, to watch the artist Jack Gilbert finish his picture of the lake with a flashy whitewater lily.

That night Dad and I, along with the Harpers, ate dinner at the restaurant favored by our cousins and Uncle Russ. After his visit to Aunt Helen, Dad felt frisky and ready to rock and roll to an appreciative audience. Many of his jokes were at my expense, but I'd given him a dispensation that would last for the rest of his life.

"How was a guy to know he was raising Judas Iscariot in his own house?" he asked my cousins. "I mean, have some pity on an old man who fathered a boy who got his nose out of joint whenever Daddy raised his voice to him or gave him a little tap on the fanny."

"That's why I didn't teach my boys to read or write, Don," Uncle Russ said. "I sure didn't want that to happen when one of my boys got his feelings hurt by me."

"When I heard how much money Pat made," Cousin Mike said, "I've been trying to get my nose out of joint, but I just can't crack the code."

"It's easy, Mike," my father said. "Just get your nose out of joint when you're about ten and keep it that way for the next forty years. You won't believe all the shit you can make up."

We left the next day, because a strange restlessness plagued my father, who believed that keeping constantly on the move could calm all the mysteries and storms in his nature. His kids all knew he was stealing off in morning darkness to confuse his cancer into believing that he was too adept in all the chicaneries of movement ever to be caught and brought down from behind. Not once did it occur to him that his cancer had booked first-class passage on his grand ship of state, no matter where he ran or tried to hide. A short time later I would join him at the weddings of my two cousins Colleen and Bridget Conroy, both daughters of Aunt Carol and Uncle Ed Conroy—a happy wedding in Naples, Florida, and one in Davenport, Iowa. Dad was at the dead center of each one and danced more than anyone at the reception parties for the two pretty girls. Always full of life, he lived the last part of his with exuberance, ready for any new adventure, singing the praises of both morning sun and the rising of a new moon. He seemed to have the energy of a thousand lesser men, and his oldest son could only watch in exhausted admiration. In the year he spent dying, he ran his kids into the ground.

His children met together in secret and made clandestine phone calls in which we talked about the brevity of Dad's future. We all decided (although Carol Ann was not a part of these planning sessions) to make Dad's going out as easy and comfortable as we could. Since brother Jim was working in Dallas at the time, he flew in many weekends to visit Dad, who was staying in Beaufort. Tim and Mike were down frequently; Kathy and Bobby Joe lived in Beaufort, but on most weekends we would find ourselves at my house on Fripp Island. If we needed to talk in private, without Dad's overhearing and interference, we could always go to the lagoon and slip secret documents and passwords about Dad's condition, his prognosis, or his mood. All of us longed for Dad to have a good death, surrounded by his children. Our love had been hard-won with screams and scars and battlefield commissions, but we were past that now.

So we began a year of submitting to Dad's whims as he made a final tour of the most significant places in his life. He planned visits to every person he'd ever considered a friend, paying special attention to my daughters, who had worshiped him ever since they had learned to talk. He made two visits to stay with Colonel Joseph and Jean Jones, the parents of Barbara's first husband, who was killed in Vietnam. They lived on a farm near Dyersburg, Tennessee, and opened it to me and my family without condition after our families merged into one. They and their Tennessee family, the Gauldins, were special additions to my life, and the entire group fell in love with my family, but especially with my father. They became a pit stop on his annual trek to Chicago and Iowa. Falling in love with Barbara had linked my destiny with dozens of histories I wouldn't have had if we'd never met. A hundred new moons would appear in my horizon whenever my daughters had a child. Because of fate, love was a million-footed thing, and so was hatred. My father was behind the wheel of his car, urging it down the peripheries of blue highways, and he carried what was killing him as an honored guest in his liver. He connected himself to Chicago, to Atlanta, and the surprising realm of Beaufort, where his children had planted their own flags of belonging and home.

In the winter of 1995, I was editing *Beach Music* in New York City when I received a summons to receive a lifetime achievement award from the Hoover Library outside Birmingham, Alabama. Both my father and the Joneses attended the ceremony. Jean Jones later told me that when I stood Dad up and introduced him to the audience, he waited for his standing ovation to be over before he sat down to dry the tears from his eyes. Dad was always a big hit at writers' conferences, and his bloviating descriptions of himself pleased whatever crowd he was addressing.

"To me, my son's writing puts him in the fourth or fifth rank of American writers, but under my tutelage, the kid's getting better," he would boast to a crowd of Southern women. "I tell him, 'Son, until you learn to write like I flew a fighter plane, you're always gonna be a tail gunner and nothing else. You got to break a few sound barriers, sink a few aircraft carriers, bring down an enemy squadron—that kind of stuff, if you get my drift. Pat writes for homosexuals, lesbians, and people of that milieu [he pronounced it "mill-lu"], when he needs to find a way to make it popular among truck drivers and factory workers, the real people who make this country run."

When I listened to this rant of his, I grew in admiration for that fixed star who had the stamina to teach me the alphabet in the home of such a proud philistine. "Thank you, Mama," I would send a prayer aloft. "I can't thank you enough."

For the next year, Dad was running on fumes as he put thousands of miles on his car each month. As he pursued redemption in the freedom of the road, the cancer was always waiting for him well rested in Beaufort. It nested in the eaves of the attics of the Fripp house. It warmed itself during the cold winter at Kathy's house. It matched Dad's volatile impatience with a mineral stillness of its own. It was always on call and always at the ready. My father was the madcap voyager of those days and could not see what his children could see so clearly. But Dad was weakening, breaking down, losing the use of his once powerful legs, suffering from shortness of breath, and falling asleep in the middle of games long before bedtime. Yet no one mentioned a word to him about the progression of his illness.

The family would discuss him almost nightly by phone, and we would find out his itinerary of the day, or the symptoms of his long fade-out of health toward the time of senescence we all knew was coming. Once he fell in Bobby Joe and Kathy's shower, and Bobby Joe had to lift him out, clean him up, and get him dressed. Bobby Joe was not thanked for his services. As he needed us more and more, Dad grew more contentious at our availability or wanting to help him. There was a whole platoon of proud men trapped in this one ornery man who passed in review with a scowl on his face when his own kids lined the parade route.

Over the long year, we learned to hide our deep concern by hosting great parties with Dad in the prow, always ready to assume his work as the centerpiece in the great circle of blood his family represented. On April 4, 1997, we planned what we thought would be the last birthday party we threw for Dad, and we planned it down to its last detail.

Dad had spent a couple of days in the hospital as they put him through several rigorous tests. I picked my unsuspecting father up from Beaufort Memorial and drove him out toward Fripp on a perfect sea island day in the low country. I had found him arguing with his doctors, saying, "Hey, Sinbad. They got any medical schools in Iran?"

"No, Dad," I said, "they just let 'em work on dogs and cats. Then they get to practice on guys like you. Hey, Doc, why don't you just put him down—like a rabid dog?"

"Hey, he took an oath, son. The hypotenuse oath, I believe it's called."

"The Hippocratic Oath, bookworm," I said to my father as I helped him leave the hospital.

When Dad drove up to the house on Fripp that day, there were more than fifty guests waiting for his arrival. His brother Ed had come down from Iowa with Aunt Carol and several of their children. My father's nephew, young Ed, came with his wife Ginny and their kids; at the time young Ed was an assistant college coach at North Carolina State. It would have thrilled Dad to know that Cousin Ed is the head coach of Tulane University today. Dad's brother, Father Jim, was there, as was his helper in the faith, Sister Ludmilla. Aunt Marge came, accompanied by two Chicago nuns from the Dominican Order in Chicago. The Harper boys showed up en masse. All of us remember how splendid and pacific that day was, and how Dad's birthday lacked the usual fireworks displays or meteors flashing across the skies of our gatherings.

As we drove up to the house, the guests serenaded Dad with a timeless rendition of "Happy Birthday," sung by two families that had never produced a good singing voice. I heard a sob come out of Dad's throat.

"Get yourself together, Dad," I said.

"How?" he asked.

"Just wing it," I advised. "Pretend you're still the shit who raised us."

When the song ended, Bobby Joe drove Dad's birthday present out of the garage. It was a spanking-new red Ford. We knew Dad loved the color red, and he'd never owned a new car. Bobby Joe said, "Don, this car is a present from your kids to the Great Santini. I picked it out myself and guarantee you this is a great car that'll run forever." When he handed the keys to Don, I thought my dad would lose his balance and fall to his knees. I'd never seen my father more surprised by a gift in my life.

Nor had I ever surprised myself by my own falling apart at my father's receiving this gift with his children present. Moving toward the back of the semicircle, I watched Dad painfully sitting in his new vehicle, happy as a mockingbird. Something in the scene got to me, and I felt a raw and animal thing forming inside me that I could not control. Making it to my front door undetected, I closed the door behind me and broke down with a swift completeness. Only my daughter Megan saw me break out of the gathering, and I found myself in her arms weeping out an emptiness I would never be able to explain. Megan held me and told me all the soft things necessary to soothe the raw places of a broken father. I'd always worried that I didn't teach my girls the simple ways of loving, but their natures were so fine and meticulous that they picked it up without my help. Through the last year or so of my father's dying, I felt cherished and appreciated by the daughters I helped raise.

A whole pig was cooking in the backyard, and a family friend, Morgan Randel, helped me make shrimp and grits for fifty people in the kitchen. Mrs. Randel served iced tea to all the guests and came up to kiss me and tell me the party was beautiful. Ever since their son Randy had fallen dead on a baseball field in front of me when he was fifteen, the Randels and I had been inseparable. My father, mother, and sister became part of their family circle, and it had proven to me how something grand could grow out of the wreckage of a ruined house. Three of my daughters, Jessica, Melissa, and Megan, all were so pretty they looked unrelated to me. They made over Don in a big Atlanta-girl way, and he had been as wonderful to them as he'd been a disappointment to us. There was a surfeit of food with great mounds of potato salad and drifts of coleslaw and the crackling goodness of crisp pig still steaming from the vinegar mop on the grill. Biscuits came out of the oven calling for fresh butter. Corn and tomatoes and onions wrapped in aluminum foil and cooked with soy sauce and a touch of sesame oil opened up in curls of sudden steam. Even the smoke tasted good.

When we waved good-bye to our father that night, his children thought we'd pulled off the perfect party. It was one of those nights when a lot of people stayed behind to clean up. It was satisfying to hear the stories being built after the party was over. Toward the end of the evening, my brother Jim called from his home in Dallas. He had not been able to break out of his work schedule, and his son, Michael, was too colicky as a baby to make the long trip back to the coast. I heard my brother Tim's overgilded version of the day's events.

"Yeah, we gave Dad a brand-new Ford. Terrye and I fought for a Mercedes, but we were overruled by the others. All cheap bastards, if you ask me. Terrye and I did the best we could, Jimbo. We took five thousand dollars from our life savings to contribute our share. I don't know what you or Kathy or Mike gave. I'm not even sure Pat gave a cent, but Dad knew we did our damnedest to make the party a success. How much did you and Janice give, Jimbo, if I'm not prying?"

"Let me speak with Pat," Jim demanded, then asked me, "How much did Tim and Terrye give for the car, Pat?"

"I don't know for sure, but around five grand, as near as I can remember."

"You're as full of shit as they are," Jim said. "Is Mike there?"

"Yeah, he's across the room. That cheapskate didn't give a cent," I said, calling out to my brother.

. . .

Time becomes a trickster and a necromancer whenever it gets serious about the job of killing your parents. Then time speaks only to taunt you with the inevitable, with the hard knowledge that there is nothing to do but prepare for the remorseless day when the hurt for your parent reaches its grand finale.

In the last year of his life we learned how to arrange Dad's pillows, turn the television to his favorite channels, take him to his favorite restaurants whenever we found ourselves passing through Atlanta. I watched the Chicago Bears, the Chicago Bulls, and the Chicago White Sox with him. In the winter after the Christmas of 1997, he began staying over at my house on Fripp Island all day. He grew exhausted, so I'd let him fall asleep in his chair while I went back to work. Working at my desk, I would hear the angry thumping of his cane on my door, and I would answer his summons with false aggravation.

"What do you want, Pop?" I would yell at him.

"Make me a sammich," he'd say. "Make me a sammich like you did when I was in Rome."

"Want some pasta with that?" I'd ask.

"Yeah, hit me with that shit too," he'd say. "I eat better at Kath's home."

"Well, hell. Jump in that red car and get your ass over to Kath's house, then," I'd say, always rising toward the fresh bait.

Each night Dad would go to sleep at Kathy and Bobby Joe's house, because Kathy, a registered nurse, was in charge of his medications and hygiene. Because his two bad hips had made any locomotion painful to him, it would often take him five minutes to make it from his car to the inside of my house. His one duty that he insisted on doing was to check my incoming mail each day. Afterward he would steal more than half the mail I received and boast when he got to Kathy's. "A great day for the Archives," he'd tell her. "I really racked up some great Arcs material." That Kathy went along with this blatant theft bothered me somewhat, but we both knew it caused much pleasure in my father's larcenous heart.

That summer, the entire world of the Great Santini made plans to visit during what was most likely his last summer. His Marine friends from three wars came to reminisce about his battles fought about fifty years before. Col. Brown Pinkston came with his pretty wife, Salina, and I remembered the first time I saw Capt. Brown Pinkston in a baseball uniform at Cherry Point when I was six years old. He hit a double off the wall and became heroic to me for my entire life. I had a crush on his daughter Gail before I was in grade school, and the family Pinkston were the most solid neighbors we made in our shifting lives in the Marine Corps. It was with a sense of genuine pleasure that I watched the two fighter pilots talk about their experiences in the Pacific Theater. I wonder whether old soldiers in Athens came together to celebrate their parts in the fall of Troy. The soldiers came with their wives and families, and my house filled up with visitors as the days grew longer and my father's life grew shorter. My sister Kathy told me that I averaged feeding fifteen or twenty people a day during those final days of Santini. As he lost weight, the fire inside him began to dim and his coloring became pale as an altar cloth. Yet he exulted in the attention his illness brought him, and the shameful ease he took in shining on center stage was never so apparent as it was in that fall of 1997.

By then, the lovely Cassandra King had come into my life and joined me in the daily care and feeding of Santini. Always embarrassed about talking about the rivers of emotions his children carried with them, Dad never spoke directly of his affection for Cassandra. Cassandra, whom I usually call Sandra, had been living with me for a while, and I'd finally found the woman I wanted by my side at my own deathbed. Dad had no desire to study these deeper currents within himself, but he noticed and approved of Sandra's composure as the Conroy thunderhead formed on the horizon ahead. Dad spoke of her by indirection.

"Your friend. What's her name? You know the one. She seems to be camping out here. You invite her, kid?"

"No, Dad," I said. "She put a shotgun to my left ear and promised to blow my brains out if I didn't let her live here. And her name's Sandra King."

"I read her book," he said. "Not bad. I especially liked her portrait of Tim and Kim."

In Cassandra's first novel, *Making Waves*, two high school boys conduct an unconsummated homosexual affair. I was stunned that Dad had read her novel, and told Sandra that was "high praise indeed."

"I figured Don would love great literature," she said. "I wasn't worried."

Dad would speak about Sandra in the third person. "Did she get my birthday present?"

"You mean that cheap piece of shit—the ugliest jacket in the world with the purple pants that glow in the dark?" I asked.

"That outfit set me back quite a few pesos, son," he said.

"It's the ugliest piece of clothing she's ever seen," I said.

"She's from Alabama. I'm sure she's not accustomed to owning the top of the line. I scooped this up from the latest couture of the month."

"Please, Dad," I said, "leave it alone."

"Next time I'll buy your little friend some jewelry of note."

"Please don't," I asked.

"Your little friend deserves the best. Nothing else is good enough for her," he said.

On Thanksgiving Day, my good friend from Atlanta, the journalist Larry Woods, brought down a television crew from CNN to do a family special on the great healing that had taken place since Don Conroy announced that he had a fatal case of cancer. Somehow, Larry had talked to the antisocial and uncommunicative Carol Ann and convinced her that this would be a celebration of the strength and inviolability of family. How he convinced my sister to partake in such an un–Carol Ann–like event, I have no idea. Still furious with Carol Ann's ruinous pullback from her family, I took little interest in anything resembling a television-induced reconciliation. But Larry convinced me that I was doing my father a huge favor, because it upset Dad that such divisions and fault lines had cracked through the solidarity he hoped we could achieve by his death.

My father made his own pitch one day when I took him to the Shrimp Shack for lunch. "This thing about Thanksgiving, Pat," Dad said, eating his shrimp burger while gazing at one of the loveliest salt marshes on the planet. He applied the ketchup and horseradish on his burger and then said, "I know you said no to Larry when he called, but I'd like a reconsideration filed at my desk at oh eight hundred tomorrow."

"I already said no, Dad. I've been eating Carol's shit for twenty years, and I'm getting not to like the taste."

"It'd make it easier on everyone else if you'd change your mind," he said.

In anger I said, "What are the ground rules, Dad? Carol doesn't do anything without a list of things she won't tolerate."

"Piece of cake," Dad said. "She doesn't want to be seen on-screen with you unless it's at Thanksgiving dinner, with you sitting at one end of the table and her at the far end. She doesn't want any of your work read aloud, but she'll allow herself to read one poem of her own choosing." Larry was also not allowed to film Carol Ann and me together in conversation, and he could refer to our long separation only fleetingly.

"What do I have to do?" I asked.

"I think you're supposed to look kind of worshipful when Carol's mug appears on the tube," he said.

"I'd like to take a tire tool and hammer her head against the brick fireplace," I said.

"You always had a violent streak," Dad said. "It used to worry me when you were only a wee little lad."

The weekend before Thanksgiving there was another gathering of the troops to man the campfire as Dad grew weaker and weaker before our eyes. Larry did long interviews with Dad, Carol Ann, and me, and when I saw the results, I could see death forming like low-lying clouds in Dad's pale blue eyes. Though Carol Ann refused to exchange a single civil word with me, Larry conducted his interviews with her far away from my house. Larry had lost his wife, Dee Woods, to cancer the previous year, and he was still reeling from the aftermath of that terrible grief. Since Larry had lost his own father when he was a boy, he always followed my explosive relationship with Dad with a troubled but exhilarated eye. Larry, a handsome but careworn man, was trying to repair some head-on collisions in his own life by putting my family together. He wanted the characters of his chess set to form lines of communication as we dealt with the empty spaces on our board, even as we prepared to enter our last battle together. Larry was shooting the piece for the sake of his own troublesome past. But that's what artists do, and I had no problem with the urgency that he brought to his task.

When the film appeared on Thanksgiving Day my family watched with both moans and silence. All of us were amazed to hear that Carol Ann had a job selling organic herbs at a farmer's market in the East Village.

Mike asked, "Did anyone know Carol had a job?"

Jim answered, "Where the hell is the East Village?"

"She lives there in New York," Tim said.

"Jim's out of the loop," Dad said.

"Did you know she had a job, Dad?" Jim asked him.

"Naw. She kept us all out of the loop," Dad said. "She's closer to Kathy than any of her brothers."

"I've never heard the mention of a farmer's market," Kathy said.

"It's all bullshit. Complete bullshit," Tim said.

"I love it. I gotta get Larry on the phone and thank him," Dad said. "I mean, that's a heavy theme there. How a father helps bring his whole family together after his son writes a lying piece-of-shit book about him. There's greatness in that story."

Tim's wife, Terrye, poked two fingers down her throat as though to induce vomiting. "God, what a horseshit family." But she winked at me in conspiracy and smiled.

Jim said, "Tell me once again, Dad, whose writing do you prefer, Pat's or Carol's?"

Dad, playing to his audience, paraphrased what he had said on national TV: "I far prefer Carol's poetry to Pat's cruddy prose. I taught all of my children that poetry was a much higher art form than prose ever could be."

The whole family jeered at Dad, who bellowed with laughter, pleased with himself beyond all comprehension.

Then cold weather came to the low country. The shrimp and crabs disappeared from the rivers, and oystermen came back from the dark flanges of mud banks in search of the swollen oyster or to interrupt the commerce of quahogs. The marsh that had darkened with the deepest green, then ripened into a tawny, palomino gold as the winter surged into our sounds and rivers, turned brown in its seasonal death. It was a year my father's illness became congruent with the cold season's passage. The palmettos rattled in northwesterly winds, and the birdsong had forsaken the woods beside our house. Now the chemotherapy that once seemed like it was saving Dad had reached the point where the returns were limited, and the cancer began to assert its hegemony over my father's entire life. He awoke each morning, turned the day into a feast of joy as Christmas came and went, and Dad, Cassandra, and I stayed up to watch the coming in of 1998.

"This may be the last one I'll ever see," my father said, and we approached the realm of deepest philosophy in his one-celled life.

"That's the spirit, Dad," I said.

"No, I've been thinking about it," he said. "I was born an Irish dope. Grew up starving. Was happy my whole life. Then the Japs attacked Pearl Harbor, and it turns out to be the luckiest thing that ever happened to me. I enlisted in the Marine Corps and they made me a fighter pilot and sent me to Atlanta for further training. I see your mother crossing the street. She and I had never seen nothin' and they send us moving all over this country, pay us good money, put a roof over our heads, and we get seven wonderful kids in the process. I fight in three wars. I couldn't wait to get to work in the morning. My daughter writes a book of great poetry and my oldest son writes a few horseshit novels. When I die, I'll know I'm a literary figure for the rest of time."

"Please, Dad. I puke easily," I said.

"A literary figure, how you like them bananas, son?" he said.

"I trust literature to be more selective," I said.

"No, you made me too powerful to ignore," Dad said. "Who wants to read about those bellyaching pussies when you're diving toward a battleship with the Great Santini leading your ass?"

As March approached, Dad made elaborate plans to attend the St. Patrick's Day parade in Savannah. Though I did not know it, Savannah had an annual parade that was the second-largest in this country after New York City. More surprisingly, we learned that my father had marched in this parade for the last twenty years of his life.

"Who in the hell do you march with, Dad?" I asked in astonishment.

"I march by myself. I represent the great family of Conroy out of Galway, and I do a damn good job of it."

Dad pulled out a faded photograph taken by the *Savannah Morning News* of him marching alone down the streets of Savannah. It was a marvelous, definitive photograph of my shamrock-covered father's wearing of the green from his spiritual homeland.

"I won't be marching this year," he said, a plain statement of fact.

"Good decision," I said, and made some calls to my friends in Savannah.

On March 17, we gathered on the balcony of Jack Leigh and his wife, which was on Oglethorpe Street and directly over the parade route. Jack had been a photographer of great note when his life received a lightning bolt that made him one of the most famous photographers in America for a while. The photograph he shot will set him down with the immortals. A young journalist named John Berendt had come south to write an extraordinary book about Savannah entitled *Midnight in the Garden of Good and Evil*. John had hired Jack Leigh to take a photograph for the book jacket, and Jack went down to one of Savannah's celebrated cemeteries to take a haunting image of a slim young woman holding two bowls in perfect equipoise. Overnight, the photograph made Jack Leigh famous.

Once I took my father to an opening of a Jack Leigh exhibition, and it was one of the rare moments when I could study my father's seduction by the silent world of the contemplative arts. He even asked me whether he could buy one of Jack's photographs for himself.

"Sure. All the photographs are for sale," I said. "That's why he's having an exhibition of his work."

"I'll give him a buck for that one," Dad said, checking his wallet.

"Keep your money, Dad," I advised.

"My money ain't no good in this joint?" he asked in surprise.

"He has this bad habit," I said. "He likes to feed his family."

On the way back to Fripp, I could still tell Dad was musing over his response to Jack Leigh's work. "That stuff," Dad said, "I liked it. I mean, I've seen a lot of trees and a lot of rivers. But not like that. What was it I was seeing?"

"Art, Dad," I said. "You were feeling the art."

"So, that's the deal for you guys," said Dad. "For you and Carol, too."

"That's what we try for, Dad," I said.

But his disease was taking dominion as Cassandra, Don, and I sat on a crowded balcony, watching and applauding as the nation of Ireland passed in sweet review. The Irish families of Savannah, their ranks swollen to the thousands, threw trinkets and candy to the onlookers. The horses of the Savannah police kept order along the lines of crowd-heavy boulevards, and seventy bands barked out the anthems of a country with a ruthless, indomitable history. As I watched the parade, I said to myself that I came from a fighting people who could not be appeased or made to bow to an enemy's flag, and that was the blood the Conroy family brought out of Galway and into the steerage of what America held for us. Please attack me, English lord, and one of my grandsons will take up my cudgel and meet you at the edge of the Irish Sea. There is plenty wrong about the Irish, but forgetfulness is not one of those things.

That marvelous day when my father stood up for Ireland one last time, he also remembered and honored the country that had taken in his clan and given them the great brave keys of their redemption in a new land. Each time an American flag would pass, my father would struggle to his feet and salute that flag smartly, the way it's done by a Marine officer. Most times I had to rise and help him to his feet, lifting him out of the chair until he could control his balance. He saluted every flag that passed us that day, and a hundred must have passed in front of the colonel. When he almost fell with one of his last salutes, a young woman who was watching him came over.

"You don't have to stand for every flag, Colonel," she said. "You're the Great Santini."

Dad nodded to her, then said to me and Cassandra as he rose to salute once again, "You know why I stand every time it passes by? I fought for that flag."

Later that night, the Great Santini began to die in earnest.

CHAPTER 20

Hurrah for the Next Man to Die

I t was a lovely April morning in 1998 when a cry of distress woke me. I reached over in bed to find Cassandra gone. I threw on my khaki pants, striped shirt, and Docksiders, then found her cleaning my father's blood from the bathroom to a trail he left as he fled, trying to escape the summons of his own destiny. As I raced for my Buick, Cassandra yelled out the back door, "He's heading for the naval hospital emergency room. Kathy just called."

Down Highway 21, I drove faster than I'd ever driven before, roaring through St. Helena Island and what had begun to be called the Gullah-Geechee Corridor and the dead center of black culture as it developed through the years before and after the Civil War. I was driving toward my father's last days, and doing it at unsafe speeds.

With my father's natural inclination for embracing all that was military, I would've been happier had he signed into a veterinary clinic than the old warhorse of a naval hospital located on Ribaut Road. I wasn't sure the naval hospital even had an emergency room, which proved to be right. Their facilities were primitive at best, and Dad was bleeding like a wounded water buffalo, and every time his heart beat, a new rush of blood would burst out of his body. His eyes were dazed and helpless with what I saw to be a resignation to his fate.

Kathy and I drove him to the real emergency room at Beaufort Memorial Hospital, though I don't remember a thing about the transfer. But an hour later, his hemorrhaging was under control, and they were making plans to admit him.

"I thought I'd bought the farm," Dad said to us.

"If you survived this, you could survive anything," I said.

I was reminded of a conversation I'd had with Dad years before. During the outbreak of the first Gulf War, he and I had heard on the news that the Iraqi air force had flown to the safety of Iran to avoid the annihilation of its warplanes. When Dad made a sound of disgust, I turned to him for some explanation of his contempt for the Iraqi pilots.

He said, "If my country was at war, and we were attacked by enemy pilots, I'd take a six-shooter and a Piper Cub up into the sky. I guarantee I'd bring two or three of those assholes down before they got me." But our pilot was going down now, quickly. Since his birthday was the following day, we managed to put a last birthday party together, and the hospital released him to attend. Afterward, he would be at Kathy's home, and in her care. This birthday was a far more sedate ceremony than last year's. This was a time of saying good-bye. His relatives from Chicago came en masse, and large groups of the cousinry from both branches also came. Having lost an enormous amount of body weight, Dad was a wisp of the glorious man who once walked through the Carolina sunshine every inch the soldier, every corpuscle a building block that created the fighter pilot. There were three cakes that Cassandra made, as well as a small shipload of food that came as if by magic into our house for what everybody knew was a final chance for farewell. Though Dad looked terrible, he was game, and put on a convincing show of having the time of his life. In the middle of their gallant charade, Kathy gave me a sign, and we helped Dad stumble into our back bedroom. Since Dad was covered with a light blanket, I had failed to notice that he was bleeding copiously. Kathy removed his pants that were drenched in blood, and gave him medicine that would control the bleeding; then I took him to the bathroom.

Watching our father die was a tearless, wordless vigil because we had no capacity to coax out the words that would bring peace to his last hours. That evening, we put Dad into his fire-engine-red Ford as a passenger, and Kathy drove him to her house in Beaufort. I watched them leave, knowing that Dad was going out of my life on Fripp Island forever.

Since the time of Dad's extinction was upon us, we held family meetings, dividing up time when we could be on call for anything that came up. Again the refrain was heard: "Pat and Carol don't have jobs. They're both writers, so they can be with him twenty-four/seven."

"Don't have jobs!" Carol said, jumping at the bait. "I'll have you know that writing is the hardest work you can do. And unappreciated, unless you write crap, like Pat."

"Jim," I said, "you've got a point. Carol and I can be full-time caretakers. The rest of you guys get down here when you can. You're always welcome at the Fripp house."

Tim said, "I feel nothing. Yet I feel something. It's unbelievable. I feel like I should go talk to Dad, but I'm afraid I'll upset him."

The dark one replied, "He doesn't give a shit what you have to say, Tim. He doesn't care what any of us thinks. That's the way it's always been and how it's always going to be."

"Gosh, Jimbo, what a happy prospect you've added to all of our good-byes to Dad," I said.

"You know I'm right. I'm always right," Jim replied.

"I'm working on a poem that'll make Dad as immortal as Achilles," said Carol Ann.

Carol Ann lit a cigarette in the front yard of Kathy and Bobby Joe's house and began smoking it while carrying on an imaginary conversation with an invisible tribe who lived in the secret aurora above her head. After I said good night to Dad that evening, I walked back into Kathy's living room and saw Bobby Joe and my teenage nephew Willie staring out of a slat in their venetian blinds, a hostile audience to Carol Ann's animated one-woman parade. There was no amusement in their secret surveillance of Carol Ann's free fall into the arms of her own roiled forces of demons.

"She gets crazy when something like this happens," I tried to explain.

"Why's she talking to herself, Uncle Pat?" Willie asked.

"She can't help it," I told him.

Carol Ann was walking her post in a military manner, just like it said to do in all the military guard manuals. But her gesticulations were wild thrusts into the air, moving her cigarette like a Fourth of July sparkler, and she spoke to me when Kathy and I went outside to join her.

"My father will die in my arms just like my mother did. I'll be by his side every second. The tie that binds a female poet to the sperm that begat her is impossible to sever. I feel closer to Dad at this moment than I ever have. It'll be an ancient story fulfilled by one of the daughters of Agamemnon," she said to me.

"You might want to take your act to the backyard, Carol. You're freaking Willie and Bobby Joe out," I suggested.

"They can't stop a poet's work," she scoffed. "All the battalions on earth are helpless when a poem is being formed."

Kathy said, "The house across the street is empty, Carol, and the owner has offered you the run of her home for as long as you need it."

"To have both parents die in your arms . . . how extraordinary," Carol Ann said.

"I wouldn't try it for a while," I told her. "I'd wait until he goes into a coma. By the way, your watch will begin here at eight tomorrow morning. I'll take the second shift."

So the deathwatch over the Great Santini began the next day. My brothers took vacation days to ease my father's path toward darkness. I bought a new tape recorder and began to interview Dad about his career in the Marine Corps. It turned out to be a story I'd never heard before. Suspicious about my motives, he concluded that I had already sold the book and movie rights to the tale of how Don Conroy had lived the life, on how to conduct yourself in a manly fashion in a universe being dominated by pussies and women. His powers of fantasy took over, and he imagined that I was working on a textbook of how a man of action lived at the fullest pitch imaginable.

"God, those Hollywood fruitcakes must be creaming all over themselves thinking about such a role coming up for grabs," he said. "Tell me again why Hollywood men are such short little squats?"

"Dad, even God can't make a face so handsome and put it in a large body," I said.

"They're short as shit," Dad said, fumbling with the tape recorder, "but they've got some good-looking heads."

For an entire week, I recorded Dad trying to tell the real stories of his life, the ones that shaped him into the man and father he became. I wanted him to reveal the keystones of his journey that caused the high, watertight esteem he brought to his own assessment of his life. His ego had always seemed like an inverted iceberg to me, three-quarters of it exposed to sunshine. Yet he had emerged with that overinflated ego from an Irish slum during the Depression, and that feat alone astonished me. From knowing Dad for so long, I knew that he was savvy enough not to reveal a thing about his emotions as he grew up in that tumultuous household of his. According to Dad, all was swell in his Chicago family, although no one seemed to have enough to eat. But his parents were flawless vessels of rectitude. His brothers and sisters were in all ways Olympian creatures at play in the moonlight of Bishop Street. There were no revelations of breakdown or drift or even a hint of despair. All was a cause of wonderment and joy in that perfectly coiled nautilus of a home on the South Side of Chicago.

Since I knew the basic outline of his early life and his accidental meeting with my mother in Atlanta, I asked him mostly about his career as a Marine Corps pilot. He told me about the forty-five missions he flew in the Pacific as Bill Lundin's wingman. Every time he mentioned Bill Lundin's name it was with great respect, even reverence. He and Bill later flew with the Black Sheep Squadron, the first of the Marine flyboys to drop bombs in the Korean theater.

"Korea was my war," Dad said. "The North Koreans and the Chinese made a bet that they could win the war by the sheer force of numerical superiority. They thought airpower wouldn't play much of a role. Man, were those people wrong! Bill and I came across a formation of North Korean tanks trying to make their way into Seoul. We blew every one of those tanks off the road. I was hell on tanks, son. Horses, too."

"Horses?" I said, surprised.

"I was on a reconnaissance mission over the north—this was after the Chinese had come into the war—talk about ants! I thought the earth was moving when the Chinese crossed the border. I must've killed a thousand of them with napalm, but they just kept coming."

"But you mentioned horses?" I said.

"I always told you I had real good peepers. Guys used to love to fly with me, because I could spot something going on downstairs. One day, we were flying in clear weather, and I see something odd taking place below. So I go down just for curiosity's sake and see about ten thousand horses in a camouflage city. The Chinese were using them to carry supplies."

"So what did you do?"

"I called in for a carrier strike; then I went down and emptied all my ordnance on those horses. The noise they made was pathetic," he said.

Though he told me about annihilating a company of North Korean regulars on the Naktong River at the onset of the war, and besieging a battalion of enemy soldiers hiding in ambush as an American squad made their way up a mountain north of Seoul, I thought I was used to my father's recitals of tongues of napalm scouring the countryside of Korea. But in my nightmares, it's not the dying men set on fire by my father that disturb my sleep. Instead it's the wordless death of those conscripted horses that would die a hideous death for reasons not even the combatants could've explained to them. Why the killing of horses upset me far more than the wholesale slaughter of men is a question I've never come up with any satisfactory answer for.

For several days, Dad gave me interviews and filled in details of his career previously unknown to me or my family. He told me about my playing for the Old Dominion Kiwanis baseball team, and how he knew several of the fathers on that team who worked for the CIA.

"You called them Mr. Smith or Mr. Jones when you talked to them on the practice field," Dad said enigmatically. "I called them Mr. Brown or Mr. Black when I met them at work."

"I don't get it," I said.

"You're not supposed to," Dad said. "A Marine's got two areas of expertise. I knew some fighter pilots who were experts in transportation or supply. I was assigned to naval intelligence. I was a spook."

I was shocked. "But—you always hated spies."

"That's what I'm telling you," Dad said. "I had good reason to hate spooks. There's not one of them you can trust."

"When we were at Arlington?"

"Bingo, pal. I was on duty when Francis Gary Powers's spy plane was shot down in Russia. I had to give a briefing at the White House early that morning. I was tired for the three years I was a spook."

"You were mean as shit for those three years."

"Man, talk about pressure. I was involved in trading secrets with the Brits and the Jew boys during the Suez Canal crisis."

"So that explains Offutt Air Force Base," I said, and it pleased my father that I made the connection.

"I thought you might become a spook," Dad said. "You always were one step ahead of your peers."

A Marine fighter pilot at a celebrated Air Force base in the middle of the Midwest had never made sense to me. I was still at the stage in my life when I was looking to be a career Marine. Each day in our first two weeks there, Dad would drive me to a secluded region near the main runway, where we would watch the thrilling spectacle of a B-52 taking off as another B-52 came in for its ominous and somewhat portentous homecoming.

"Here's the drill, sports fans," Dad explained. "The B-52 that just landed has an Air Force general on it. So does the bird that just took off. If the Russkies wipe out Washington in a nuclear attack, the general in the sky becomes the commander in chief and takes his plane to drop a nuke on Moscow."

"Nice world, huh, Dad?" I said, watching a huge plane heading toward the western sky.

"The real world," he said.

As Dad was relating this secret life to me, something deep within him was breaking apart, capillary by capillary, bloody cell by bloody cell, as his voice weakened and his coordination began to fail him. As I was talking to him, I was an eyewitness to his minute-to-minute dying. There were things I needed him to tell me, but knew those words would never pass his lips. I was born to the father I was supposed to be born to, and anything else was commentary of the most frivolous, senseless kind.

"Here was my job at Offutt, son," he said in one of his last days of lucidity. "I was sent out there to plot the nuclear destruction of China."

"What in the living hell!" I said. Dad could often shock me, but it was rare for him to surprise me in such a way.

"You heard me right, jocko," Dad said. "I spent a year working on that plan."

"You think it would've been effective?" I asked.

"It'd sure hurt the sale of moo shu pork in that part of the world," he said in his deadpan way.

"My God, the Marine Corps is so smart. To send the biggest ass-hole in the world to plan the destruction of the most populated country on earth!"

"I got a personal letter from Secretary Robert McNamara for my good work," he said.

"Yeah, that guy'll live for a long time in the history of great military leaders."

"Don't fight a war in Asia," Dad said. "That's the Conroy rule."

"It ain't caught on," I said.

My cousin John Harper held a morbid curiosity about Don Conroy and his ability to talk about nuclear weapons as though they were only carburetors for his Ford. Like the rest of us, John had read the books about the destruction of Hiroshima and Nagasaki at the end of World War II. John was certain that Dad's nonchalance about talking about nuclear weapons was uncensored bravado and nothing else. I proceeded to ask Dad the same set of questions that Cousin John had once laid out before his favorite uncle.

"Okay, Dad," I said, studying my notes. "If you got a lawful order from the president that you were to drop a nuclear bomb on Atlanta, could you do it? Now, remember, me and my family, Jim and his family, and most of your friends also live there. Could you really execute that order?"

"Boom," my father said matter-of-factly. "Next question. That was too easy."

"Let's go to New York. If you drop a bomb in the New York met-ropolitan area, you're sure of wiping out up to eight million people, and the greatest cultural center in the world. Your daughter Carol lives there. Could you do it?"

"Boom," he said.

"Okay, let's go to Chicago, the city where you grew up and that you love more than anyplace on earth. All your relatives live there, and all would be destroyed if you dropped the bomb."

"Boom," said Dad. "Hey, this game is getting boring, son. I'm a Marine, and I do what I'm ordered to do. End of story."

That night I called up and told all my brothers, sisters, and daughters that Don was going to be dying soon. They'd better make plans to say their good-byes. The next day he struggled with the recorder, with his quavering voice, the power running out of him as the cancer ate him from the inside out. Though it was awful, it was part of his life's cycle, as immutable as the tides that ran by Parris Island and the flight paths along the air station. The Conroy tribe began gathering again in Beaufort. We instituted a schedule where one of Don's children would always be within call.

Unsurprisingly, my sister Carol Ann was avoiding all encounters with me. She would not come over to Kathy and Bobby Joe's house unless my car was nowhere in sight. She bristled like a guard dog whenever I passed through her angle of vision. Even when we exchanged pleasantries, hers were barbed and loaded with mistrust. Whenever she looked at me, her contempt filled the distance between us. Finally, we were reduced to being two writers who could not find the language to soften the history we shared from different battle stations.

But five days before Dad's death, Carol Ann and I were forced into a conversation that we had not prepared or planned in the elaborate architecture we designed to avoid each other. I came to Kathy's house to relieve Carol Ann after she had pulled an early morning shift. I'd arrived to assume my duties for the next six hours, when Tim would take over my watch. When I drove into the driveway, pandemonium had broken loose. I heard Carol Ann screaming, with her voice carrying all over the neighborhood.

"Dad, you've got to tell me you love me. I need it so badly, Dad. I need to hear you say it before you die. You've never said it to me! You've never said you're proud of me. I have to hear it from your lips. Tell me you love me, Dad. Tell me you're proud of me! I need it. I have to have it, Dad."

I gestured to Carol Ann that I needed to speak to her and gently led her out of Dad's bedroom to the couch in Kathy's living room. Dad was disheveled and rattled by Carol Ann's assault, but like me, he took it in a spirit of recognition of what an impossible life Carol Ann had led, with madness and genius clashing against her spirit. I let her scream and cry for a few minutes more. Then I finally spoke to her in a voice I hoped was conciliatory and loving at the same time.

"Carol, it's important for you to know this," I said. "Dad's dying. He's not going deaf. You don't have to scream at him."

"He's got to do this for me, Pat," Carol Ann cried, shifting up toward hysteria. "He's never told me once that he loved me. That he was proud of my work as a poet."

"He's always telling me he far prefers your poems to my work," I told her.

"Talk about damning with faint praise," she said.

"Carol, just don't scream at Dad. You've got him very upset."

"Has he ever told you he loved you, Pat? Tell me you've ever heard him say he's proud of you."

"As a matter of fact, he has," I said. "Every day of my life Dad calls me and tells me how much he loves me and how proud he is of the career that I've made for myself. Then he pauses and says, 'I wish I felt the same way about Carol, but I just don't feel shit for her.'"

Carol Ann threw a pillow at my head, and we both began laughing. Finally, I said, "Carol, that's Don Conroy dying in there, not Bill Cosby. That's the Great Santini in there, and he's just not put together like other men. Though he can't say it, he sends you money every month to support his daughter, the poet. He loves us with action, not with words. He's done great by you."

"I still need him to say it," Carol Ann said, her jaw set in a cast of pure stubbornness.

So I took Carol Ann by the arm and led her back to the room so she could say good-bye to Dad. For several minutes, Carol Ann composed herself, looking up only when our brother-in-law, Bobby Joe Harvey, walked in from his huge workplace in the backyard. Bobby Joe was known as the "Conroy family redneck," because that's how he identified himself to the rest of Beaufort. He thought a couple more rednecks in the family would improve it immensely. As for our politics, Bobby Joe would scoff and call us pinko liberal communists. Over the years we all had grown fond of Bobby Joe. There was nothing he couldn't do with his hands, from building a boat's motor to assembling a wrecked car into a collector's dream. Though there'd been some fireworks in the initial years of his marriage to Kathy, he was now solidly ensconced as family. He and my father had hit it off big when they first met, and Dad had become the father figure Bobby Joe had needed his whole life.

Bobby shuffled into the bedroom with his white beard immaculate and his grooming impeccable. He paused by Dad's bedside to say, "Hey, old man. You feeling any better?"

And my father, with his voice weak as a fawn's, looked up at his son-in-law. I spotted that vile, impish laugh go off in my father's head as he said, "I love you, Bobby Joe. I'm proud of you, Bobby Joe. I've always loved and been prouder of you than my loser children."

I caught Carol Ann in midair going for my father's throat. I'm sure she meant to kill him as he lay helplessly on his bed. Wrestling her out the front door and onto the lawn, I watched Carol Ann break into a run and disappear into her loaned house across the street. Bobby Joe came up behind me and said, "I don't know what I did, bro. I didn't mean to upset Carol so much."

"You were perfect, Bobby Joe," I said. "Remember that Carol is a wounded bird and always will be."

"I think the whole family is fucked-up," he said. "So does everyone else in Beaufort."

"That could serve as a one-sentence history of the Conroy family," I said. Bobby Joe put his arm around me, and we went back inside to be with Dad. All the commotion had exhausted him, and he was sound asleep when I returned to my post.

My father's entire world sprang into amazing life as each of his children took over some role in his slippage into unconsciousness. Checking with one another on an hourly basis, we compared notes on how much Dad was running down after the cancer had begun to wreak havoc on his brain. Though he still had lucid moments, the end was clearly visible, and we filed our reports with the far-flung array of friends and relatives who awaited our notes from the field.

On our first full shift together the following day, Cassandra and I interrupted a strange, improvised rite that Carol Ann had made up in her long march through the mythologies of the world. There was some kind of incense burning that struck me as Roman Catholic in origin.

As we entered the room, Carol Ann was pouring oil onto Dad's head, and it was streaming down his face, causing him great discomfort and, I believe, embarrassment.

"What in the living hell are you doing, Carol?" I said, trying to control my temper as I touched a drop of oil coming like a tear from my father's face.

"This is an ancient Indian ceremony," she said, "that I took from a Pueblo Indian ceremony, but also borrowed from the Sioux and the Apache."

"Funny, Carol," I said after tasting the oil on my fingertip, "I never knew that Apache Indians used extra virgin olive oil in their sacred rites."

"That's a chrism of mystery that our woman-hating Catholic Church uses for their worthless last rites of extreme unction. It's a bow toward Dad's own nonsensical religion."

"Dad's a lot of things, Carol," I said through thin, trembling lips, "but quit using him as a tossed salad."

"This incense may effect a cure," she said.

"It's our watch, Carol," I said. "If your oil works, I'll have Dad sprint over to your house across the street."

"Always the funny man," she snarled.

Cassandra went into the bathroom and came out with a towel rinsed with warm water, and one dry towel. She cleaned off and dried Dad's head and face.

"Tell your little friend thanks," Dad said about Cassandra. "Doesn't she remind you of your mother?"

"Yep, Dad," I said. "She sure does."

Two days before his death, Cassandra and I appeared for our shift, with my brother Tim coming straight down after school to relieve us for the late-afternoon shift. Kathy seemed to be a member of every shift, since Dad was in her house. But we were having trouble with our hospice group, who was often late showing up and slow on the trigger finger about getting an ample supply of morphine to relieve the agony Dad was now going through. As I entered the house, I heard Dad desperately gagging. Sprinting around the corner, I saw Carol Ann holding Dad's head on her shoulder, popping in morphine pills that he kept spitting out. Undeterred, Carol Ann would throw another pill down Dad's throat, and he would strangle it out in a blue foam.

I pulled Dad away from Carol Ann, and did it roughly. I turned his head toward the floor and a discolored wave of saliva came flooding out; then he gasped in a desperate convulsion and started to breathe again. His eyes held pure terror. Cassandra ran to the sink for a glass of water, and as I was wiping his foaming blue mouth, he swallowed for the last time in his life.

"Carol, you're killing Dad. You're drowning him. He can't swallow anymore. He's losing the ability to," I said.

"How the hell was I supposed to know that?" she said, furious.

"Look," I said; then I turned toward Dad. "This hospice shit didn't work out, Dad. Your kids don't know what we're doing. But I know what to do, okay? I'm going to take charge of this right now."

I picked up the phone and called 911 and got an immediate response.

"Hello, ma'am. This is Pat Conroy on Azalea Drive. My father has colon cancer and needs immediate help. Please send an ambulance here as soon as possible." Thirty seconds later, I heard the cry of an ambulance being sent out from the hospital.

When Carol Ann heard the sound, she roused herself from some form of trance and began screaming in my face. "Did you hear that, Cassandra? Did you hear the sound of the slave master in Pat's voice? That's what I had to endure all my childhood—the horrible sound of the patriarchy making demands. The chauvinist's crumbs are all I was thrown. A woman's opinion was worth less than dirt in Santini's house. We weren't given human status at all. We were chattel and nothing else."

"Hey, Carol," I said, "shut the fuck up."

I then went outside to meet the ambulance, which was coming down the street. Cassandra stayed behind and tried to minister to Carol Ann, who was caught in the tight netting of an agony that was a lifelong affliction to her. My sister Kathy followed the ambulance, then got Dad set up in a room in the oncology ward, where a morphine drip was started right away. He was breathing hard and overwhelmed by the scene his kids had just caused him to live through. When the morphine began to cut into his suffering, he looked up at Kathy and said, "I love morphine, sissy."

And those were the last words my father spoke.

CHAPTER 21

The God of Last Things

My brothers Tim and Mike sat with my father during the first night shift at his deathwatch, the first week in May. Dad had not spoken to them since they assumed their duties as watchmen. Flying in from Dallas, my brother Jim was already airborne, and he'd been scheduled to take over the second night shift. Carol Ann was so distraught in her lostness and her inability to balance her precarious hold on reality that we all feared to leave her alone with Dad.

My brothers Mike and Tim have never seemed related by blood. Certainly Mike could pass as part of a cousinry tenth removed from Tim, but there have always been canyons of difference pulling them apart by centrifugal, invisible forces. Mike gives off an aura of repose and self-containment that hides the fact that he is the most tightly wound of the Conroy siblings, his leg tapping away like a runaway motor as he sits on a couch, or appraises a situation, or renders an opinion about politics. He is the most trustworthy Conroy and has served as the executor of Mom, Dad, and Tom's affairs. He throws himself into these deadly dull conundrums with resignation and follows each of them through to its final conclusion. Though cheapness is his most egregious flaw, he considers it a great virtue and wishes the rest of us could develop similar tendencies. Mike was reading the sports section when my father drew his last breath.

My brother Tim is overemotional, excitable, and passionate. From his birth, the Bermuda Triangle—the family name for the three middle children—has picked on Tim and worried him to the point of hysteria. Mike, Kathy, and Jim could find something to criticize in every breath Tim drew. He would react with a cloistered rage, since he found our family as maddening and dangerous as I did. When Dad's labored breathing came to an abrupt stop, Tim began leaping about, hopping up and down, feeling Dad's pulse, checking his temperature, listening to his chest, but jumping in tiny three-step hops as the reality of the moment overcame him.

"Mike, Mike, Mike!" Tim cried out. "What happened? What just went wrong? What's going on with Dad?"

Then Tim leaped to the other side of the bed to see whether the situation looked any better from that angle. Motionless, Mike continued to check the baseball scores until Tim yelled at him, "Hey, Mike, let's talk about the important things. Did the Yankees beat the goddamn Red Sox last night? I couldn't sleep, I was so worried about that game."

Mike, not looking up, said, "The Red Sox won."

"What's happened to Dad?" Tim yelled. "You cold son of a bitch."

"It looks like Dad just died, monkey boy," Mike said. "Why do you keep jumping up and down like a little monkey boy?"

"What a cold, loathsome monster you are, Mike," Tim said.

"Keep jumping around, monkey boy," Mike said, finally putting the paper down and approaching Dad's bed, eyeing his motionless form carefully. "Better tell the nurses that Dad died," he ordered.

The nurses confirmed that Dad was dead and, after preparing the body for removal, left Mike and Tim in the room to say good-bye to him. That's when it caught up with them. They both fell apart and wept in the penned-in closures of their own silence. Mike and Tim were the first to realize in the thunderclaps of pure grief how much the children of the Great Santini had come to love him.

Tim said, "We'd better intercept Pat before he gets up here. He'd go nuts if he walked in now."

"You're right," Mike agreed. "Pat won't do well with this. I might even have a second monkey boy on my hands."

My brothers took the elevator down to the front of the hospital, then assumed positions to intercept me when I turned off Ribaut Road into the hospital parking lot. They saw me as I was driving north on Ribaut, but I surprised both of them by gliding right past them and not even glancing at the hospital where my father had just died. According to Tim, I nearly ran over Mike, who tried to step in front of my car to inform me about Dad.

"Pat doesn't give a shit about his own father," Tim said, in both surprise and disgust.

"Pat's going somewhere," Mike said. "He's probably buying new panty hose at Walmart."

"He didn't even glance over here," Tim said.

Though I'd departed from Fripp early to go see Dad, it hit me that I'd forgotten to bring Julia Randel my annual Mother's Day gift, and Mother's Day was the next day. When I visited Anne Rivers Siddons and her husband, Heyward, in Maine for three straight summers, I'd discovered that Morgan and Julia Randel were crazy about boiled lobsters. Since then, I brought Mrs. Randel live lobsters each Mother's Day, yet this year the day had crept up on me. Mrs. Randel had taken over the job of mothering me after the death of my own mother. Few people have ever loved me with such a soft laying on of hands, or asking for so little in return. My father died while I was lifting forlorn lobsters from a tank at Publix.

By the time I drove the five blocks to the Randel house, Cassandra had arrived at the hospital with my sister Kathy, and heard from my puzzled brothers about my strange dereliction of duty. Cassandra explained about Mrs. Randel and Mother's Day. When I arrived at Mrs. Randel's house, she was waiting for me in her driveway, having gotten the call from my brothers. The Randels were leading a youth group in a prayer meeting inside their house, and Mrs. Randel took me by the hand and walked me into their overgrown front yard, which was lush and azalea-covered. On her seldom-used front porch, she told me my father died and that it would probably do me good if I cried. She had often brought me to cry at this site, and she was an easy woman for me to shed tears in front of. When her son Randy died, I wrote my first poem in honor of his death. When her thirty-four-year-old son Darrell died of neurofibromatosis, a form of Elephant Man's disease, I flew in from San Francisco to deliver his eulogy. As the years passed, I composed eulogies for both Morgan and Julia Randel. When I die, their only surviving child, Julie, has to read a prayer at my funeral. As the tears made their way down my face, slowly at first, then at flood levels, Mrs. Randel soothed me. I lost control, and Mrs. Randel whispered prayers for me and my father. Something inside me realized that my faith had come from an ancient source, and I let myself be comforted and reconciled by it.

Then the business of Dad's death held us all by the throats as we tried to organize the events surrounding the funeral. Our Beaufort closed ranks around us once again. We lived in a house full of cut flowers and home-delivered meals and notes of both condolence and appreciation. The Marine Corps information department at both the air station and Parris Island called to tell us they would help the family in any way they could. Marine Corps headquarters checked in to note the passing of a legendary Marine aviator.

Though Dad's death was not a surprise to any of us, it still had the power to shock us into stupefaction. None of us performed at the top of his or her game during the stressful times leading up to his funeral, but we all forgave ourselves for doing so. *The New York Times* did a semisweet but disapproving obituary of Dad the next day, and Carol Ann had her first meltdown over the *Times*'s reference to Dad being an abusive father.

"That's not the man who raised me," she said in a histrionic voice. "I was raised by a gentle, kind man who never raised a hand to any member of his family."

Jim said, "You must've been raised by a different father."

"Give us a break, Carol," Tim added.

Carol Ann fought back. "To me, Dad was the perfect father. We loved each other in a way the males of this family will never understand. I've lost my closest friend, and God knows he loved me best of all."

The rest of us prepared ourselves and our children to accept any way Carol Ann reacted to her grief as her natural right. That night as the family fixed dinner, there was a shout from the den of my house, where the TV was on CNN. We ran in there to see a wonderful photo of Dad in his dress uniform, and a voice on the TV letting the world know that the Great Santini had died. His children fell silent, but a feeling of pride was let loose in the room, the unnameable sense of belonging that comes to a family that has always suffered from the stigmata of being the new strangers in town. It was a lovely moment for all of us.

Meanwhile, the world of Santini began to move south, as a large contingent of the Irish Conroys were heading toward Beaufort. My publishing world was sending its representatives too, and it was a thrill for me to show my editor, Nan Talese; my longtime agent, Julian Bach; and Marly Rusoff, who would one day become my agent, the small town I'd been writing about for thirty years. During my tour of Beaufort, Nan looked around and said, "What on earth do you *do* here, Pat?" And Julian echoed her question several times. Because Marly had visited Beaufort on a number of occasions, I did not have to make my sales pitch on the illimitable, river-braceleted charms of Beaufort to her. Long ago I had pitched my tent in the marsh-possessed town enclosed by tidal creeks that smelled like some eau de cologne of oyster beds and salt. It was here we were going to bury my father, and I couldn't have been happier that this would be his final resting place.

The next night was the viewing, and the saying of the rosary. The rosary was the idée fixe of the Chicago Irish, whose muscular Catholicism overpowered the weak-kneed, tepid religion of the Southern branch. Father James P. Conroy came in his priestly collar yet again, and took over the call for prayer, with Sister Marge Conroy in loud-voiced attendance. Looking at Dad's open casket, I stared at his ghastly, mummified face and thought of a story Jim and Tim had told me the night before.

Jim began, "It was at Dad's birthday party last month. . . ."

"And Aunt Marge and Father Jim were in the living room with Dad," Tim picked up. "Someone told Dad that he looked a little yellowish."

Jim finished the story. "Dad asked if anyone else thought he looked yellow. Sister Marge looked at her brother and said, 'Like a fucking banana, Don.'"

My eyes traveled upward, where I saw for the first time a cartoon my great friend Doug Marlette had drawn for my dad's funeral. It had been placed near the casket. It depicted a jet plane crashing through the pearly gates of heaven, with Saint Peter and several terrified angels running low to avoid the flight plan of the jet. Below the cartoon were the words "Stand by for a fighter pilot." On the cockpit of the plane, Doug had stenciled, "The Great Santini." Doug's gift cartoon was all the prayer we needed. Its quiet elegance eased our way through a fire-eating week of leavetaking.

The night before the funeral, Carol Ann came to my room looking troubled and mad-dog at the same time. Thus far, Carol Ann had behaved splendidly, with only a couple of outbreaks to remind us of past detonations of her jumpy spirit. But she and I found ourselves alone in my writing room off the master bedroom, where she had come with a stonewall agenda on her mind.

"Are you going to write a eulogy for Dad tomorrow?" she asked.

"I'm thinking about it, Carol. I haven't written a word yet," I said.

"Oh, you'll write one," she said. "Your ego is much too big to let such a golden opportunity pass by."

"Well, thanks. Guess I'll write one for sure now," I said.

"I've written a poem. A very great one, I think. But I'll not read my poem until you're finished with your prose. Dad always agreed with me that poetry was a much higher art form than prose."

"He even shared that sentiment with me. Dad, that aficionado of refined taste. I'll be glad to read a eulogy if I can think of anything to say."

"You're an egomaniac," she said. "You'll come up with something."

For a long time after the lights went out, Cassandra and I talked about all the enervating events that had led up to this ceremony. In the darkness I confessed to her that I wasn't sure I could write a single word praising Dad's life—that I was still caught up in the unhealable rancor I brought from my memory of my childhood. She said it didn't matter. I'd written the novel *The Great Santini*, and that would always stand me in good stead as my valediction to my father. We went to sleep holding hands.

At three in the morning, I awoke and walked to the writing desk as if in a trance. As sometimes happens to me, I dreamed out what I was supposed to write. I wrote the first paragraph of Dad's eulogy, then broke down. The second one came easily, until I broke down again. I knew what I was supposed to say and what I was required to say. Because it was the right thing to do, I went at it in a straight line that never wavered. I finished before dawn on the day I would attend my father's funeral.

When I walked out of my room dressed for the ceremony, the house had turned into a maze of breakfast and showering and dressing in close quarters. I had rented the house next door for overflow, and it too was brimming with people in different states of dress. At nine o'clock a fleet of limousines from the Copeland Funeral Home parked in the circular drive. They began to fill up with Floridians, Georgians, South Carolinians, Iowamen, and the brash Chicago tribesmen. In silence we rode to St. Peter's Catholic Church on Lady's Island, me sitting in amazement at the easy beauty and spirit of my daughters—something that was beyond words to me on this strangely immortal day.

There was a huge crowd awaiting us at the church. The parking lot was overflowing and spilling into the parking area of a nearby shopping center. Folks were heading toward the church at a rapid pace. In the lines ahead of me, I witnessed one false note that filled me with a nameless dread. Yet again, Carol Ann had leaped from her limo before it came to a stop, causing the driver to panic and step on the brakes, sending the other passengers lurching forward. When she regained her footing, Carol Ann sprinted into the church and down the center aisle.

My Fripp friends Gregg and Mary Wilson Smith described the scene to me later. Gregg said, "You don't usually see women doing wind sprints at a funeral, but that girl was flying."

Mary added, "As soon as Carol was convinced that every eye in the church was on her, she began a slow unpacking of jars and bottles she had in this huge purse. She set out water, then poured a glass for herself and drank it down. Nobody knew who she was or what in the living hell she was doing. But she unpacked lotions and oils and stuff, then spent ten minutes arranging them near the pulpit. Then she went to sit in the first seat on the front row—nearest the aisle."

"Goddamn, you Conroys sure know how to put on a show." Gregg laughed.

We waited with the patience of cattle to be lined up by the funeral directors, who were working from typed lists of family and pallbearers. There was a bovine serenity in our milling around, ready for our call. One of the problems in our orderly lineup was Carol Ann's sudden and unexplained disappearance.

Then the herd began to move, and we moved with a lack of grace, following the flight plan of Dad's casket's circuit through the church. The crowd was big and lively and ready for a show. It felt like a gaggle of well-wishers who had bought tickets to some private circus. I spotted Carol Ann already seated only when I heard Jim say to her, "Why don't you move to the end of the pew, Carol? Then the rest of us wouldn't have to climb over your ass to get to our seats."

Carol Ann possessed the voice of an aggrieved thespian when she answered, "Because I was closer to Dad by far than any of the other children. Our love for each other was boundless. As deep as the ocean. As mystical as poetry itself."

Jim, Janice, and their children then crawled over Carol Ann's knees; so did Cassandra and I, and so did Kathy and Bobby Joe and my nephew Willie, along with the rest of the immediate family. Mercifully, we filled up the first pew. The next five pews filled up with relatives at a brisk, efficient pace.

I opened the daily bulletin of the church, which was specially printed for the funeral. To myself, I whistled when I saw they were giving Dad a solemn high mass, usually reserved for the most highly regarded members of a church community.

A phalanx of priests came out of the rear of the church, including the pastor, Father Cellini, Dad's personal confessor; who was followed by Dad's brother, Reverend Jim Conroy; and our cousin the Reverend Jim Huth. The priests made an elaborate circumnavigation of the church with smoke pouring out of censers, reminding everyone that the Catholic Church had emerged from the Middle Ages and still believed in ancient rites of purification and submission to God's will. The priests gave the Protestants of Beaufort quite a show that day. They held nothing back from the mysterious origins of the Roman Church banished to caves beneath the Appian Way.

As I was checking the program to see my prescribed order in the ceremony, I saw my name as eulogist, with Carol Ann next in line with her poem written for the repose of Dad's soul. Whoever was sitting to my right—I believe my brother Tim—handed me a note written by Carol Ann from her watch-post at the end of the pew. I had never received a note from a sister at my father's funeral, but I'd never attended my father's funeral before, so my surprise turned to curiosity as I unfolded the note and began to read.

"Pat, I have glasses of water on the ledge beneath the podium. Also Kleenex, and lip balm, and some moisturizers if you need them. Also, I think you should know . . . I don't plan to read my poem until the priests are finished with their mumbo jumbo bullshit. Only then will I read the sacred poem I've written for our father's memory. Love, Carol."

I moaned out loud, but not enough to draw much attention to myself. Looking up to the ceiling, I thought of all the repercussions her supercilious and untimely note could cause. The scene played out in my head in all its nightmarish clarity. After I finished my eulogy, Father Cellini would announce to the audience that Carol Ann Conroy would now read a poem to honor her father. He would then take his seat as the chief celebrant. All eyes of the church would look to the first row, expecting to see Carol Ann rising out of the pew with paper in her hand and a love song for her father in her heart. Carol Ann had now changed the choreography of the whole service, and no one or nothing would move toward the altar from our contingent. At this moment, there were exactly two people in the church who knew Carol Ann's plans—the two of us. I was fully aware that Carol Ann had an infinite capacity for the reptilian stillness required by such an unconventional move. In my mind's eye, I could hear the audience stir with impatience, the undertakers checking their watches, and Carol Ann's rowdy family start to hoot and hurl abuse at her for her inappropriate showmanship. This was a problem I didn't know how to control or avert. Finally I leaned forward in the pew, shaking with fury, and pointed my finger at Carol Ann. I whispered in a rage, "Hey, Carol Ann, you're doing your poem as scheduled. Give me a goddamn break. Just one goddamn break."

Wheeling around and sitting with my back turned away from Carol Ann, I missed what I'm assured by many was the high point of the passion play we were all caught up in—a whirlwind no one could escape.

Ready for my assault, Carol Ann launched an immediate counterattack. She went down on one knee and started pumping the air with two-handed salutes of middle fingers directed at me and me alone. There were also sound effects as she accompanied every middle finger with a rapid-fire growling of "fuck you," while the funeral mass for our father moved toward the reading of the Epistle. Some of the church heard Carol Ann's intemperate tirade against me. Later, my brothers estimated that at least half of the mourners heard the chant of "fuck you" echoing through the church. If I had heard or seen her, there would've been a fistfight in pew one. But the town of Beaufort received a legitimate Conroy thrill of combat. Mike later told me Carol Ann had shot me forty birds, but Tim insisted it was nearer sixty, and Jim claimed more than one hundred. Cassandra, who had been a Methodist minister's wife for nearly twenty years in her previous life, thought she had seen everything when it came to family feuds erupting at funerals. She told me that the Conroy family was in a league of its own.

But I learned all this later. My task rose before me: to calm down before I read what I'd written about Dad only hours before. I was so distraught that I tried to bring my breathing back to normal, my blood pressure to a survivable level, until my temper folded like linen in some storehouse deep inside of me. The important thing was Dad and his legacy. I closed my eyes and thought of my father's life. It was time for the eulogy and I heard my name called. I moved down the aisle toward Carol Ann and whispered to her, "Please read your poem when your name is called." And I walked to the podium and delivered my eulogy.

When I returned to my seat, I passed Carol Ann and leaned down to whisper, "Do you need help getting to the podium, Carol?"

She did not, but walked to the microphone with a stiffness and formality that surprised me. As if in some ritual trance, she poured a glass of water and drank it slowly. She moistened her lips with an aromatic balm, and she took a lozenge to clear her throat.

Then she began to speak in her poet's voice. Her first sentence began, "Our father, who art in the air." It was a very moving and short poem, and she had promised to send us all a copy after her return to New York. Not one person, that I know of, has ever seen a copy of that poem, which remains precious to me because it was our family poet's farewell to Dad.

They stopped traffic on all of Beaufort's streets that intersected with the slow caravan that drove my father's body to its grave site at the national cemetery. The town held my father in the highest honor. The Marines were perfect, as I fully expected them to be, as they fired their volley of rifles into the air and a handsome senior officer handed me the crisp, folded flag that had covered his casket, which I accepted for the children of the Great Santini. The beauty of things military takes nearly all of its children prisoner in its primal love of order, its ceremonies that are timeless and changeless—they buried Dad with honors in the same cemetery where my mother was laid to rest.

Mom and Dad, I leave you now. I'll have no reason to return to the dresser where my mother prepared herself for her gowned balls at the homes of ambassadors. Dad, I release you to command your squadrons. I've been hard on you. But that's what literature requires, what the South requires, and what the corps always insists upon. For years, I made a study of Javanese shadow play, which I stumbled upon while looking for another book. In it, I thought I discovered a perfect metaphor for our family life. In Java the play is called Wayang, and it tells of terrible, bloody battles where the slaughter is indescribable. These are made-up stories between gods and kings, good and evil. The common people have to watch breathlessly, helpless in their meaningless and powerless awe. The play was acted on an immense stage as a mythical encounter, fortified by tradition, as a vehicle for the trembling villagers to view the events in a terrifying way. The dalang was a puppet master disguised in grotesque masks. This puppet master whose power was limitless controlled the destinies of everyone in the world.

I was born to the house of a puppet master, the dalang under the guise of Don Conroy. His wife and children were servants to the terrible dreamscape of his most bizarre qualities. He came at us like a lord of the underground, his rule disfigured. His family grew up around him, and we made our own judgments and told our own stories. By writing my novels, I tore the mask of the dalang out of your hands, Dad, and I decided to wear it myself. I've written about my family more than any writer in American history, and I take great pride in that. But your spirits deserve a rest, and I'm going to grant you a long one, one that lasts forever.

Mom and Dad, though I won't come this way again, I hope that your strong souls rest in peace. Though I will not write about you again, I would like you to take note that I still find both of you amazing, my portals into the light, and a myth and a narrative told in the rich mysteries of art.

Cassandra King and I were married the week following my father's death. It was my first step of a long repair job on the shape and architecture of a troubled soul. But I needed sweetness in my life and an infinite source of understanding. Cassandra and I had become inseparable as we cared for Dad in the final year of his life. I had fallen in love with a woman who'd fallen in love with the Great Santini. I could do no better in this life, and Cassandra has brought me a portion of love I never thought I'd find on this earth.

Now, fifteen years later, I count my days by the number of warplanes I hear from jets returning to the home field in Beaufort. Cassandra and I bought a house on Battery Creek, and we sometimes hear the distant roar of Marine sharpshooters practicing on Parris Island's rifle range. At sunset we watch the saltwater tides rising with perfect congruence to the rising moon. No matter the time of day, the creek spreads out in the thrown coinage of sunset, bright as a centerpiece in the transcendental green of the great salt marsh. Everything we notice is a timepiece calling out the muffled drumroll of our own mortal days.

I've come home to the place I was always writing about. Fishermen wave as they come in with their catches of sheepshead or triggerfish. Battery Creek returns to the sea, passing Parris Island, where Marines on the rifle range are practicing their accuracy skills. The Beaufort River sweetens the flow as it moves through the town where the mansions look like the summer homes of the creatures of a misused tarot deck. Born homeless, I've tried to make Beaufort, South Carolina, my own. To me, these islands didn't exist until I found them. I invented the marshes, the oyster banks, and the ink-dark creeks that divide the marshes until salt water runs up against solid land. This year, the shrimp have already made their migration, and the Canada geese are returning to the pond on a road that leads into Beaufort. In the distance, the air fills with warplanes. The sound is soothing to me, the chamber music of my boyhood. I embrace it as something that belongs to me. I know a lot about circles now.

Epilogue

Pat Conroy's Eulogy for the Great Santini

Colonel Don Conroy, USMC

The children of fighter pilots tell different stories than other kids do. None of our fathers can write a will or sell a life insurance policy or fill out a prescription or administer a flu shot or explain what a poet meant. We tell of fathers who land on aircraft carriers at pitch-black night with the wind howling out of the South China Sea.

Our fathers wiped out aircraft batteries in the Philippines and set Japanese soldiers on fire when they made the mistake of trying to overwhelm our troops on the ground.

Your dads ran the barbershops and worked at the post office and delivered the packages on time and sold the cars, while our dads were blowing up fuel depots near Seoul, were providing extraordinarily courageous close air support to the beleaguered Marines at the Chosin Reservoir, and once turned the Naktong River red with the blood of a retreating North Korean battalion.

We tell of men who made widows of the wives of our nation's enemies and who made orphans out of all their children.

You don't like war or violence? Or napalm? Or rockets? Or cannons or death rained down from the sky?

Then let's talk about your fathers, not ours. When we talk about the aviators who raised us and the Marines who loved us, we can look you in the eye and say, "You would not like to have been America's enemies when our fathers passed overhead."

We were raised by the men who made the United States of America the safest country on earth in the bloodiest century in all recorded history.

Our fathers made sacred those strange, singing names of battlefields across the Pacific: Guadalcanal, Iwo Jima, Okinawa, the Chosin Reservoir, Khe Sanh, and a thousand more. We grew up attending the funerals of Marines slain in these battles.

Your fathers made communities like Beaufort decent and prosperous and functional; our fathers made the world safe for democracy.

We have gathered here today to celebrate the amazing and storied life of Col. Donald Conroy, who modestly called himself by his nom de guerre, the Great Santini.

There should be no sorrow at this funeral, because the Great Santini lived life at full throttle, moved always in the fast lanes, gunned every engine, teetered on every edge, seized every moment and shook it like a terrier shaking a rat.

He did not know what moderation was or where you'd go to look for it. Donald Conroy is the only person I have ever known whose self-esteem was absolutely unassailable. There was not one thing about himself that my father did not like; nor was there one thing about himself that he would change. He simply adored the man he was and walked with perfect confidence through every encounter in his life. Dad wished everyone could be just like him.

His stubbornness was an art form. The Great Santini did what he did, when he wanted to do it, and woe to the man who got in his way. Once, I introduced my father before he gave a speech to an Atlanta audience. I said at the end of the introduction, "My father decided to go into the Marine Corps on the day he discovered his IQ was the temperature of this room."

My father rose to the podium, stared down at the audience, and said without skipping a beat, "My God, it's hot in here. It must be at least a hundred and eighty degrees."

Here is how my father appeared to me as a boy. He came from a race of giants and demigods from a mythical land known as Chicago. He married the most beautiful girl ever to come crawling out of the poor and lowborn South, and there were times when I thought we were being raised by Zeus and Athena.

After happy hour my father would drive his car home at a hundred miles an hour to see his wife and seven children. He would get out of his car, a strapping flight-jacketed matinee idol, and walk toward his house, his knuckles dragging along the ground, his shoes stepping on and killing small animals in his slouching amble toward the home place.

My sister Carol Ann, stationed at the door, would call out, "Godzilla's home!" and we seven children would scamper toward the door to watch his entry.

The door would be flung open and the strongest Marine aviator on earth would shout, "Stand by for a fighter pilot!"

He would then line his seven kids up against the wall and say,

"Who's the greatest of them all?"

"You are, O Great Santini, you are."

"Who knows all, sees all, and hears all?"

"You do, O Great Santini, you do."

We were not in the middle of a normal childhood, yet none of us were sure, since it was the only childhood we would ever have.

For all we knew other men were coming home and shouting to their families "Stand by for a pharmacist" or "Stand by for a chiropractor."

In the odd, bewildered world of children we knew we were in the presence of a fabulous, overwhelming personality, but had no idea we were being raised by a genius of his own mythmaking.

My mother always told me that my father had reminded her of Rhett Butler on the day they met, and everyone who ever knew our mother conjured up the lovely, coquettish image of Scarlett O'Hara.

Let me give you my father the warrior in full battle array. The Great Santini is catapulted off the deck of the aircraft carrier *Sicily*. His Black Sheep Squadron is the first to reach the Korean Theater, and American ground troops had been getting torn up by North Korean regulars.

Let me do it in his voice: "We didn't even have a map of Korea.

Not zip. We just headed toward the sound of artillery firing along the Naktong River. They told us to keep the North Koreans on their side of the Naktong. Airpower hadn't been a factor until we got there that day. I radioed to Bill Lundin—I was his wingman—'There they are. Let's go get 'em.' So we did."

I was interviewing Dad, so I asked, "How do you know you got them?"

"Easy," the Great Santini said. "They were running—it's a good sign when you see the enemy running. There was another good sign."

"What was that, Dad?"

"They were on fire."

This is the world in which my father lived deeply. I had no knowledge of it as a child.

When I was writing the book *The Great Santini*, they told me at Headquarters Marines that Don Conroy was at one time one of the most decorated aviators in the Marine Corps. I did not know he had won a single medal. When his children gathered together to write his obituary, not one of us knew of any medal he had won, but he had won a slew of them.

When he flew back toward the carrier that day, he received a call from an army colonel on the ground who had witnessed the march of the North Koreans across the river. "Could you go pass over the troops fifty miles south of here? They've been catching hell for a week or more. It'd do them good to know you flyboys are around."

He flew those fifty miles and came over a mountain and saw twenty thousand troops hunkered down in foxholes. He and Bill Lundin went in low so these troops could read the insignias and know the American aviators had entered the fray.

My father said, "Thousands of guys came screaming out of their foxholes, son. It sounded like a World Series game. I got goose pimples in the cockpit. Get goose pimples telling it forty-eight years later. I dipped my wings, waved to the guys. The roar they let out. I hear it now. I hear it now."

During the Cuban Missile Crisis, my mother took me out to the air station, where we watched Dad's squadron scramble on the runway on their bases at Roosevelt Road and Guantánamo.

In the car as we watched the A-4s take off, my mother began to say the rosary.

"You praying for Dad and his men, Mom?" I asked her.

"No, son. I'm praying for the repose of the souls of the Cuban pilots they're going to kill."

Later I would ask my father what his squadron's mission was during the Missile Crisis.

"To clear the air of MiGs over Cuba," he said.

"You think you could've done it?"

The Great Santini answered, "There wouldn't have been a bluebird flying over that island, son."

Now let us turn to the literary career of the Great Santini.

Some of you may have heard that I had some serious reservations about my father's child-rearing practices. When *The Great Santini* came out, the book roared through my family like a nuclear device. My father hated it; my grandparents hated it; my aunts and uncles hated it; my cousins who adore my father thought I was a psychopath for writing it; and rumor has it that my mother gave it to the judge in her divorce case and said, "It's all there. Everything you need to know."

What changed my father's mind was when Hollywood entered the picture and wanted to make a movie of it. This is when my father said, "What a shame John Wayne is dead. Now, there was a man. Only he could've gotten my incredible virility across to the American people."

Orion Pictures did me a favor and sent my father a telegram: "Dear Colonel Conroy: We have selected the actor to play you in the coming film. He wants to come to Atlanta to interview you. His name is Truman Capote."

But my father took well to Hollywood and its byzantine, unspeakable ways. When his movie came out, he began reading *Variety* on a daily basis. He called the movie a classic the first month of its existence. He claimed that he had a place in the history of film. In February of the following year, he burst into my apartment in Atlanta, as excited as I have ever seen him, and screamed, "Son, you and I were nominated for Academy Awards last night. Your mother didn't get squat."

Ladies and gentlemen—you are attending the funeral of the most famous Marine that ever lived. Dad's life had grandeur, majesty, and sweep. We were all caught in the middle of living lives much paler and less daring than the Great Santini's. His was a high-stepping, damn-the-torpedoes kind of life, and the stick was always set at high throttle. There is not another Marine alive who has not heard of the Great Santini. There's not a fighter pilot alive who does not lift his glass whenever Don Conroy's name is mentioned and give the fighter pilot toast: "Hurrah for the next man to die."

One day last summer, my father asked me to drive him over to Beaufort National Cemetery. He wanted to make sure there were no administrative foul-ups about his plot. I could think of more pleasurable ways to spend the afternoon, but Dad brought new eloquence to the word "stubborn." We went into the office and a pretty black woman said that everything was squared away.

My father said, "It'll be the second time I've been buried in this cemetery." The woman and I both looked strangely at Dad. Then he explained: "You ever catch the flick *The Great Santini*? That was me they planted at the end of the movie."

All of you will be part of a very special event today. You will be witnessing the actual burial that has already been filmed in the actual setting. This has never happened in world history. You will be present in a scene that was acted out in film in 1979. You will be in the same town and the same cemetery. Only the Great Santini himself will be different.

In his last weeks my father told me, "I was always your best subject, son. Your career took a nosedive after *The Great Santini* came out." He had become so media savvy that during his last illness he told me not to schedule his funeral on the same day as the *Seinfeld* farewell. The colonel thought it would hold down the crowd. The colonel's death was front-page news across the country. CNN announced his passing on the evening news all around the world.

Don Conroy was a simple man and an American hero. His wit was remarkable, his intelligence frightening, and his sophistication nonexistent. He was a man's man, and I would bet he hadn't spent a thousand dollars in his whole life on his wardrobe. He lived out his whole retirement in a two-room efficiency in the Darlington apartments in Atlanta. He claimed he never spent more than a dollar on any piece of furniture he owned. You would believe him if you saw the furniture. Dad bought a season ticket for himself to Six Flags Over Georgia and would often go there alone to enjoy the rides and hear the children squeal with pleasure. He was a beer drinker who thought wine was for Frenchmen or effete social climbers like his children.

Ah! His children. Here is how God gets a Marine Corps fighter pilot. He sends him seven squirrelly, mealymouthed children who march in peace demonstrations, wear Birkenstocks, flirt with vegetarianism, invite cross-dressers to dinner, and vote for candidates whom Dad would line up and shoot. If my father knew how many tears his children had shed since his death, he would be mortally ashamed of us all and begin yelling that he should've been tougher on us all, knocked us into better shape—that he certainly didn't mean to raise a passel of kids so weak and tacky they would cry at his death. Don Conroy was the best uncle I ever saw, the best brother, the best grandfather, the best friend—and my God, what a father. After my mother divorced him and *The Great Santini* was published, Don Conroy had the best second act I ever saw. He never was simply a father. This was the Great Santini.

It is time to leave you, Dad. From Carol Ann and Mike and Kathy and Jim and Tim and especially from Tom. Your kids wanted to thank Kathy and Bobby and Willie Harvey, who cared for you heroically. Let us leave you and say good-bye, Dad, with the passwords that bind all Marines and their wives and their children forever. The corps was always the most important thing.

Semper Fi, Dad.

Semper Fi, O Great Santini.

Acknowledgments

To my great wife, Cassandra King. It's a high honor to write books in the same house with you. You have brought loveliness, order, a sense of calm, and joy into my life, and I can't thank you enough for your ceaseless love.

The long-distance runners: Nan Talese, my editor for thirty years, winner of the first Maxwell Perkins Award for lifetime achievement in editing, who has brought my books under control. Nan, I thank you with my heart; and to my agents Marly Rusoff and Mihai Radulescu.

To my first readers and editors: Maggie Schein and Jonathan Hannah; Janis and Wendell Owens and the beautiful Owens daughters; Judy and Henry Goldman; with special thanks to Katherine Clark.

To the families, Jessica, Melissa, Megan Conroy; Jim, Jason, Jacob Ray. And the Grands: Elise, Stella, Lila, Wester, Molly Jean, Jack, Katie (mine); Alessandra, Alina, Tyler, Michael, Sophia, Henry, Anna Jane, Amelia, Lucas, Harper (Cassandra's).

And to my lost daughter Susannah Conroy, the door is always open and so is my heart. You have a whole Conroy family ready to love you.

In memory of Nancy Jane King, Elton King, Milbry Gnann, Julia Randel, Kate Bockman, Hammond Smith, Sarah Ellen Harper, Jane Lefco, Nugent "The Boo" Courvoisie, Julian Bach, Emily Sickternam, Ria D. Hughs, Jay Harbeck.

As always, Gay Talese; Bernie and Martha Schein; Scott and Susan

Graber; John and Barbara Warley; Cliff and Cynthia Graubart; Ann and Heyward Siddons; Terry and Tommie Kay; Ann Torrago; Hope Bach; Wendy Weil; Carolyn Krupp; Todd Doughty; Eddie Birnbrey; Rachel Perling; Tricia Shannon; Ron and Ann Rash; Jim Landon; Tim Belk; Gregg and Mary Wilson Smith; Dot and Walt Gnann Jr.; Wilson McIntosh; Beckie, Reggie, and the Schuler boys; Will Hare; Barbara Conroy; the Harper boys; Willie Harvey; Rachel and Michael Conroy; Jonathan Haupt; Alex and Zoe Sanders; Zoe Caroline and the boys; Theresa Miller; Sallie Robinson; Jo Anne Smith; Ricardo and Laura Bonino; Liz and Christian Sherbert; Lucius and Daryl Laffitte; Mike and Pat Roberts; Wendell and Florence Minor; Melinda and Jackson Marlette.

The Death of Santini

Pat Conroy

A Reader's Guide

My dear friends and fellow lovers of Santini,

You have written so many letters of condolence since my father died that I've been overwhelmed at the task of answering them. But know this: All of them meant something, all of them moved me deeply, all were appreciated, and all were read. Don Conroy was larger than life and there was never a room he entered that he left without making his mark. At some point in his life, he passed from being merely memorable to being legendary.

In the thirty-three years he was in the Marine Corps, Colonel Conroy concentrated on the task of defending his country, and he did so exceedingly well. In the next twenty-four years left to him, he put all his efforts into the art of being a terrific father, a loving uncle, a brother of great substance, a beloved grandfather, and a friend to thousands. Out of uniform, the Colonel let his genius for humor flourish. Always in motion he made his rounds in Atlanta each day and no one besides himself knew how many stops he put in during a given day. He was like a bee going from flower to flower, pollinating his world with his generous gift for friendship.

Don Conroy was a man's man, a soldier's soldier, a Marine's Marine. There was nothing soft or teddy-bearish about him. His simplicity was extraordinary. He died without ever owning a credit card, never took out a loan in his life, and almost all the furniture in his apartment was rented. I think he loved his family with his body and soul, yet no one ever lived who was less articulate in expressing that love. On the day the doctor told him that there was nothing more to be done for him, my father told me,

"Don't worry about it. I've had a great life. No one's had a life like me. Everyone should be so lucky."

Don Conroy died with exemplary courage, as one would expect.

He never complained about pain or whimpered or cried out. His death was stoical and quiet. He never quit fighting, never surrendered, and never gave up. He died like a king. He died like The Great Santini.

I thank you with all my heart.

Pat Conroy

Questions and Topics for Discussion

1. Certain members of the Conroy clan viewed Pat's writings as a betrayal of the family, exposing their dirty laundry to the public and tarnishing their reputation. Do you agree? How would you react if someone close to you novelized your life?

2. How do you think the real-life Conroys compare to their fictional counterparts in the Meecham family?

3. Conroy describes the lessons about love that he learned from his parents' marriage in startlingly vivid terms, writing: "[Love] was a country bristling with fishhooks hung at eye level, man-traps, and poisoned baits. It could hurl toward you at breakneck speed or let you dangle over a web spun by a brown recluse spider" (pages 2–3). How do you evaluate this assessment of love and marriage? Do you think Conroy's attitude shifts at all throughout the book? How did the example of his parents' relationship influence his own marriages?

4. Conroy writes of his "high contempt" for literary critics, claiming that "no writer has suffered over morning coffee because of the savagery of my review of his or her latest book, and no one ever will" (page 46). How do you reconcile this attitude toward literary critics with the suffering his writing caused the members of his family? Do the two positions contradict each other, or are they compatible? Why?

5. In the Introduction to this book, Conroy claims that other writers

often consider autobiographical fiction to be a low form of literature. What do you think of this claim?

6. Conroy writes "I don't believe in happy families," going on to explain that "A family is too frail a vessel to contain the risks of all the warring impulses expressed when such a group meets on common ground" (page 144). Do you agree with this claim? Is there such a thing as a happy family?

7. Conroy describes his mother as playing the part of Scarlett O'Hara throughout her life. What part does Conroy play? Do we all play a role different from who we really are? If so, what part do you play?

8. Conroy sometimes describes his parents and childhood in mythic terms, comparing his father to Thor and to Ares, the Greek god of war. Is it human nature to make myths of our childhoods and deify our parents? What myths exist in your family lore?

9. *The Death of Santini* explores the impact of Conroy's Southern and Irish heritage on his upbringing. Discuss the importance of family heritage and ancestry in Conroy's life and in your own.

10. Conroy eloquently writes that "Your birthplace is your destiny" (page 100). What do you think of this statement?

11. The Conroy children sometimes have very divergent perspectives on their shared childhood memories. What do you think of this phenomenon? Can you think of similar instances in your own life? Is it possible to avoid editorializing memories?

12. In a much-discussed scene from *The Great Santini*, Bull Meecham's son chases his father around the Beauford green yelling "I love you!" Why do you think Bull/Dan runs away from this onslaught of affection?

13. Peg stuck with her marriage to Dan through some terrible times,

yet the marriage could not survive the publication of *The Great Santini*. Why do you think that is?

14. In what ways did the filming of *The Great Santini* change Pat's relationship with his father?

15. Conroy experiences the rare pleasure of watching his novel come to life on the silver screen. Who would play you in the movie of your life?

PAT CONROY is the author of ten previous books: *The Boo, The Water Is Wide, The Great Santini, The Lords of Discipline, The Prince of Tides, Beach Music, My Losing Season, The Pat Conroy Cookbook: Recipes of My Life, South of Broad,* and *My Reading Life*. He lives in Beaufort, South Carolina.

A Note About the Type

This book was set in a modern adaptation of a type designed by
the first William Caslon (1692–1766). The Caslon face, an artistic,
easily read type, has enjoyed over two centuries of popularity in the
English-speaking world. This version, designed by
Carol Twombley for the Adobe Corporation and released in 1990,
ensures by its even balance and honest letterforms the continuing
use of Caslon well into the twenty-first century.